THE CANONICAL CONCEPT OF CONGRUA
SUSTENTATIO FOR THE SECULAR CLERGY

THE CATHOLIC UNIVERSITY OF AMERICA
CANON LAW STUDIES
No. 302

The Canonical Concept of *congrua sustentatio* for the Secular Clergy

A DISSERTATION

SUBMITTED TO THE FACULTY OF THE SCHOOL OF CANON LAW OF THE CATHOLIC UNIVERSITY OF AMERICA IN PARTIAL FULFILLMENT OF THE REQUIREMENTS FOR THE DEGREE OF DOCTOR OF CANON LAW

BY
REVEREND PHILIP M. HANNAN, S.T.L., J.C.L.
PRIEST OF THE ARCHDIOCESE OF WASHINGTON, D. C.

THE CATHOLIC UNIVERSITY OF AMERICA PRESS
WASHINGTON, D. C.
1950

Murray & Heister
Washington. D. C.

Printed by
Times and News Publishing Co
Gettysburg, Pa., U. S. A.

To

MY PARENTS

TABLE OF CONTENTS

TABLE OF CONTENTS (Continued)

TABLE OF CONTENTS (Continued)

PART II

Canonical Commentary

TABLE OF CONTENTS (Continued)

FOREWORD

There is some confusion today about the kind and amount of support that is owed to the secular clergy. One reason for such confusion is the feeling that the sacrificial and self-denying nature of the priestly life demands that a priest has a right only to a scanty and minimum standard of living. This trend of thought identifies the counsel of poverty—so strongly expressed by St. Paul, "but having food and sufficient clothing, with these let us be content"—with a prerequisite for the priesthood. It is true that in conformity with this counsel the clergy, in the first centuries of Christianity, led a life of poverty by sharing in the common goods of the Church.

However, it is no less true that it was recognized even by the Apostle who exhorted the clergy to practice poverty that "the laborer is worthy of his wages," and therefore has a right to a fitting compensation. Although poverty was rightly considered very befitting in those who aspired to the priestly life, it was not accepted as a necessary condition for ordination. Later, when Christianity was recognized and its once-hunted clergy became, next to the civil rulers, the most influential citizens of the State, the clergy accepted a standard of living more consonant with their popular influence and dignity. Although the former *gens lucifuga* had now become the rulers of the temporal City of God, the memory and value of the apostolic poverty was never forgotten. The cultivation of a spirit of detachment from worldly goods was always urged upon the clergy, and the recognition of the duty of charity coined the magnificent phrase, *"Quidquid clerici est, pauperum est."*

When the first priests came to the territory of the present Eastern United States, they came almost as did the Apostles to the pagan nations—without the support of a system of sustenance or aid by the state, without any particular protection of law, without the prospect of popular support by those to whom they would minister. The Church in the United States began as it did in the first centuries; the Jesuits in Maryland were conscious of this parallel and did not try to institute a system of support similar to that then current in the Catholic regions of the world. Naturally, as the fortunes of the Church improved, the system of support of the clergy improved. However, even after the United States had become the wealthiest nation in the world, the concept of the fitting support owed to the clergy was and remains, in many sections, conditioned by the circumstances and history of the clergy in colonial days. It is therefore the purpose of this dissertation to consider the concept of fitting support of the secular clergy as contained in the Code of Canon Law, and independently of the popular concept.

The writer takes this occasion to express his gratitude to the late Archbishop Michael J. Curley for making it possible to commence the study of Canon Law, and to his Excellency, the Most Reverend Patrick A. O'Boyle for his permission and encouragement to complete that course of study. A debt of gratitude is also acknowldeged to the members of the Faculty of Canon Law for their gracious and unfailing assistance, especially to Dr. Jerome Hannan for his patient and wise counsel. The writer is likewise indebted to the librarians of the University Library, particularly to Dr. Stephan Kuttner, as well as to those of the Congressional Library, the Peabody Library in Baltimore, and the Harvard College Library, for their assistance. Acknowledgment is also made to the Belgian Embassy in Washington, the Chanceries of the Archdioceses of Paris, Vienna, Limerick, Dublin, Westminster, Malines and Cologne for the information they so graciously afforded. Particular thanks are also due to the secretarial staff of the Chancery for their assistance in preparing the manuscript.

PART I

Historical Development

CHAPTER I

From the Apostolic Age to the Carolingian Era

Just as the Jewish Law had accorded to the Levites and the spiritual superiors of Israel a fitting and competent support, the Christian Law also taught that the ministers of the new religion were to be accorded a decent support. St. Paul's actions and writing epitomized the teaching of the Christian Church:

> For you yourselves know how you ought to imitate us: for we were not unruly while with you, neither did we eat any man's bread at his cost, but we worked night and day in labor and toil, so that we might not burden any of you. Not that we did not have the right to do so, but that we might make ourselves an example for you to imitate us.[1]

St. Paul thus staunchly propounded his right to support from his disciples, and just as staunchly insisted on providing an example of industry and self-support.

As the Christian Church increased in numbers with the consequent increase in the work of the spiritual ministry, the robust self-sufficiency of a St. Paul was no longer universally practicable. St. Peter was the first to propose that the manual labor of caring for the dependents of the Church be entrusted to lower ministers of the Church, the deacons; the bishop, however, the highest ecclesiastical authority in the community, retained the right to appoint and ordain deacons, thus exercising a controlling power over the administration of the goods of the Church.[2] The clergy, in the Apostolic Age, were supported as members of the Christian community who shared their goods in common.[3] Hence there was no specific determination of the amount of support due the clergy.

---

[1] Thessalonians, III: 7-10.

[2] Acts of the Apostles, VI: 1-7.

[3] Acts of the Apostles, II: 44.

In the first few centuries the Church defined those who were to be supported by the Church—the widows, orphans, poor, visiting Christians—and thus determined the extent of the obligations resting on the clergy.[4] Thus, although the clerics were urged to be satisfied with only what was necessary for the most modest living, they needed a considerable income to satisfy all their obligations.[5] It is interesting to note how extensive and binding was the law of hospitality; all Christian visitors to the community were accorded lodging and meals, especially those who were forced to flee from persecution.[6]

During these first few centuries when the bishop continued to supervise the distribution of the tithes, first-fruits and offerings, through his lower clergy, the priest received these distributions at frequent intervals; the clergy did not receive enough to support themselves for a considerable amount of time.[7] The spread of Christianity to the rural areas necessitated separate "parishes" (which did not enjoy the juridical position of a parish today) with separate incomes for the pastors; these churches were placed under the direction of "rural bishops" appointed by the urban bishops.[8]

At a later date the rural bishops were called *"chorepiscopi,"*[9] and they were approved and confirmed as an institution in the I General Council of Nicaea (325).[10] The *chorepiscopi* received their

[4] *Didascalia et Constitutiones Apostolorum* (2 vols., ed. F. X. Funk, Paderborn, 1905), lib. II, XXV, 2 (hereafter cited *Didascalia*).

[5] "Satis ergo vobis sint, quae sufficiunt, victus et vestitus et quae omnino necessaria sunt."—*Didascalia,* lib. II, XXV, 1.

[6] *Didascalia,* lib. V, III, 1.

[7] *Didascalia,* lib. II, XXVII, 1-2; lib. II, XXVIII, 2; *Constitutiones Apostolorum,* L. VI, XXIX, 1-3. It is evident from both these works that the Church depended primarily on the gifts of food and goods rather than on returns from landed estates during the first two or three centuries.

[8] These rural bishops are mentioned in a synodal letter written by the bishops of the Council of Antioch (269). Cf. Eusebius, *Historia Ecclesiastica,* Lib. VII, c. 30—Migne, *Patrologiae Cursus Completus, Series Graeca* (161 vols., Parisiis, 1857-1866), XX, 709-720 (hereafter cited with the initials *MPG*).

[9] Council of Ancyra (314), c. 7—Bruns, *Canones Apostolorum et Conciliorum Saeculorum IV-VII* (2 vols., Berolini, 1839), I, 69 (hereafter referred to as Bruns).

[10] C. 8—Bruns, I, 16.

support in the same manner, though not in the same style, as the urban bishops, even though they were subordinate to them. Later, to prevent the lowering of the dignity of the episcopal office by the creation of a *chorepiscopus* for every rural parish, visiting priests, called "*periodeutai,*" were appointed. They performed many of the duties of the *chorepiscopi.*[11] The *periodeutai,* although they enjoyed a certain degree of independence of action and support, were dependent on the urban bishop, and did not have the same authority and functions as a pastor enjoys these today.

The great increase in the number of Christians after the peace of Constantine necessitated a development of the "parish" system, and consequently also a closer definition of the means of support for the clergy. There was at least a modified parochial system in Egypt in the latter part of the fourth century,[12] and the Council of Elvira in 305 referred to deacons ruling over churches under the supervision of priests, thus showing that there was a kind of parochial system in Spain.[13] The Church in Africa also defined, in the fourth century, the duties of priests in charge of churches which were certainly separate from the bishop's church or cathedral.[14] There are also one hundred and five canons attributed to a IV Council of Carthage (398), or a council of 419, which give a rather vivid account of what was claimed to be the concept of the African Church concerning the support of the clergy.[15] According to these

[11] Council of Sardica (343), c. 6—Bruns, I, 90.

[12] Cf. St. Athanasius, *Apologia contra Arianos,* I, 74—*MPG,* XXV, 385.

[13] C. 77—Bruns, II, 12.

[14] II Council of Carthage (390), c. 4—Bruns, I, 119; III Council of Carthage (397), c. 36—Bruns, I, 128; IV Council of Carthage (398), c. 10—Bruns, I, 142.

[15] These canons constitute the famous *Statuta Ecclesiae Antiqua,* which Christopher Justel (1580-1649) and other scholars maintain cannot be attributed to the IV Council of Carthage. For a discussion of the authenticity of the canons, cf. Hefele-Leclercq, *Histoire des Conciles de l'Eglise* (10 vols. in 19, Paris; Letouzey et Ané, 1907-1938), II, 201-209, where 133 canons are ascribed to the African Church under the title, "*Codex Canonum Ecclesiae Africanae.*" The canons are contained in Hardouin, *Acta Conciliorum et Epistolae Decretales ac Constitutiones Summorum Pontificum* (12 vols., Parisiis, 1714-1715), I, 975 ff. (hereafter cited as Hardouin); Mansi, *Sacrorum Conciliorum Nova et Amplissima Collectio* (53 vols. in 60, Parisiis, 1901-1927), III, 945 ff. (hereafter cited as Mansi); Bruns, I, 140.

canons, the Church owned considerable property under the administration of the bishop.[16] Every cleric was given a regular stipend for his support,[17] but this stipend was evidently insufficient, since each cleric, even the learned, was required to gain a living by trade or by agriculture.[18]

Even if this austere life for all clerics was prevalent in Africa, it was not legislated for the universal Church. The next century reveals the specific legislation of the Council of Chalcedon (451), namely, that the ordination of clerics was forbidden unless each one had an appointment to a church, or a chapel, or a monastery, and thus could be supported; thus, each cleric received a *titulus* for his support.[19] It is evident from the same canon that priests were assigned to churches in the city, in the country (in villages), to chapels of martyrs, and to monasteries as chaplains. The clergy remained under the jurisdiction of the bishop,[20] and the bishops seemed to be particularly desirous of maintaining their jurisdiction over the village churches or parishes.[21]

The same Council furnished definite information on the concept of a fitting salary for the support of a bishop. Maximus, Bishop of Antioch (449-455), requested the Council to permit him to allot a certain portion of the goods of his Church for the support of Domnus, deposed predecessor of Maximus; the Council approved an annual pension of 250 *solidi* for Domnus, even though he was to live *"in communione laicali."*[22] There was, apparently, considerable doubt about the culpability of Domnus. The same Council (Twelfth Session, Oct. 30, 451) granted to two bishops, contenders for the same see, an annual pension of 200 gold pieces, but another bishop was appointed to the see of Ephesus, the contested see.[23] The granting of these pensions, involving separate sustenance at the expense of the Church, was considered a great innovation, and

---

[16] C. 31—Bruns, II, 144.
[17] C. 49—Bruns, II, 146.
[18] Cc. 51, 52—Bruns, II, 146.
[19] C. 6—Bruns, I, 27.
[20] C. 8—Bruns, I, 27.
[21] C. 17—Bruns, I, 30.
[22] Mansi, VII, 722.
[23] Mansi, VII, 294; Hardouin, II, 558.

the papal legate was asked for his specific approval of these acts, particularly the assigning of the pension to the deposed Domnus.[24]

A liberal allowance for the maintenance of clerics was necessary, since the same Council had decreed that no cleric or monk should engage in any business or trade, even as a means of securing the necessities of life; a cleric was forbidden even to be the legal guardian of infants, orphans and widows, unless it was required by law or specifically permitted by the bishop.[25]

Contemporary with the Council of Chalcedon (451) there developed a customary division of the income of the churches in order to insure a decent support for the clergy assigned to the churches. Pope St. Gelasius (492-496) sanctioned this existing law or custom in a letter to the Christian Church of Brindisi and Sicily, in which he instructed the bishop to divide the revenues of the Church into four shares: one for the construction and maintenance of the church buildings; one for the poor and dependents of the Church; one for the bishop, and the fourth for the clergy. The Pope referred to this existing custom as *"dudum rationabiliter decretum."*[26]

The support due the clergy was not judged by spartan and austere standards. Support meant a decent livelihood, and the income of the clergy depended to some extent upon their merit. This rule of equity had been established before the reign of Pope St. Gelasius, by Pope St. Simplicius (468-483).[27]

The Church's generous concept of the support due the clergy is especially evident from the penal decisions of those centuries. Bishop Perpetuus of Tours (461-491) decreed in 474 that two deposed clerics were to receive their sustenance from the Church by

---

[24] Mansi, VII, 722; cf. Hefele-Leclercq, *Histoire des Conciles de l'Eglise,* III, 382.

[25] C. 3—Mansi, VII, 393.

[26] Migne, *Patrologiae Cursus Completus, Series Latina* (221 vols., Parisiis, 1844-1855), LIX, 47 (hereafter referred to as *MPL*) ; Jaffé, *Regesta Pontificum Romanorum ab Condita Ecclesia ad annum post Christum natum MCXCVIII* (editionem secundum correctam et auctam auspiciis Gulielmi Wattenbach curaverunt F. Kaltenbrunner, P. Ewald, S. Loewenfeld, 2 vols. in 1, Lipsiae, 1885-1888), n. 636 (hereafter referred to as JK, JE and JL respectively) ; Mansi, VIII, 856-857; c. 26, C. XII, q. 2.

[27] Mansi, VII, 973-974; it was later quoted by Gratian in c. 28, C. XII, q. 2. Cf. the Council of Agde (506), c. 36—Bruns, II, 153.

sharing in the daily distributions (*sportulae*) from the church income.[28] The II Council of Macon (585) deposed Faustianus, Bishop of Aix, and ordered his consecrators, Bishops Bertramnus, Orestes and Palladius, each to provide one hundred gold coins (*aurei*) every year for the support of the deposed bishop.[29] Pope St. Agapetus I (535-536) ordered that a Bishop Contumeliosus (who apparently had deserved his name), deposed by a provincial council, should be supported from the funds of his diocese.[30] The same Pope also ordered that the African bishops who abjured the Arian heresy should be received back into the Church, and should share in the daily distribution of goods (*sportulae*).[31]

The Church also showed a keen solicitude for the proper support of bishops and clerics who had unjustly been forced to leave their offices. Pope St. Gregory the Great (590-604) commanded the bishops of Italy to receive generously their persecuted confrères of Illyria, who had been driven into exile.[32] Likewise, bishops who because of ill health were forced to resign from the active ministry were supported from the income of their former sees.[33] Although most of these decisions applied to bishops, they naturally would also have applied, *mutatis mutandis,* to clerics other than bishops.

The principle of the early Church to provide fitting support for all clerics, even those who had shamefully betrayed their sacred office, found its legal expression in the Roman Law institute, called the *beneficium competentiae,* which guaranteed to one found guilty of a charge enough goods for his bodily support.[34]

---

[28] D'Achery, *Spicilegium sive collectio veterum aliquot scriptorum* (2. ed., 3 vols., Parisiis, 1723), I, 303.

[29] Mansi, IX, 960.

[30] JK, n. 890; Mansi, VIII, 856-857.

[31] Mansi, VIII, 849.

[32] Joannes Diaconus, *Vita Gregorii, MPL,* DXXV, 140.

[33] *Op. cit.—MPL,* LXXV, 201, 202.

[34] "A type distinct from these (actions) is found in actions in which the *condemnatio* was limited to the dependent's means: *'in id quod facere potest',* the so-called *beneficium competentiae* . . . *'Quod facere potest'* was not the same in all cases; in general it was literally taken, but a donor was allowed to retain the necessaries of life, 42. 1, 19. 1, and this may have been generalized under Justinian."—Buckland, *A Textbook of Roman Law* (Cambridge: University Press, 1932), p. 693. The Christian Church broadened

Thus, by the end of the sixth century, the Church had firmly established the principle that clerics were to be accorded a decent livelihood from the income of the Church, that this income was to be graded to some degree according to the merit of the cleric, that at least one-fourth of the income of the Church was to be devoted to the support of the clergy and one-fourth to the Bishop, that even delinquent clerics were to receive sustenance from the Church.[35] The imperial Roman law also acknowledged that the clergy deserved a respectable support, and in the East the Emperor gave a generous amount for their support.[36]

The situation in Constantinople was indicative of the fluctuating conditions of ecclesiastical support. Before the reign of Justinian (527-565), a number of churches had been built and endowed by generous Christians; the endowment consisted of property or property rights sufficient for the maintenance of the church and the clergy. In a series of misfortunes and misdemeanors the churches had lost their endowments. In this unfortunate situation, Justinian (desirous of controlling the Church through his governmental bureaucracy) decided to stabilize the income for the clergy and also the number of the clergy. The cathedral was to have the following complement of clerics, who were to take care of the religious services and spiritual needs of all the Christians in the city: 60 priests, 100 deacons, 40 deaconesses, 90 subdeacons, 110 lectors, 25 cantors,

---

the application of this principle, especially to cases involving delinquent clerics; cf. S. Riccobono, "*Cristianesimo e Diritto Privato,*" *Revista di Diritto Civile,* N. 1 (Milano, 1911), pp. 15, 49. Cf. also A. Levet, *Bénéfice de Competence* (Paris, 1927), pp. 239-241, who disagrees with Riccobono on the amount of goods left to the convicted person through the *beneficium competentiae,* but who readily admits that daily sustenance was included. C. (5. 18), 8; D. (50, 17), 173. The principle of the *beneficium competentiae* is incorporated in canon 122 of the present Code of Canon Law.

[35] In some localities, generous bishops divided the income of the Church into thirds, according one-third for the support of the clergy. Cf. Thomassinus, *Vetus et Nova Ecclesiae Disciplina circa Beneficia et Beneficiarios* (10 vols., Magontiaci, 1787), Pars III, L. 2, c. 11, n. 7 (hereafter referred to as Thomassinus).

[36] *Novellae Iustiniani,* (3.1) 2—*Corpus Iuris Civilis* (3 vols., Vol. III, *Novellae Constitutiones,* ed. stereotypa quinta, recognovit R. Schoell; opus Schoelli morte interceptum absolvit G. Kroll, Berolini: apud Weidmannos, 1928), III, 18-20 (hereafter referred to as *Novellae*).

100 door-keepers (*ostiarii*). These clerics were to live a community life, and no one could be ordained to replace them until a vacancy by death or a disability had actually occurred.[37]

To maintain the proper level of support for the clergy in the city, Justinian forbade the ordaining of any clerics in excess of the established number, despite his dubious argument that the law did not forbid the ordinations, but forbade only any additional emolument for the clergy.[38] Any protest that the legal number of clerics could not care for the existing churches in Constantinople was met by the order that they were to circulate and alternate in serving the various churches throughout the city.

The Church in the West, during the sixth century, had fared better than in the East in establishing landed wealth. The IV Council of Orleans (541) decreed that oratories could not be erected in the homes or estates of the wealthy unless the oratory was endowed with sufficient land to support the clergy attached to the oratory.[39] The Church in Gaul gradually acquired considerable land property which provided a secure endowment.

It is certain that by the end of the sixth century the principal resources of the Church in Gaul were large estates equipped with all the necessary buildings. In accordance with the contemporary economic system, the estate generally had a retinue of serfs.[40] These large estates were called *villae,* and the whole estate was divided into two sections: one reserved to the proprietor, the *mansus indominicatus,* and the other divided into tenures, called *hobae, casatae, mansi-serviles ingenuiles.*[41] The clergy, supported by the income from the *mansus* and the dependent tenures, had as stable

---

[37] *Novellae* (3. pr. 1).

[38] *Novellae* (3.2).

[39] Cc. 26, 33—Bruns, II, 206, 207.

[40] "*Dès la fin de l'époque romaine, les bien-fonds en deviennent l'élément principal . . . les établissements religieux feront necessairement figure de grands propriétaires terriens.*"—Carlo de Clercq, *La Législation Religieuse Franque de Clovis à Charlemagne* (Louvain, 1936), p. 303 (hereafter referred to as *La Législation Religieuse Franque*). Cf. Emile Lèsne, *Histoire de la Propriété Ecclésiastique en France* (3 vols., Lille, 1922), I, 205 (hereafter referred to as *La Propriété Ecclésiastique*).

[41] Lèsne, *La Propriété Ecclésiastique,* I, 211.

and sufficient a support as the landed gentry—as long as they were left unmolested in their rights.[42]

There were, by law, other sources of income for the Church, such as the tithes, the first-fruits, and the offerings, but the income from these was apparently very minor compared with that which accrued from the property of the Church. In fact, the payment of tithes had long been neglected by the time of the important II Council of Macon (585), an indication that the Church did not depend upon them as it had in the East in the earlier centuries.[43] Even in sections where the tithes were paid, it was done very irregularly and spasmodically.[44]

Hence, in Western Europe where the generosity of the laity endowed the Church with landed property, the clergy enjoyed a suitable and secure income. This situation prevailed at the end of the sixth century in most of Gaul, of Spain, and also in those parts of Germany and Italy where the Lombards did not harass the Church.[45]

---

[42] Although the Church profited from the labor of the serfs, as other landowners, it accorded them generally far better treatment than they secured at the hands of lay lords.—Lèsne, *La Propriété Ecclésiastique,* I, 229.

[43] C. 5: "Unde statuimus ac decernimus ut mos antiquus a fidelibus reparetur et decimas ecclesiasticas famulantibus ceremoniis populus omnis inferat."—Bruns, II, 250.

[44] Lèsne, *La Propriété Ecclésiastique,* I, 187.

[45] A. T. Fliche-V. Martin, *Histoire de l'Eglise* (9 vols., incomplete, Paris: Bloud and Gay, 1935), V, 38, 53 (hereafter referred to as *Histoire*).

CHAPTER II

The Carolingian Era

During the eighth century, Gaul (which today comprises France, Belgium, the Netherlands and part of Germany) became the strongest Catholic nation in the West. This political pre-eminence naturally brought with it a pre-eminence also in the affairs of the Western Church, with a consequent effect on the development of the canonical law of the Church.

The Church had grown sufficiently affluent during the Romanic and Merovingian periods in Gaul (henceforth more conveniently referred to as France) to excite the cupidity of the lay nobility. During the eighth century there occurred in France a steady confiscation of Church property on the part of the strong and greedy nobility, abetted by the weak royal power. This confiscation, chiefly wrought through the influence of Charles Martel, Frankish ruler of Austrasia (715-741), was partially justified by the necessity for ready resources to meet the onslaught of Islam which was storming France from Spain.[1]

After the victory of Poitiers (732) had relieved the Mohammedan threat to France, Charles Martel rewarded his adherents by ceding to them bishoprics and Church benefices, which then were either filled with unworthy candidates or allowed to remain vacant, while the court favorites pocketed the income. The condition of the Church was chaotic.[2]

As a consequence of this chaos and confiscation, the clergy in many instances were left destitute. The chronicler of the great

---

[1] Lèsne, *La Propriété Ecclésiastique*, II, 56.

[2] The Church in France, one learns on the authority of St. Boniface (1754), did not during part of the seventh and eighth centuries have any archbishop, any councils or synods, or any formation of canon law for seventy or eighty years!—*Letter of St. Boniface*, n. 50—*Monumenta Germaniae Historica* (MGH), *Epistolae Selectae*, I (ed. M. Tangl, Berolini, 1916), 81; De Clercq, *La Législation Religieuse Franque*, p. 111; Lèsne, *La Propriété Ecclésiastique*, II, 14 ff.

Abbey of St. Wandrille at Fontenelle lamented that Teutsindus, the illegally installed abbot, had so dissipated the wealth of the Abbey that its resources had been expended to feed dogs instead of monks. Later, Archbishop Hincmar of Rheims (845-882) complained that the few clerics who remained for the service of the cathedral were forced into business to support themselves.[3] This pillage of property extended even to small rural parishes, many of which had been robbed of almost everything.[4]

The complaints of pillage furnish an idea of the amount of property held by the small and rural parishes. Three rural parishes, whose property was later restored, had owned respectively two, six, and forty manses. A manse (*mansus*) was generally of variable extent, just as a farm today can be of almost any size, but the presumption is well-founded that those rural churches were well supported.[5]

After the death of Charles Martel, Pope Saint Zachary (741-752) and the great St. Boniface (673-754) set about to restore the means of maintenance of the Church in France. Carloman (741-747), the successor of Charles Martel, convoked a national council, the German Council—the territory of Germany and France constituted only one kingdom—to recover the ancients rights and possessions of the Church. Carloman courageously ordered the despoilers of the Church to return the wealth of the Church to its rightful owners.[6]

The degree of the King, supported by the enactment of the Church council, was not enough to cure immediately the vice of a generation. The following year, at the Council of Lessines (743), Carloman recognized the widespread non-compliance with the decree of the preceding council, and made a compromise necessitated by his need for money to finance his efforts to restrain the turbulence in the kingdom. By this compromise, Carloman allowed

[3] Lèsne, *La Propriété Ecclésiastique,* II, 24.

[4] Lèsne, *op. cit.,* II, 32.

[5] Lèsne, *loc. cit.* In the ninth century, each parish was to have an estate (*mansus*) consisting of twelve acres.—Hincmar, *Capitula Synodica,* II, c. 2—*Collectio Sirmondensis, Concilia Antiqua Galliae* (3 vols., Parisiis, 1629), III, 623.

[6] *Letter of Boniface,* n. 50—*MGH, Epistolae Selectae,* I, 81; *Capitulary of Carloman* (742), c. 1—*MGH, Leges* (5 vols., Vol. I, ed. G. H. Pertz, Hannoverae, 1835: Neudruck, Leipzig, 1925), I, 16.

the laity to retain temporarily their possession of Church property (seized by them) by paying the *precarium* and *census* to the Church —thus also enabling them to maintain their contributions to the support of the royal army. By this arrangement every small tenure (*casata*) was bound to pay a *solidus* (which consisted of twelve *denarii*) to the Church for its support. If this sum was not sufficient to provide for the maintenance of the Church which actually owned the property, the *precarium* was to be subscribed again. If this second payment still proved incapable of saving the Church and its clergy from penury, the possessions were to be restored to the Church—a very unlikely eventuality.[7]

As with all successful compromises, the compromise of Carloman tended to preserve a system it had hoped eventually to abolish. Hence, to understand the financial system of the Church in the Carolingian era, one must understand the concept of the *precarium* and the *census*. The *precarium* was the payment of a sum of money acknowledging the cession by the bishop (or a competent ecclesiastical authority) of the use and income of lands belonging to the Church; the *precarium* was important, not only as a substantial contribution to the support of the Church, but also as a recognition of the Church's right to its despoiled property. Originally the bishop had the right to revoke the concession at will, and at the death of the beneficiary the property reverted to the bishop, the proprietor. Though the immediate proprietor was considered to have the exclusive right, by Roman Law, to grant concessions on his property, the feudal concept, with its pyramiding of the rights of over-lords, which culminated in the supreme right of the kind over all the land in his kingdom, brought a change; by right of might, the king could cede the Church's property to someone without consulting the ecclesiastical proprietor. This illegal procedure was dignified by the title of *precarium verbo regis, precarium* by royal command.[8]

---

[7] Council of Lessines (743), c. 2—Mansi, XII, 371; *MGH,* Legum Sectio III (*Concilia*), II (*Concilia Aevi Karolini*), Pars I (ed. A. Werminghoff, Berolini, 1906), 7.

[8] It is not to the present purpose to discuss at length whether the ecclesiastical *precarium* was the direct derivative of the *precarium* in Roman Law. Undoubtedly the Church and the State added further elements to the original

The *census* was much smaller than the *precarium,* and was widely used as a tax. It often denoted a tribute or a payment for the use of land, and was thus understood in the Carolingian era.[9]

Carloman finally abdicated in 747, retiring to a monastery on the bleak but famous Mt. Soracte. He left the government to his brother Pepin (747-768), who succeeded in formally ousting the impotent Merovingian King, Childeric III (+755). Pepin, with the approbation of the reigning Pope Stephen III (752-757), became the acknowledged king.

Pepin enforced the payment of the *precarium* and *census,* for he considered it a necessary mollification of the Church's rightful demand for support in the absence of its rightful possession of its lands.[10]

The Frankish bishops assembled in 755 at Verneuil-sur-Oise and petitioned that the King restore the rights of the Church.[11] Ap-

concept, which was the grant of the possession and use of property, generally of land, to someone without any demand for a fee; the medieval *precarium* had the added element of payment for the usufruct of the property. In the Roman Law concept of *precarium,* the proprietor could regain possession at will; the medieval *precarium* always preserved, at least nominally, the essential element of the proprietor's right to the land and the revocability of his cession of the use of his property—even if the king or lord never budged from his ill-gained church property. Lèsne, *La Propriété Ecclésiastique,* I, 314. There was also a confusing looseness of terminology in regard to the *precarium.* Often the words *"precaria"* and *"precaturia"* were used; they referred generally to the letter written by the person imploring the concession of the use of the property.—Lèsne, *La Propriété Ecclésiastique, loc. cit.*

[9] Council of Frankfort (734), c. 25—*MGH,* Legum Sectio II (*Capitularia Regum Francorum*), I, (ed. A. Boretius, Hanoverae, 1883), 76; *Council of Chalon sur Saône* (813), c. 15, 17—*MGH,* Legum Sectio III (*Concilia*), II (*Concilia Aevi Karolini*), Pars I, 277.

[10] Though Pepin in general favored the vindication of the rights of the Church, he was not above occasionally winking at the sacrilegious seizure of a church benefice; he installed a favorite, Remi, in the Church of Langres, who then gave the dependent Church of Bèze to his courtesan.—Lèsne, *La Propriété Ecclésiastique,* II, 24. On the other hand, after his conquest of Aquitaine, Pepin ordered that the possessions still held by the Church in that territory be left undisturbed, and that the *precarium* be paid on the Church possessions seized by laymen. Cf. *Capitulary of Aquitaine,* c. 3, 11—*MGH,* Legum Sectio II (*Capitularia Regum Francorum*), I, 43.

[11] Council of Verneuil-sur-Oise (755), Preface—Mansi, XII, 579.

parently Pepin realized that his temporizing in returning the possessions of the Church, despite his insistence on the payment of the *precarium* and the *census,* was a grievous injustice. At any rate, he decided to assist the Church, but not at the price of estranging the nobility; as usual, he compromised, decreeing that everyone should pay the long neglected tithe, but allowing those who held Church property still to continue in possession of those lands. At the end of a letter addressed to the bishops of his realm in 764, in which he ordered the recitation of the litanies in thanksgiving for a beneficial harvest, he suddenly and peremptorily ordered the payment of the tithe. Everyone, not only the wealthy, was obliged to pay the tithe.[12]

Then, shortly after he had commanded everyone to pay the tithe, Pepin further decreed another payment to the Church in recompense for its despoiled property. The new levy, called the double title (*nona, novalia*), was imposed only on those who occupied lands belonging to a church. It is difficult to determine when this double-tithe was first levied, but it is probable that it was imposed by Pepin at the same time he imposed the tithe, or shortly thereafter.[13]

This double-tithe, also called a ninth, was actually a ninth of the revenue which remained after the subtraction of the tithe. The tithe and double-tithe amounted to two-tenths of the revenue, regardless of which way it was computed.[14] The double-tithe, since it was a recompense for the means of sustenance taken from a church, was paid to the church which was despoiled of its property,

---

[12] "Et sic previdere faciatis et ordinare de verbo nostro ut unusquisque homo, aut vellet aut nollet, suam decimam donet."—*Encyclica de Litaniis Faciendis (764)—MGH, Leges,* I, 32. The concept of the tithe was applied to almost everything; some considered the season of Lent a tithe of the year to be rendered to God.—VIII Council of Toledo (653), c. 9—Bruns, I, 282.

[13] Lèsne, *Le Propriété Ecclésiastique,* II, 108. Agreeing with Lèsne on this surmise is E. Perels, Die Ursprünge des karolingischen Zehntrechtes, *Archiv fur Urkundenforschung* (Berlin & Leipzig, 1908), IV (1911), 203. Another opinion holds that the double tithe was instituted later.—U. Stutz, Das karolingische Zehntgebot, zugleich ein Betrag zur Erklärung von c. 7 und 13 des Kapitulars von Heristall," *Zeitschrift des Savigny Stiftung für Rechtsgeschichte, Germanistische Abteilung* (Weimar, 1880-), XXIX (1908), 202.

[14] Lèsne, *La Propriété Ecclésiastique,* II, 108.

not to the bishop (unless he was the direct administrator of the land, that is, if the land belonged to the cathedral or a church dependent on the cathedral). Since in some cases the bishop permitted the tithe to be paid directly to the parish, instead of to the bishop (who made the distribution of the portions), some parishes received both the tithe and the double-tithe.[15]

The granting of the tithe and the double-tithe, though they delayed the return of the Church's property, enabled the Church to maintain the clergy and the ecclesiastical buildings in a fitting manner.

It was during this time that the great Bishop of Metz, Chrodegang (742-766), acting as apostolic legate at the Council of Verneuil-sur-Oise in 755, drew up his famous Rule for the community life of the secular canons in his diocese. Owing to his reputation both at the royal court and at Rome, the policy of Chrodegang enjoyed singular favor.[16] The Rule was so specific concerning the duties, rights, and sustenance of clerics, that from it one can gather a rather comprehensive idea of the current concept of a fitting support for the clergy.[17] The purpose of the Bishop

---

[15] Lèsne, *La Propriété Ecclésiastique,* II, 108, 109.

[16] Chrodegang is supposed to have been the secretary of Charles Martel, later his chancellor, and finally, in 737, his prime minister. On March 1, 742, he was appointed bishop of Metz, but at the request of Pepin retained his civil post.—Mansi, XIV, 313; *Life of Chrodegang—MGH, Scriptores,* X (30 vols. in 31, Vol. X, ed. G. Pertz, Hannoverae, 1852; Neudruck, Leipzig, 1925), X, 552-572.

[17] The original Rule of Chrodegang was short, consisting of only thirty-four canons or chapters. At a later time interpolations were added, presumably by Angilramnus, successor to Chrodegang in the See of Metz (768-791). Finally the Rule, with further additions, was promulgated for the canons of the whole kingdom of France by the Council of Aachen (816). ". . . eine früher allein bekannte Form war alledrings interpoliert und mit späteren Zusätzen, besonders aus den Aachener Statuten, versehen. Indes enthält ein von Heidelberg in die Vatikana gekommener Codex, 'ziemlich deutlichen Anzeichen nach,' die ursprüngliche Regel, zu welcher bereits Chrodegangs Nachfolger, Angilran, einen Zusatz machte."—Max Heimbucher, *Die Orden und Kongregationen* (2. ed., 3 vols., Paderborn, 1907-1908), II, 4; Mansi, XIV, 332. To distinguish the provisions of the three different editions of the Rule of Chrodegang, the writer will refer to the original Rule simply as "*Rule,*" to the later rule as the "*Enlarged Rule*" and to the other regulations

was to draw up a practical rule, not so strict that it would discourage any except the ascetical, but not so lax that it would not insure compliance with a high priestly standard.[18] The Rule was intended for all the secular canons—those clerics who lived a community life *secundum canones*—and the good Bishop used all his paternal influence to prevail on his priests to become canons, but without complete success.[19]

First, the Rule enjoined the performance of a great deal of charitable work. The parish church was not only the center of the religious life of the community, it was also the center of all the charitable and social work of the community, and cared especially for the poor, the sick, and the pilgrims.[20]

Pastors and ecclesiastical superiors were commanded to prepare a place of reception or refuge (*hospitale*) for the poor, and to allocate enough goods for their care. The impoverished lesser nobility were a special type of poor (*matricularii*), who were entitled to have a representative collect alms at the door; they also performed certain services for the church, such as protection.[21] The only portion of the church's income that could not be diverted to this work of charity was the tithe paid to the church from its estates (*villae*).[22]

The canons, as well as all parishes, were to afford hospitality to the sick and to pilgrims. For this purpose hospices (*xenodochia*) were to be built and maintained.[23] These hospitals provided care

---

as canons of the Council of Aachen (816). The Rule of Chrodegang is printed in Mansi, XIV, 314 ff.; the Enlarged Rule is found in Mansi, XIV, 332 ff.

[18] ". . . ut quantum possumus, si non quantum debemus, ad rectitudinis lineam, Deo inspirante, clerum nostrum reducamus."—Introduction to the Rule—Mansi, XIV, 314.

[19] Mansi, XIV, 314.

[20] "Le budget des églises absorbant toutes les dépenses d'un caractère religieux, social, charitable, leur temporel devient le vaste reservoir des ressources destinées à y faire."—Lèsne, *La Propriété Ecclésiastique,* I, 146-147; Fliche-Martin, *Histoire,* V, 563.

[21] *Rule,* c. 34—Mansi, XIV, 332; Lèsne, *La Propriété Ecclésiastique,* II, 380-389; Fliche-Martin, *Histoire,* V, 564.

[22] Council of Aachen (816), c. 141—Mansi, XIV, 242; *MGH,* Legum Sectio III (*Concilia*), II (*Concilia Aevi Karolini*) Pars I, 416.

[23] Council of Aachen (816), c. 141—*MGH, op. cit., loc cit.;* Fliche-Martin, *Histoire,* V, 564.

for incurables, and were accessible also to pilgrims, who apparently found them such a boom to making pilgrimages that some never stayed home.[24]

Hospitality to visiting clerics was also a strict duty. The Rule provided that all clerics who attended the Divine Office and High Mass on major feast days were to be fed in the refectory of the canonry.[25]

Thus the duties of charity were so great that they normally required one-third of the income of the canonry or the parishes; but the only part of the income that could not be diverted to meeting these expenses was the revenue from the estates of the church.[26] The importance that the Rule attached to the performance of these duties by the canons is seen from the penalty meted out to a cleric who was negligent in the performance of them—he was to be punished worse than other delinquents, and was to be removed from office.[27]

It is obvious then that a parish needed a large income to enable it to discharge its obligations of charity (besides the contributions due to the bishop)—duties which could never be ignored.

The Rule imposed no obligation of poverty upon the canons. It was presumed that each priest, before entering the canonical life, enjoyed a benefice or owned some private property; upon entering the canonical life, clerics agreed to donate their goods to the community, but retained the right to the income from their property during their lifetime.[28] At least some of the canons owned considerable property, since the Rule alludes to donations of fields, forests, pasture lands and other valuable assets.[29]

---

[24] Gougaud, *Les Chrétientés Celtiques* (Paris, 1911), pp. 166 ff.; Council of Meaux (845), c. 40—Mansi, XIV, 827.

[25] *Rule,* c. 30—Mansi, XIV, 327.

[26] Council of Aachen (816), c. 141—Mansi, XIV, 242; *MGH,* Legum Sectio III (*Concilia*), II (*Concilia Aevi Karolini*), Pars I, 416.

[27] Council of Aachen (816), c. 141, ". . . severius quam ceteri delinquentes a prepositis iudicandus est, et a ministerio removendus."—Mansi, XIV, 243; *MGH, loc. cit.*

[28] *Rule,* c. 31, ". . . de rebus quas possidet ad ecclesiam beati Pauli Apostoli solemnem donationem per praesentem faciat, reservato tamen tempore vitae suae usufructuario ordine."—Mansi, XIV, 328.

[29] *Rule,* c. 31—Mansi, XIV, 328. The insistence on the right of the private administration of the income from property finally led to the abandonment

The canons also augmented their income by accepting stipends offered for the celebration of the Mass, on the occasion of the conferring of the sacraments, or by way of bequests.[30]

It is apparent that the founder of the Rule and also other ecclesiastical authorities had no thought of reducing all clerics to a uniform income, nor did they think that all clerics would have the same financial obligations—though they later stated that all clerics should have the same quantity of the necessities of life, i.e., food, dress, and drink. There was a consciousness of the ancient rule of Pope Simplicius, namely, that clerics should be rewarded according to merit, though all were required to give excess goods to the poor. This attitude had received recognition much earlier in the Council of Merida (666), which allowed the bishop to reward deserving clerics with a greater income, thus to encourage others to greater efforts. Obviously, clerics who had achieved some eminence, by rank or by personal effort, were to have a greater income than others.[31]

The ecclesiastical authorities were so intent on affording a decent livelihood to every canon that they strictly condemned those who for vain glory erected canonries which did not yield an income sufficient to sustain the canons.[32]

The canons were obliged to live a community life, which included sleeping in dormitories, but some canons were permitted to have separate apartments or rooms (*mansiones*) distinct from the common dormitory.[33]

---

of the canonical life in some areas, since community living and private ownership seemed psychologically incompatible.—Heimbucher, *Die Orden und Kongregationen,* II, 7.

[30] *Rule,* c. 32—Mansi, XIV, 330. The word "*stipendium*" seems to have been used in an equivocal sense—to denote an offering made to the priest for the celebration of Mass and the administration of the sacraments, and also for the portion given by the bishop to the priest for his sustenance.—De Clercq, *La Législation Religieuse Franque,* pp. 11-12.

[31] C. 13: ". . . haec enim causa et majoribus majorem praestat gratiam et minores excitat ut ad melius tendant."—Bruns, II, 90.

[32] *Enlarged Rule,* c. 3—Mansi, XIV, 332; Council of Aachen (816), c. 118—Mansi, XIV, 230; *MGH,* Legum Sectio III, (*Concilia*), II (*Concilia Aevi Karolini*), Pars I, 398, 399.

[33] *Rule,* c. 3—Mansi, XIV, 316.

There was also a common refectory, and the Rule was almost as precise as the Army in prescribing the menu. The daily fare included bread, meat, cereals, vegetables, relishes, and wine or beer (when available).[34] Ordinarily the canons ate two meals daily, but on fast days, in conformity with the discipline of the Church, there was allowed only one principal meal, which consisted of cereals (*cibaria*), cheese or fish, vegetables and relish.[35]

Since wine was one of the staples of life, the Rule also provided for it in the daily fare. A more liberal allowance was approved for regions where vineyards abounded, but the superior was obliged to procure beer or another substitute if no wine was available.[36] When no wine or beverage was available, the canons were exhorted to bear the trial patiently, and they were strongly cautioned against drunkenness.[37]

The Rule also provided, with the same spirit of discretion and practicality, for the adequate but unostentatious dress of the canons. Any immoderate or unusual mode of dress was to be avoided; this included wearing either worldly dress or affecting the habit of a monk.[38] Also, at regular intervals, new clothing was provided the canons.[39]

---

[34] *Rule,* c. 22—Mansi, XIV, 324. The first Rule decreed that each canon was to receive as much bread as he needed (c. 22), "quod sufficiet accipiat," but later a definite amount, three pounds in our weight, was allotted each day as the maximum.—*Enlarged Rule,* c. 7—Mansi, XIV, 333; Council of Aachen (816), c. 122—Mansi, XIV, 233; *MGH,* Legum Sectio III, (*Concilia*), II (*Concilia Aevi Karolini*), Pars I, 301.

[35] *Rule,* c. 22—Mansi, XIV, 324.

[36] At first the *Rule* (c. 23) provided for a difference in the allotment of wine according to rank, priests and deacons receiving three goblets (*calices*) of wine at the noon meal, and two in the evening—Mansi, XIV, 325. Later (c. 8 of *Enlarged Rule*) all the canons were given five pounds (*libras*) of wine a day, which possibly corresponded to the former allotment for priests and deacons; each "pound" consisted of twelve ounces.—Mansi, XIV, 333; Council of Aachen (816), c. 122—*MGH, loc. cit.* Those who disliked wine were to have an equal amount of beer.—Mansi, XIV, 324.

[37] *Rule,* c. 23—Mansi, XIV, 324.

[38] *Enlarged Rule,* cc. 52, 53—Mansi, XIV, 338.

[39] The original *Rule* (c. 24) provided that the older canons were to receive new capes and woolen gowns, thus enabling them to pass down their worn

Finally, the Rule provided security and adequate treatment for any of the infirm or aged canons. If a canon fell sick, he was to receive immediate care, which included having a separate room assigned to him and a cleric attending to his needs. The infirm canon was allowed to have his meals at any time he desired if it was not possible for him to receive his meals at the regular hours.[40]

Although the Rule secured a decent and assured sustenance for the canons, it also interposed an effective bar to avarice and greed by embodying the law that a priest could be pastor of only one church.[41]

The more liberal allowances as made in the later additions to the primitive Rule were evidence of the improvement in the material prosperity of the Church during the reign of Charlemagne (768-814). Charlemagne accomplished his great aid to the Church by insisting on the observance of the statutes made by his predecessors, and especially by encouraging gifts to the Church.[42]

These gifts, which gradually built up a considerable patrimony for the Church, came from all classes of society.[43] Charlemagne cut through the mesh of feudal law that entangled property ownership, and made it possible for the Church to be the undisputed proprietor of goods given or bequeathed to it. This bold action not only conveyed the property to the Church, but it secured it legally against the avarice of the lords. Charlemagne drew up a list of things that could be given to the clergy, and the list is so extensive that it

---

capes and gowns to the younger clergy.—Mansi, XIV, 325. Later, according to c. 41 of the *Enlarged Rule,* new clothes of all types, including outer garments, underwear, and shoes were to be provided each year to all the canons.—Mansi, XIV, 325. Curiously, even the time for issuing the items of clothing was determined: the cape and gowns were to be received at the beginning of the winter, on the feast of St. Martin; the shirts were issued at Easter, and the shoes in the middle of September.—Mansi, XIV, 325.

[40] *Rule,* c. 28—Mansi, XIV, 326.

[41] *Enlarged Rule,* c. 67—Mansi, XIV, 340.

[42] The Council of Chalon-sur-Saône (813), in c. 18 commanded the payment of tithes under pain of excommunication.—*MGH,* Legum Sectio III (*Concilia*), II (*Concilia Aevi Karolini*), Pars I, 277.

[43] Lèsne, *La Propriété Ecclésiastique,* I, 158.

strains the imagination to find something of real value that was not included in it.[44]

These gifts to the Church could be divided into those that were offered on the occasion of the conferring of a sacrament, and those that were bequeathed by testamentary disposition. The clergy received a stipulated portion of the goods or of the revenue from the gifts (such as lands and pastures).

Offerings were made every Sunday at Mass, and in some places at daily Mass.[45] Doubtless the generosity of the faithful was stimulated in some places by the practice of announcing aloud in church the name of the donor before he contributed—until the Church forbade this practice.[46] The stipends which the priest received for celebrating Mass could be kept entirely, as also the offerings made on the occasion of the conferral of the sacraments.[47]

The great increase in the material prosperity for the Church during the reign of Charlemagne was due primarily to his legislation on gifts by will and to his personal example of generosity.[48] In his will Charlemagne gave eleven-twelfths of his movable goods to his children.[49] The immovable goods, namely, the lands of his realm, naturally fell to his successors.

The custom of leaving goods and property to the Church through one's will became so universal that the Church was led to decree

---

[44] *Capitulare Legibus Auditum* (803), c. 6—*MGH,* Legum Sectio II (*Capitularia Regum Francorum*), I, 113; Ansegisus, *Collectio Capitularium,* L. I, c. 135—*MGH,* Legum Sectio II (*Capitularia Regum Francorum*), I, 399 (hereafter referred to as *Collectio*).

[45] Thomassinus, Pars III, L. 2, c. 14, n. 5.

[46] Council of Frankfort (794), c. 51—*MGH,* Legum Sectio III (*Concilia*), II (*Concilia Aevi Karolini*), Pars I, 171. Most of these offerings of food were distributed by the priest to the poor, but frequently an extra portion was given explicitly for the use of the priest.—Regino, *Libri Duo de Synodalibus Causis,* lib. I, c. 1, n. 65—*MPL,* CXXXII, 187, 204 (hereafter referred to as Regino); Thomassinus, Pars III, L. 1, c. 14, n. 6; Council of Frankfort (794), c. 51—Mansi, XII, 908.

[47] *Rule,* c. 32—Mansi, XIV, 330.

[48] Thomassinus, Pars III, lib. 1, c. 23, n. 6; Lèsne, *La Propriété Ecclésiastique,* I, 161.

[49] Baluzius, *Capitularia Regum Francorum* (2 vols., Paris, 1780), I, 487; *Gallia Christiana* (16 vols., ed. D. Sammarthanus—P. Piolin, Romae et Parisiis, 1870), II, 254.

that no one was to be forced to conform to that custom.[50] Those who tricked or circumvented people into bequeathing them property were considered guilty of seizing the possessions by violence, and therefore were bound to restore such goods.[51] Although at one time, under the Frankish law, one could give all his possessions to the Church,[52] it was finally enacted that two-thirds of the deceased person's estate was to belong to his family heirs, and only one-third could be willed to the Church; in a later period, no more than one-third could be given to the Church without the consent of the heirs.[53]

Although this legislation and personal generosity of Charlemagne aided primarily the canons, who were extolled by both Church and State as the exponents of the ideal clerical life for seculars,[54] the parish priests who were not canons were also aided thereby. The laws which aided canons, who often held benefices other than canonries, aided equally the parish priests who were not canons.[55]

A series of laws during the reign of Charlemagne made secure the income of the parish priests who were not canons. The Council of Aachen (789) renewed the legislation that no one could be ordained unless he was assigned to a church for his support.[56]

---

[50] Council of Chalon-sur-Saône (813), c. 6—*MGH,* Legum Sectio III (*Concilia*), II (*Concilia Aevi Karolini*), Pars I, 275.

[51] Council of Chalon-sur-Saône (813), c. 7—*MGH, op. cit., loc. cit.*

[52] *Capitula Legibus Addenda* (*818-819*), c. 6—*MGH,* Legum Sectio II (*Capitularia Regum Francorum*), I, 282.

[53] Synod of Worcester (1240), c. 50—Mansi, XXIII, 541; Thomassinus, Pars III, L. I, c. 22, n. 1.

[54] Council of Aachen (816), c. 115: "Quia evidenti auctoritati liquet, canonicam institutionem ceteris praestare institutionibus."—*MGH,* Legum Sectio III (*Concilia*), II (*Concilia Aevi Karolini*), Pars I, 397.

[55] Actually, at this period, there was a fostering of contrary concepts towards the secular clergy. The canonical life with its emphasis on sharing common property, was extolled as the ideal life for the clergy, yet the legislation and generosity of the faithful rightly conferred a secure and sufficient income for the parish priests who were not canons. The opposition between these concepts was only psychological, not real, since a priest could own a great deal of property and still elect the community life of a canon; eventually the improved status of the parish clergy proved a detriment to the development of the canonical life.

[56] Ansegisus, *Collectio,* I, c. 25—*MGH,* Legum Sectio II (*Capitularia Regum Francorum*), I, 399.

Also, clerics were not allowed to leave the church for which they had been ordained, nor could they care for souls at more than one church.[57] All support was to come from the church to which they were assigned, since no cleric was allowed to engage in secular business.[58]

With characteristic thoroughness, Charlemagne decreed the amount of property required for the minimum decent support of a parish church. The property naturally consisted of land, the most stable form of wealth. Each church was to have at least one estate, or farm, which was to be absolutely free of all obligations to civil authorities. These immunities from taxation were not left to the interpretation of the local civil authorities—they were specified; no levy was to be made on the tithes, offerings of the faithful, houses belonging to the estate, or orchards. The only taxes or obligation to be paid from this estate (*mansus integer*) were those due to the ecclesiastical authorities.[59] Thenceforth the *mansus integer* became the recognized unit of property as required for the support of a church; even the priests in private churches on manorial estates were to have at least one plot of land (*mansus*) free of obligation.[60]

---

[57] Ansegisus, *Collectio, loc. cit.;* II General Council of Nicaea (787), cc. 10, 15—Hardouin, IV, 769, 770.

[58] *Ecclesiastical Capitulary* (789), c. 23—*MGH,* Legum Sectio II (*Capitularia Regum Francorum*), I, 55; Ansegisus, *Collectio,* I, c. 22—*op. cit.,* I, 399.

[59] Ansegisus, *Collectio,* I, c. 85: "Sancitum est ut unicuique ecclesiae unus mansus integer absque servitio alio attribuatur, et presbyteri in eis constituti non de decimis neque de oblationibus fidelium, non de domibus neque de atriis vel ortis juxta ecclesiam positis neque de praescripto manso aliquod servitium faciant praeter ecclesiasticum. Et si aliquod amplius habuerit, inde senioribus suis debitum servitium impendant."—*MGH,* Legum Sectio II (*Capitularia Regum Francorum*), I, 407. This famous decree was often quoted and has been attributed to the Capitulary of Worms (829), c. 4—*MGH,* Legum Sectio II (*Capitularia Regum Francorum*), II, 12; it was also included in the Council of Aachen (829), according to Jacques Sirmond's *Concilia Antiqua Galliae,* II, 431, but the canon appears earlier, in the *Ecclesiastical Capitulary* (818-819), c. 10—*MGH,* Legum Sectio II (*Capitularia Regum Francorum*), I, 277.

[60] *Ecclesiastical Capitulary* (818-819), c. 10—*MGH,* Legum Sectio II (*Capitularia Regum Francorum*), I, 277.

Of course there had been other royal and ecclesiastical laws concerning the rights and immunities of the clergy and their property, but they had been unsuccessful. The Council of Verneuil-sur-Oise (755) decreed that "all ecclesiastical immunities" should be preserved, but this general canon proved ineffective.[61]

Since this immunity from civil taxes and obligations was granted only to that unit of property, the *mansus integer,* which was required for the support of the clergy of the parish, it was necessary to estimate the extent of a *mansus.* A mansus was an estate, including lands and buildings, large enough to support a free man and his dependents; the income was large enough to enable him to discharge all his obligations both ecclesiastic and civil.[62] The Council of Metz (888) determined that the property of the *mansus* immune from obligations consisted of the farm lands, cemetery, four serfs and their children. The land of the mansus was therefore large enough to require the services of four serfs—a sizable estate.[63]

Archbishop Hincmar of Rheims (845-882) enjoined his judges and deacons, in making their investigations, to determine if each parish possessed a *mansus* consisting of twelve acres (*bunnuaria*) besides the land for the cemetery, the necessary farm buildings, the home, and four serfs. Obviously Hincmar considered this a minimum amount of property for the support of a church.[64] The relative value of such an estate in those days can be learned if one compares it with the estate of six acres (*bunnuaria*) allotted by the

---

[61] C. 19—Sirmond, *Concilia Antiqua Galliae,* II, 33; *MGH,* Legum Sectio II (*Capitularia Regum Francorum*), I, 36.

[62] *Glossa* s.v. *manso,* ad c. 25, C. XXIII, 98; Gonzalez-Tellez, *Commentaria Perpetua in Singulos Textus Quinque Librorum Decretalium Gregorii* IX (5 vols. in 4, Venetiis, 1699), III, 582 (hereafter referred to as *Commentaria*); Cardinalis Hostiensis (Henricus de Segusio), *Commentaria in Quinque Libros Decretalium* (5 vols. in 3, Venetiis, 1581), III, 149 (hereafter referred to as *Commentaria*); Cujaccius, *Omnia Opera* (13 vols. in 12, Prati, 1840), X, 856.

[63] C. 4—Sirmond, *Concilia Antiqua Galliae,* III, 526. The words *"pro quattuor mancipiis"* refer to serfs, although the word *mancipia* could refer to small tenures of land, since it was used to denote both the serf and the tenure of land worked by him.

[64] Hincmar, *Capitula Synodica,* II, c. 2—Sirmond, *Concilia Antiqua Galliae,* III, 623.

Monastery of Corbeil to a miller, a well-to-do member of the community in those days.[65]

The amount of land required for a *mansus* differed somewhat according to the fertility of the region and the prevailing standard of living in that section. There was a very liberal allowance for the support of the parish clergy in Hungary; by royal decree, each church had two *mansi* equipped with serfs, horse and cattle, six oxen and two cows, and thirty-four domestic fowl. A church thus equipped was to be built by every ten large estates (*villae*).[66]

The Church in Spain, a century before Charlemagne, had decreed that, unless a church was supported by at least ten households or small estates, it was not to have a resident pastor, but was to be joined with another parish. Such parishes were so indigent that the portion of income normally due the bishop was used for the repair of the church.[67]

All property in excess of this *mansus integer* belonging to a church was to be subject to the obligations and taxes due to the civil authorities, or to those who had donated the lands.[68]

Besides the obligations due to the lay authorities or lords, the *mansus* owed certain obligations to the bishop. Besides the one-fourth of the tithes due the bishop,[69] and the cathedraticum, which usually amounted to two *solidi*,[70] the parish priest was also bound to make an offering on the occasion of the visitation by the bishop. To prevent any abuses, the amount of this offering was fixed at

---

[65] *Statuta Antiqua Corbeiensis Monasterii*, I, c. 7—quoted from DuCange, *Glossarium* (9. ed., 10 vols., Paris, Librairie des Sciences et des Arts, 1938), V. 208.

[66] S. Endlicher, *Die Gesetze des heiligen Stefan* (Wien, 1849), Lib. II, c. 1, p. 47.

[67] XVI Provincial Council of Toledo (639), c. 5—Bruns, I, 370.

[68] The commentators generally agree that the words "*senioribus suis debitum servitium impendant*" refer to the civil authorities or to those who donated the land in excess of the *mansus integer.*—Gonzalez-Tellez, *Commentaria*, s.v., *senioribus*, ad c. 1, X, *de censibus, exactionibus et procurationibus*, III, 39; Hostiensis, *Commentaria*, s.v., *senioribus*, c. 1, X, *de censibus, exactionibus et procurationibus*, III, 39.

[69] Hincmar, *Capitula Syndica*, II, c. 16—Sirmond, *Concilia Antiqua Galliae*, III, 624.

[70] II Council of Braga (572), c. 2—Bruns, II, 40: C. 1, C. X, q. 3.

two *solidi,* or its equivalent; the equivalent was reckoned at a peck of barley, a measure of wine, and a small pig or sheep worth half a *solidus.* This decree simply revived a canon of the VII Council of Toledo (646), which in turn had repeated a canon from the II Council of Braga (572).[71] The bishop was forbidden to collect this offering for a visitation more than once a year, regardless of how many visitations he made.[72] If the bishop made no visitation, he could not demand the offering. To obviate any possible circumvention of this law, the bishop also was forbidden to divide the parishes simply for the sake of securing contributions from more parishes. The law, therefore, effectively protected the parish priest from the avarice of the prelates.[73]

Actually, a great proportion of the income of the church was devoted to the support of the poor and dependents of the church. Each parish was obliged to have its hospice, and this support of the poor was such a heavy drain on the parish finances, that in affluent parishes two-thirds of the offerings were devoted to the poor; in poorer parishes the priest was required to give only a half of the offerings for the poor—thus to allow the priest enough for himself and for the other members of his household.[74] The priests were required to support their indigent near-relatives from their own income, and were specifically forbidden to support them from funds destined for the other poor of the parish, unless there were exceptional circumstances.[75] The parish clergy were expected to be particularly generous in times of famine, even to the point of devoting all possible resources, including the *annona* (contribution of grain by the parishioners) to the relief of the poor.[76]

---

[71] Council of Toulouse (843), c. 2.—Sirmond, *Concilia Antiqua Galliae,* III, 2; VII Council of Toledo (646), c. 4—Bruns, II, 263; II Council of Braga (572), c. 2—Bruns, II, 40.

[72] Council of Toulouse (843), c. 5—Sirmond, *Concilia Antiqua Galliae,* III, 2.

[73] Council of Toulouse (843), c. 6, 7—Sirmond, *Concilia Antiqua Galliae,* III, 2.

[74] Ansegisus, *Collectio,* I, cc. 70, 80—*MGH,* Legum Sectio II (*Capitularia Regum Francorum*), I, 403, 404.

[75] Hincmar, *Capitula Synodica,* II, c. 16—Sirmond, *Concilia Antiqua Galliae,* III, 624.

[76] Ansegisus, *Collectio,* I, c. 126—*MGH,* Legum Sectio III (*Capitularia Regum Francorum*), I, 411.

Although, as ever, the power of the bishop over all ecclesiastical property in his diocese was acknowledged,[77] there was an increased independence of the parish priest in the administration of the parish funds—which was a further guarantee of at least an equitable share of the income for the pastor. Instead of receiving an allotment from the bishop (as in the early centuries), the parish priest collected and divided the income. There was a prescribed procedure for the division of the tithes, which procedure postulated the presence of qualified witnesses of the division and the issuance of a written receipt to those who contributed.[78] If one accepts literally the provisions of the law, the priests were allowed to keep one-third of the tithes and double-tithes, without any payment to the bishop; the remaining two-thirds went to the support of the buildings of the church and for the support of the poor.[79]

This decree, which actually derogated from the ancient law of the division of the church income into four parts, was not unprecedented. The Frankish Church was simply following again the law and the practice of the then practically extinct Spanish Church (through the occupation of the Moors), since the Council of Merida in the year 666 had decreed that the income of the Church was to be divided into three parts, and the third was to be used for the restoration or maintenance of the churches instead of being sent to the bishop. This decree was renewed at the XVI Council of Toledo (693), which also added that, if the churches were in a state of good repair, the bishop could retain the third of the income due him.[80] The Spanish bishops realized that they were changing

[77] *Ecclesiastical Capitulary* (*810-813*), c. 4—*MGH,* Legum Sectio II (*Capitularia Regum Francorum*), I, 178.

[78] *Capitulary for Priests* (*802*), c. 7—*MGH,* Legum Sectio II (*Capitularia Regum Francorum*), I, 106.

[79] *Capitulary for Priests* (*802*), c. 7: "Ut ipsi sacerdotes populi suscipiant decimas et nona eorum et quicumque dederint scripta habeant et secundum auctoritatem canonicam coram testibus dividant. Et ad ornamentum ecclesiae primam partem eligant, secundum autem ad usum pauperum atque peregrinorum . . . tertiam vero partem semetipsis solis sacerdotes reservent."—*MGH,* Legum Sectio II (*Capitularia Regum Francorum*), I, 106. Later, at the time of Hincmar, the bishop was accorded one-fourth of the tithes.—*Capitula Synodica,* II, c. 16—Sirmond, *Concilia Antiqua Galliae,* III, 624.

[80] Council of Merida (666), c. 16—Bruns, II, 91: XVI Council of Toledo (693), c. 5—Bruns, I, 370.

the ancient law of the Church, but apparently felt empowered to change such an ecclesiastical law for the benefit of the Church in that region. In fact, they also ordered that the money offered in church on feast days be also divided in three parts.[81] The action of the bishops in Spain and in the Frankish Kingdom did not derogate from the ancient law in the other sections of Christendon, nor did it even cause that law to be forgotten before it was again revived in France and Spain.

Charlemagne, with a view to increasing the income of the parishes, requested the bishops to renew the command upon the faithful to pay the tithe, the *census* and the double-tithe (if so obligated); to facilitate this, each parish was to have clear and definite limits.[82] As a further safeguard against the spoliation of church property, Charlemagne ordered an inventory made of church possessions; hence, no despoiler could support a claim of bona fide possession.[83] The pastors were also enjoined to give an account of their administration of the funds of the parish, and to maintain a close scrutiny of the treasures of the church, for some merchants and Jewish traders had boasted that they could buy from churches whatever they wished.[84]

Besides securing substantial support for the parish clergy, the lay and ecclesiastical authorities during the Carolingian era enacted laws to discourage avarice on the part of the clergy. No church property could be alienated, for the personal gain of him who so acted, by a cleric of any rank.[85] Further, each priest was

[81] XVI Council of Toledo (693), c. 5: "Nam sicut antiquitas de causis ingruentibus edicta multimoda edidit, ita nunc nostri temporis aetas de his quae occurrunt, ut fiant, convenit. . . ."—Bruns, I, 370; Council of Merida (666), c. 14—Bruns, II, 91.

[82] Council of Frankfort (794), c. 25—*MGH*, Legum Sectio II (*Capitularia Regum Francorum*), I, 76; *Ecclesiastical Capitulary* (*818-819*), c. 9—*ibid.*, p. 277; Ansegisus, *Collectio*, I, c. 146—*MGH*, Legum Sectio II (*Capitularia Regum Francorum*), I, 412.

[83] *Capitulary of the Royal Representatives* (MISSORUM) *Promulgated at Nijmegen* (*806*), c. 3, 4—*MGH*, Legum Sectio II (*Capitularia Regum Francorum*), I, 131.

[84] Ansegisus, *Collectio*, I, c. 117—*MGH*, Legum Sectio II (*Capitularia Regum Francorum*), I, 410; IX Council of Toledo (655), c. 4—Bruns, I, 293.

[85] Ansegisus, *Collectio*, II, c. 29—*MGH*, Legum Sectio II (*Capitularia Regum Francorum*), I, 420.

required to bequeath to his church whatever he had acquired after his ordination. The Church and its dependents, not the priest or his relatives, became the recipients of whatever wealth the priest had acquired.[86]

Thus, at the end of the Carolingian era, ecclesiastical discipline and support had been restored: the clergy were under the administration of the bishop of the diocese, and not of the lay lords (who, however, retained their titles to property and the excess profit), and there was a systematized plan of income for the clergy. Bishop Chrodegang had drawn up a rule embodying the "ideal" life of the diocesan clergy—the community life of canons; he had specified what constituted decent support for the clergy, even to the particulars of food and clothing. Then, for both the canons and the secular parish priests, there was determined how much land constituted a minimum benefice for a church, and this minimum benefice was granted immunity from civil obligations. Also, as a result of the granting of parish benefices (and also from the influence of the proprietary church system), the parish priests were accorded a greater independence in the administration of the funds of the parish church.

Much of this change had been wrought by the strong arm of the civil power, which by its exercise of this power was accordingly tempted to consider the Church its ward. A cynic could say that the Church, in escaping from the spoliation of the Merovingian era to the domination of the Carolingian era, had leaped from a bottle into a jar. But the guarantee and the realization of support for the Church and the clergy during the Carolingian era, however it was accomplished and however incomplete it remained, proved valuable in that it afforded a precedent and a guide for the future. Even when the civil power later misused its sovereignty for the confiscation of the Church's wealth, the Church could justly claim that recognized rights had been violated.

Then as now, it remained easier to regain once acknowledged rights than to establish claims to rights still to be acknowledged. This does not mean that the Church regarded the Carolingian sys-

---

[86] Ansegisus, *Collectio,* I, c. 150—*MGH,* Legum Sectio II (*Capitularia Regum Francorum*), I, 420.

tem as perfectly canonical and just. The Carolingian Empire had corrected some excesses and had also curbed the further looting of the Church, but it still allowed in many cases an unjustifiable possession of church property by the lay lords, for although this possession of church property had antedated the Carolingian era, the unjust character of the possession could not confer a just title to the property.

CHAPTER III

From Charlemagne to Gratian

Within a generation after the death of Charlemagne the erstwhile protecting hand of the lay power fell like a mailed fist on the Church. The greedy nobility began to confiscate the property of the Church and to infringe on the rights of the clergy. The repeated protests of the church authorities are evidence of the state of affairs.[1] The income of the parish clergy was so reduced that in many places they could no longer maintain their wonted hospitality; in fact, even the hospices for the Irish pilgrims became very dilapidated.[2]

This rapacity of the lay power, through the evil of lay investiture, naturally ended with the introduction of unworthy candidates into many church offices. Church benefices were again used as political pawns; the only care that some unworthy bishops afforded their flock was a constant fleecing. Concomitant with this development there had been in some areas a lowering of the standards of conduct among the parish clergy. The ideal of community life for canons, as proposed by Chrodegang, was difficult to maintain. The canons gradually neglected the prescriptions of community life, though they still claimed support from the income of the cathedral or church to which they were incardinated. Separate living led to separate maintenance. Thus the common funds and property of the church, which had formerly supported the bishop and the canons, was divided and parcelled out in shares; this gave rise to the separate funds or portions called the *mensa episcopalis* (for the support of the bishop) and the individual prebends or portions of income assigned to the canons.[3]

---

[1] Council of Verneuil-sur-Oise (844), c. 12—Sirmond, *Concilia Antiqua Galliae,* II, 21; Council of Beauvais (845), c. 1, 3—Sirmond, *Concilia Antiqua Galliae,* III, 24; Council of Meaux (845), c. 17, 18, 19—Sirmond, *Concilia Antiqua Galliae,* III, 36, 37.

[2] Council of Meaux (845), c. 40—Sirmond, *Concilia Antiqua Galliae,* III, 43.

[3] Lèsne, "Les Origines de la Prébende," *Revue Historique de Droit* (fourth series, Paris, 1921-), VIII (1929), 242-290; Fliche-Martin, *Histoire,* VII, 261. Thomassinus, Pars III, L. 2, c. 23, n. 3.

This partitioning of the goods of the Church facilitated the spoliation of the Church by the law power, since a prebend could be awarded without the attached obligation of living a community life.

On the other hand, among the zealous prelates the formation of individual prebends led to a determination of how much was needed for the support of a cleric, since a cleric was allowed to receive only one prebend.[4]

The income of the individual prebend must have been roughly equivalent to the income of the parish priest, since the parish benefice, like the prebend, was intended to provide a decent support for the parish priest and clerics; at this time the system of parish benefices was almost universal.[5]

However, the system of parish benefices and prebends was distorted by the increasing demands of the bishops and abbots for large proportions of the incomes. The trend of generosity toward the parish clergy established by the Council of Merida (666), by the XVI Council of Toledo (693), and by Charlemagne's Capitulary for Priests (802) was definitely stopped. The famous collection of canons by Bishop Burchard of Worms (1000-1025) reveals that the bishop collected a third of the income of the parish from its lands and funds, and even a third of the offerings made by the faithful; besides this, a *census* was paid to the bishop.[6] At least in some places the bishops took one-half of the "altar offerings" of churches.[7] In Rome the ancient custom of the four-part division of the income was maintained, with the bishop receiving a fourth—

---

[4] Council of Piacenza (1094), c. 15—Mansi, XX, 806; Council of Clermont (1095), c. 12—Mansi, XX, 817.

[5] Wernz, *Ius Decretalium* (6 vols., Vol. II, 3. ed., Romae et Prati, 1913), II, n. 245; Thomassinus, Pars III, L. 2, c. 16.

[6] Burchardus, *Libri Viginti Decretorum,* III, c. 103, 136—*MPL,* CXL, 713 (hereafter referred to as Burchardus); Ivo, *Decretum,* Pars III, cc. 174, 202—*MPL,* CLXI, 239, 246 (hereafter referred to as Ivo). By ancient law, when the baptismal chapels were the property of the diocese, the bishop rightly claimed a third of the income.

[7] Burchardus, I, c. 229—*MPL,* CXL, 615; Ivo, Pars III, c. 202—*MPL,* CLXI, 246.

evidence that the laws of Spain and France under Charlemagne had not changed the law or practice in Rome.[8]

These regressions to the older law did not mean that the concept of a decent livelihood for the clergy had been forgotten—they only made it more difficult for the smaller parishes to save enough for that purpose. The Council of Trosly (909) had decreed that at the time of his ordination a priest was to be given a parish which was endowed and which enjoyed an income from tithes.[9]

The canonical collection of Burchard contained the statute which forbade the erection of churches until the bishop had given his permission and had determined whether there was a sufficient income for the expenses of the church and the support of the clergy. The parish buildings still included a hospice for the pilgrims and the poor.[10] According to the mind of the Church, the minimum fund for the decent support of the clergy still consisted in the *mansus integer,* so well recognized in the time of Charlemagne, and this estate was to be immune from all civil obligations.[11] Also, regardless of what may have been practiced, the estate of the parish was considered inviolable, and the parish priest was not to dispose of it in any way.[12] The bishop also was forbidden to touch the property of a parish, not being permitted even to assign the possessions of an already established parish to a newly-founded parish.[13]

The estate of the church was not the only source of income for the parish clergy; they received, as in other centuries, the tithes, first-fruits, and offerings of the faithful which were levied on all the produce of the farm, both vegetable and animal, and were levied on all classes of society.[14] Even priests who had been leading scandalous lives were to receive the offerings customarily made by the faithful when such priests conferred sacraments whose recep-

---

[8] Ivo, Pars III, c. 201—*MPL,* CLXI, 246.

[9] C. 6—Hardouin, VIa, 520.

[10] Burchardus, III, c. 6—*MPL,* CXL, 675; Ivo, Pars III, c. 8—*MPL,* CLXI, 201.

[11] Burchardus, III, c. 52—*MPL,* CXL, 682; Ivo, Pars III, c. 55—*MPL,* CLXI, 209.

[12] Burchardus, III, c. 3—*MPL,* CXL, 674.

[13] Burchardus, III, c. 7, 9—*MPL,* CXL, 675.

[14] Ivo, Pars III, c. 174—*MPL,* CLXI, 238; Council of Rome (1059), c. 5—Mansi, XIX, 898.

tion customarily involved an offering. Later the Council of Rome (1059) forbade the faithful even to hear the Mass of priests who were leading scandalous lives.[15]

Unfortunately the practice of the times belied the church law. The spoliation of the parish estate or benefice had extended to parceling out to various people, by the lay lords, the elements that constituted the total income of the parish. Some received part of the tithes, or all of the income from the pasture or vineyards, or part of the offerings.[16] Even when some of those who had received church property showed their repentance, they often made restitution by restoring the stolen property to another church or monastery.[17] Whatever was left of the parish property after it had been pared and whittled came to be called the *presbyteratus,* a wraith-like remnant of the original wealth. This *presbyteratus* or *beneficium presbyteri* was the pittance on which the priest was supposed to support himself; obviously he was now in no position to support all those who formerly had been supported by the once well-endowed church. Since the *presbyteratus* was simply the residue left after the spoliation, there was no law determining how much should be left —it depended upon the discretion of the lay proprietor of the church property. This illegality, however, frequently followed a pattern whereby a plot of land near the church was left for its support, and this was called the "altar-land" (*terra altaris*);[18] the "altar" thus belonged to the bishop or the priest, while the "church" with its income belonged by some involuted logic to the lay proprietor. Of course the Church decried such a division, but such

---

[15] Burchardus, III, c. 75—*MPL,* CXL, 689; Council of Rome (1059), c. 3—Mansi, XIX, 898.

[16] Council of Metz (888), c. 2—Mansi, XVIII, 78; Council of Ravenna (904), c. 1—Mansi, XVIII, 230; Council of Coblenz (922), c. 8—Mansi, XVIII, 346; Council of Ingelheim (948), c. 9—Mansi, XVIII, 421-422; Fliche-Martin, *Histoire,* VII, 285-288.

[17] Fliche-Martin, *Histoire,* VII, 286.

[18] Stutz, "Ausgewählte Kapitel aus der Geschichte der Eigenkirche," *Zeitschrift der Savigny-Stiftung, Kanonistische Abteilung;* vol. 2 (1937), 73 ff.; P. Imbart de la Tour, *Les Paroisses Rurales du V au XI Siècle* (Paris, 1900), pp. 265-267; 278-280; Lèsne, "Evêché et Abbave," *Revue d'Histoire de l'Eglise de France* (Paris, 1910-), V (1914), 44, 50; Fliche-Martin, *Histoire,* VII, 290.

protests were often as ineffective as the crash of cymbals against a guarded fort.[19]

Despite such flagrant and apparently widespread abuses, the Church still maintained its teaching concerning the support of the clergy. The famous Abbot Regino (+915), head of the monastery of Prüm, in his handbook for ecclesiastical judges, certainly held that the parish estate was to be as large as it had been in the days of Charlemagne; according to Abbot Regino, each church was to have a *mansus* consisting of twelve *"bunnuaria"* (a measure of land) and tilled by four serfs; besides this, there was to be a cemetery, and an enclosed courtyard in which were located the church and the priest's house. Of course he was also to enjoy the tithes contributed by the free men of his parish who possessed their *mansi ingenuiles.*[20]

The Abbot also restated that the bishop in his visitation of churches was not to exact more than two *solidi,* a very modest sum.[21]

Not all the ecclesiastical authorities followed the Abbot in his adherence to the ancient law and the rights of the Church. In fact, some councils finally restricted themselves to trying to vindicate the rights of the bishop and the clergy to the "altar," and thus left the lay lords to their ill-gained possession of the "church" and its tithes.[22]

In the midst of this chaos there arose a series of strong Popes, the most eminent of whom, the great Gregory VII (1073-1085), stoutly maintained the rights of the clergy. Gregory VII, who tried to cleanse the Church by isolating church offices from lay domination and interference, forbade any molestation of the rights of the parish clergy, and took steps to restore the independence and the support of the clergy. No one, not even an abbot, was permitted to

---

[19] Council of Ingelheim (948), c. 8—Mansi, XVIII, 421.

[20] *Libri duo de Synodalibus Causis,* lib. I, c. 1, n. 13—*MPL,* CXXXII, 187. This first chapter or canon contained very detailed instructions for the ecclesiastical judges with reference to the property and furnishings required in each church; they were to inquire if each church had a *mansus* with "bonvaria (bunnuaria) duodecim, praeter cimiterium et curtem ubi ecclesia et domus presbyteri continetur, et si habeat mancipia quattuor."

[21] *Op. cit.,* lib. 1, c. 11—*MPL,* CXXXII, 193.

[22] Council of Seligenstadt (1022), c. 20—Mansi, XIX, 399; Council of Rheims (1049), c. 2, 3—Mansi, XIX, 741-742.

take tithes or first-fruits from a parish without the express consent of the Pope or of the local bishop.[23] Also, no bishop was permitted to impose any hard or unusual exactions on the clergy.[24] Pope Gregory VII reminded all the faithful that they were obliged to render not only the tithe but also the usual altar offerings at Mass and at the reception of the sacraments.[25]

Through the influence of this great Pope, councils throughout Christendom reiterated the claims of the long-trampled rights of the Church and the clergy, and asserted the clergy's right to the income of the Church. There were many decrees against all kinds of simony, against investiture by laymen, against the seizure of the income of the Church by the laity, a renewal of the law of tithes and offerings, and insistence on the ancient law that a cleric was to have only one prebend or church, and that each church was to have enough resources for the support of the clergy.[26]

Instead of a mechanical repetition of the ancient law, there arose an interpretation according to equity. At the Council of Nîmes (1096) Bishop Isarne was obliged by Pope Urban II (1088-1099) to restore to the clergy of the church St. Sernin (St. Saturnine, the cathedral church of Toulouse) the fourth of the income he had taken—which was due him according to law—because the church could not afford that much.[27]

There were, fortunately, certain regions, like clearings in a jungle, where the discipline of the Church was enforced and where the clergy enjoyed its rightful support. The recently converted Kingdom of Hungary protected the support accorded to the clergy by the national patron, King St. Stephen (997-1038). King Colo-

---

[23] V Roman Council (1078), c. 8.—Mansi, XX, 509.

[24] V Roman Council (1078), c. 9—Mansi, XX, 509.

[25] V Roman Council (1078), c. 7, 12—Mansi, XX, 509-510. It had already been decreed by the Council of Rome (1059), c. 5, that those who refused to make the required contributions to the Church were to be excommunicated. —Mansi, XIX, 898.

[26] Council of Rouen (1074), cc. 2, 3—Mansi, XX, 398, 400; Council of Winchester (1076), c. 12—Mansi, XX, 460; Council of Poitiers (1078), c. 1, 2—Mansi, XX, 498; Council of Vienna (1080), cc. 4, 5, 12—Mansi, XX, 556, 557; Council of Clermont (1095), cc. 12, 16—Mansi, XX, 817; Council of Rouen (1095), c. 5—Mansi, XX, 924; Council of Nimes (1096), c. 6—Mansi, XX, 935; Council of London (1102), c. 16—Mansi, XX, 1151.

[27] Mansi, XX, 941-942.

man (1095-1114) revoked the grants and gifts except those made by King Stephen,[28] but he insisted that all pay tithes, and those who had no tithes to pay, as the serfs, were to pay three *denarii* a year—eloquent testimony that even the serfs must have enjoyed a measure of prosperity.[29]

Unfortunately the papal authority in its effort to relieve the condition of the parish priests often encountered an obstacle in the bishops, many of whom were hostile to a reform that would deprive them of some of their income.[30] Pope Gregory VII (1073-1085) and his immediate successors had dealt mostly with re-establishing the broad principles of church support and discipline; they had not been able to define specifically the support due to parish priests while they were occupied with the more general principles and with the reform of the status of bishoprics and exempt abbeys. The general councils dealt specifically with the problems of clerical support.

The first two Councils of the Lateran, held in 1123 and 1139, excluded the laity from interference with the appointment of pastors,[31] and the laity was forbidden to touch the offerings and tithes given to the parish churches or to any church.[32] The laity who possessed church property of any kind were obliged to return it; especially the churches, to the local bishop. This decree not only aimed at ending the laity's possession of the "churches" in contradistinction to the clergy's possession of the "altar," but it pre-

[28] *Ecclesiastical Constitutions of King Coloman (1103)*, L. I, c. 7—Mansi, XX, 1173.

[29] *Ecclesiastical Constitutions of King Coloman (1103)*, L. I, c. 24; L. II, c. 2—Mansi, XX, 1173, 1176.

[30] The I Council of Rome (1074); c. 24, reminded the clerics that the obedience which they owed to papal authority exceeded that due to the bishop. —Mansi, XX, 430. Also, the Concordat of Sutri between Pope Pascal II (1099-1118) and Henry V of Germany (1106-1125), which sought to end the evil of investiture, was wrecked with the connivance of many bishops. Even the compromise effected by the Concordat of Worms in 1122, between Pope Callixtus II (1119-1124) and Henry V, was not well received by many bishops.—Fliche-Martin, *Histoire,* VIII, 361 ff., 387 ff.

[31] I General Council of the Lateran (1123), c. 18—Mansi, XXI, 285.

[32] I General Council of the Lateran (1123), cc. 4, 14—Mansi, XXI, 282, 285; II General Council of the Lateran (1139), c. 10—Mansi, XXI, 528. Also the important Council of Rheims (1131) contained the same decrees in cc. 7, 9, 15—Mansi, XXI, 459.

vented the laity from returning parish churches and chapels to monasteries—it kept diocesan property within the diocese.[33] The Council of Rheims (1131), which was attended by bishops from beyond the borders of France, forbade the faithful to assist at Mass when it was celebrated by the married clergy, and decreed that no benefices or prebends were hereditary. This assured support for the righteous clergy and prevented the loss of church property on the part of the parishes.[34]

These general councils, especially the II General Council of the Lateran, condemned all kinds of simony, and deprived the simoniacal clergy not only of the reception of sacrilegious income but also of the tenure of their office.[35] This officially ended such disgraceful practices as paying for parishes and receiving money at the time of confession.[36]

Thus by the middle of the twelfth century the Church had succeeded in extirpating many of the abuses which had developed during the preceding centuries. The rights of the Church to the appointment of all offices in the Church as well as the right to the administration of all church property was vindicated. The parish churches were gradually freed from the illegal exactions and spoliations made by the laity and avaricious prelates. The legal protection afforded the parishes was gradually enforced and made a reality. Undoubtedly some abuses continued to exist, but they were recognized as such and were given no tacit approbation and sufferance. The great difficulty lay, as ever, in the lack of a well-defined and promulgated legal code for the universal Church. Church councils and papal decrees had provided legislation to correct abuses and to vindicate rights, but if these were to achieve their full effect there was prior need of an authoritative and thorough compilation of law which was binding everywhere throughout the Church.

[33] I General Council of the Lateran (1123), c. 10—Mansi, XXI, 283.

[34] Council of Rheims (1131), cc. 5, 15—Mansi, XXI, 459.

[35] II General Council of the Lateran (1139), cc. 1, 2—Mansi, XXI, 527.

[36] *Charta Episcopi Roberti Lingonensis* (*1101*): ". . . emolumentum ex confessionibus fidelium sacerdotibus obveniens quolibet mense, qui tricenariis aut circiter diebus constet."—*Gallia Christiana,* IV, 151. The custom of making an offering at the time of a monthly confession seems to have been accepted by the ecclesiastical authorities in some sections.

CHAPTER IV

FROM GRATIAN TO THE COUNCIL OF TRENT

SECTION 1. THE DECRETUM OF GRATIAN

Towards the middle of the twelfth century the famous Gratian finished his epochal collection of canon law, the *Concordia Discordantium Canonum.* The work was more a promise than a fulfillment in regard to the problem of the decent support of the clergy. Gratian's work, popularly known under the prosaic title *Decretum,* repeated all the laws on clerical support as enacted throughout the preceding and often contrary phases of canonical legislation.

Gratian stated the premise of the Church's doctrine on the support of the clergy, namely, that the bishop alone, under the Pope, has the authority to dispense in his diocese the ecclesiastical goods and property whereby the clergy are supported.[1]

The bishop was obliged to dispense the use of the church property in an equitable and regular manner for the clerics of his diocese, but he was not empowered to alienate ecclesiastical property, except for very definite reasons.[2] No church could be built until the local bishop had been satisfied that there was enough income for the support of the church and of the clergy and also for the meeting of other expenses.[3] If the bishop had neglected this matter, then either he or the founders of the church were obliged to support the clergy or to provide a dowry.[4] It was equally forbidden to erect a church or a chapel for the sole purpose of collecting funds which accrued from the offerings of the faithful or from any other source.

---

[1] C. 23, C. XII, q. 1; cc. 2, 3, C. X, q. 1; cc. 24, 26, C. XII, q. 1.

[2] C. 23, C. XII, q. 2; c. 19, C. XII, q. 11.

[3] C. 9, D. 1, *de cons.*

[4] C. 9, D. 1, *de cons,* c. 1; cf. *casus* in the *Glossa* on this canon. At a later time the bishop alone was held accountable for the support of a cleric ordained without a *titulus*—c. 13, X, *de aetate et qualitate et ordine praeficiendorum,* I, 14; cc. 2, 4, 16, X, *de praebendis et dignitatibus,* III, 5.

No doubt this prohibition was directed against the erection of shrines which were built more for the enrichment of a lord than for the sanctification of souls.[5]

Each priest was to be assigned to his own church, but he was to hold only one church or prebend.[6] This church was not necessarily a parish church in the sense in which it is understood now; the church to which the priest was to be assigned could be a parish church in the city or in the country, or a church built as a shrine to a martyr.[7] However, if the income from one church was so meager that the priest could not be supported by it, he could be permitted to draw his support from more than one church, generally by holding one church *in titulum* and the other in *commendam;* also the priest could hold a prebend and a parish if both were necessary to afford him decent support.[8] Rufinus (+1190) stated that conditions in Rome, with its large city parishes, gave rise to the prohibition that no cleric was to have more than one church, and that this rule was of ancient origin.[9] It was agreed, however, that no cleric should draw support from two churches or chapels if these were located in two different dioceses, since a priest or a cleric could not be simultaneously incardinated in two different dioceses.[10]

In determining how much constituted a decent support for the clergy, the ecclesiastical authorities considered the demands made upon the clergy. Pre-eminent among the demands made upon the clergy were the obligation to support the poor and the pilgrims, and to contribute to the support of the bishop. There were of course other duties incumbent upon the parish clergy, notably the repair and the maintenance of the church buildings, but since in some instances the repair of the church buildings was paid from the contribution to the bishop, and in some cases offerings were made specifically for these repairs by the faithful, the duties of furnishing

---

[5] C. 10, D. 1, *de cons.*

[6] C. 1, C. XXI, q. 1; c. 1, C. XIII, q. 1; c. 1, D. LXXXIX.

[7] C. 1, D. LXX.

[8] Rufinus, *Summa Decretorum* (ed. H. Singer, Paderbornae, 1902), p. 383 (hereafter referred to as *Summa*); c. 2, D. LXX; c. 3, C. XXI, q. 1.

[9] Rufinus, *Summa*, p. 384.

[10] Rufinus, *Summa*, p. 383.

hospitality to the needy and of giving support to the bishop were the primary ones. Consideration will be given first of all to the duties imposed on the clergy, and then to the amount and the sources of income due to the clergy. In connection with the amount of income due the clergy, we shall note the attitude of the Church towards work performed by the clergy in aid of their sustenance.

The extent of the hospitality afforded by the Church is evident from the different types of institutions maintained for the poor and the pilgrims; there were *xenodochia,* where the pilgrims were supported, *ptochotrophia,* where the poor were received, *gerontocomia,* or hospices for the indigent aged, *orphanotrophia,* wherein the orphans were cared for, and *brephotrophia,* where the infants of the poor received food.[11] Obviously, not every parish could afford to support all these specialized institutions, but each church was required to have a hospice or a guest house for pilgrims and the poor; even small churches under the administration of abbeys were required to have a hospice or a guest house.[12]

The attitude of the Church towards hospitality afforded to the poor was summed up in a very simple rule—none in need of food was to be refused.[13] Naturally, those who had a special claim on the charity of the Church, for instance, the patrons and founders of churches, were to be accorded a more generous treatment than a mere dole of food.[14]

It was also recognized by law that the clergy were obliged to support their near-relatives, and hence provision for this was to be made in the determining of their income. "No man can hate his own flesh" was quoted by the canonists in warrant of this duty.[15]

Numbered among the near-relatives who had a claim on the clergy for support were also the wives of clerics who had been

---

[11] *Glossa* s.v. *xenones,* ad c. 23, C. XXIII, q. 8.

[12] C. 68, C. XVI, q. 1; c. 10, C. XVIII, q. 2; *Glossa* s.v. *domum,* ad c. 9, D. 1, *de cons.*

[13] "Si autem quis petit pro nutrimento, tunc indistincte omnibus est danda."—*Glossa* s.v. *postulat,* ad c. 1, D. XLII. Also, although it was generally forbidden to alienate any property of the Church, it was permitted in time of necessity to sell the gold vessels of the Church to feed the poor—c. 70, 71, C. XII, q. 2.

[14] C. 30, C. XVI, q. 7.

[15] *Glossa* s.v. *ut de mercede,* ad c. 11, D. XXXI.

married legitimately before receiving sacred orders.[16] It should be noted that the support which was due to the near-relatives and to the wives was to come not from the funds allotted for the poor and the pilgrims, but from the share of the cleric. Hence such dependents could represent a considerable amount in the cleric's budget.

Another considerable item in the expenses of the parish priest was the support of his assistant cleric. The divers and numerous parochial duties demanded the presence of at least two clerics in a church. Of course, it was not necessary for both of the clerics to be priests, since many of the duties of the parish could be discharged by a cleric who was not a priest.[17] The support accorded to this assistant cleric was to be in proportion to his rank and sacred profession.

In contrast with the simple though extensive rule for hospitality incumbent on the clergy, in Gratian's *Decretum* the rule for the amount of support due to the bishop remained unsettled. Gratian simply collected the preceding laws concerning the amount due to the bishop, and left unsettled the then arising difficulties. He reiterated in many places the ancient law that the bishop was to receive one-fourth of the income of the church;[18] then in successive canons he stated other laws, which allowed to the bishop one-half of the offerings made at the altar or one-third of such offerings.[19]

Of course these varying laws had been promulgated for different times and circumstances, but no effort was made to clarify their extension or application. To confuse the situation even more, Gratian quoted the legislation of the Spanish Church, which decreed that the bishop was bound to use the third of the parish income that was due to him for the repair of the church or its buildings; the bishop was not entitled to any portion if he did not use that portion for the repair of the church buildings.[20] Still undismayed, Gratian added the canon which declared that the bishop could exact

---

[16] C. 11, D. XXXI.

[17] *Glossa* s.v. *custodum*, ad c. 9, D. I, *de cons.*

[18] C. 26, C. XII, q. 2; c. 63, C. XVI, q. 1; c. 27, 28, 29, C. XII, q. 2; c. 30, C. XII, q. 2.

[19] C. 7, C. X, q. 1—the bishop is to receive one-third of the altar offerings; c. 8, C. X, q. 1—the bishop is to receive one-half of the altar offerings.

[20] Cc. 2, 3, C. X, q. 3.

only the *cathedraticum,* consisting of two *solidi,* from each parish, and was not to be accompanied by a retinue of more than fifty persons on his episcopal visitations.[21] There was, however, a general and equitable warning which forbade bishops to treat the clergy in a harsh or a servile way by levying taxes or services on them.[22]

Small wonder that the prudent glossator limited himself to stating that the prelates should follow the reasonable custom of their region![23]

There was no specification in the *Decretum,* as in the Rule of Chrodegang, regarding the amount of food or clothing considered adequate for clerics; the *Decretum* simply urged moderation and temperance in eating, and conformity to clerical usage in clothing.[24] The *Decretum* limited itself, as will be seen, to stating general rules on income, and to determining in a vague way what constituted a minimum income.

The income from the church was supposed to be sufficient for the priest, so that there would not be any need for him to engage in secular business in order to augment his income. Occupations unbecoming to the clerical state were specified: tax collecting, banking, commerce for profit, etc.[25] If a cleric did engage in such secular trade or business, he was to be excommunicated.[26]

Since many clerics had acted as guardians or tutors for orphans, children and widows, a cleric could perform these offices when he was required by law or permitted by his bishop to do so. These works of charity were not forbidden by canonical precept.[27] Further, inasmuch as the canons forbade only such work as was "unbecoming" to the priestly state, the question was raised whether it was

[21] Cc. 1, 8, C. X, q. 3. The *casus* of the *Glossa* on canon 8 states that in France some bishops were accompanied by 250 persons during a visitation and that the whole entourage stayed several days at a church, with disastrous effects on the church's finances.

[22] C. 1, 6, 9, C. X, q. 3.

[23] *Glossa* s.v. *necessitate,* ad c. 1, C. XXI, q. 1.

[24] Cc. 4, 5, C. XXI, q. 3; cf. Rufinus, *Summa* (ad c. 4, C. XXI, q. 3), pp. 385, 386.

[25] C. 1, C. XXI, q. 3; c. 1, C. XIII, q. 3.

[26] Cc. 2, 8, C. XIII, q. 3.

[27] C. 1, D. LXXXVIII.

permitted for pastors or clerics of poor churches to engage in any extraneous occupation in order to augment their income. It was decided that a cleric could engage in such work for gaining the necessities of life as long as the work did not interfere with the duties of his office.[28]

This work could be either that of a trade or that of agriculture, but the cleric could not devote so much time to it that it would take up his whole day.[29] Under the influence of monasticism, no cleric, however learned, was thought to be lowering himself in dignity if he learned a trade that could help secure for him the necessities of life. Precluded from the list of lawful pursuits was all commercial activity—trading for profit—and even sauntering idly through the market place was strongly discouraged.[30] In fact, if the income of a church had been seriously diminished, the pastor was urged to perform manual work or to petition for the union of his church with another.[31]

Engaging in such lawful pursuits for one's support, however, was certainly not considered the duty of the clergy, and it was permitted only under unusual circumstances, that is, when the parish was poor. A church was not considered "poor" unless there was not a sufficient income for the support of the pastor, including his obligations of furnishing hospitality and of giving support to the bishop; a church which did not have an income of more than ten gold marks (*marchae*) was considered poor, although this sum was at that time a considerable amount.[32] No church was to have a resident priest unless there were ten households in the parish.[33]

The income of a church came from a number of sources, as it had in former years. The mainstay of the Church's income continued to be the *mansus integer,* the estate of the church, which was free of obligations to the lay authorities. Generally it was large enough

[28] C. 3, D. XCI.

[29] *Glossa* s.v. *officii* and *vigiliis,* ad c. 3, D. XCI.

[30] "Clericus quantumlibet verbo Dei eruditus, artificiolo victum quaerat. Omnes clerici, qui ad operandum validi sunt, et artificiola et litteras discant. Qui vero non pro emendo aliquid in nundinis vel in foro deambulant, ab officio suo degradentur."—c. 4, D. XCI.

[31] *Casus,* ad c. 1, C. XXI, q. 1.

[32] *Glossa* s.v. *necessitate,* ad c. 1, C. XXI, q. 1.

[33] *Glossa* s.v. *mancipia,* ad c. 3, C. X, q. 3.

to require the efforts of four serfs;[34] the smallest *mansus* was large enough to support a farmer and his family, and thus represented an estate large enough for the support of the parish cleric and his dependents.[35]

The church also received tithes, first-fruits, and offerings from all the faithful located in the parish.[36] The first-fruits consisted of one-fortieth of the crop (according to the computation of a pious person) to one-sixtieth (for a less pious person). The first-fruits of animals was one of every two hundred in the herd.[37] The offerings made on the occasion of a person's decease formed a considerable part of the income of the church, and those who obstructed the fulfillment of a will were punished with excommunication.[38] Though no fixed amount was required, there prevailed in some localities the pious custom of counting Christ as a son in the family and of contributing His share to the local parish church; thus, if there were three children, Christ became the fourth, and so one-forth of the estate was given to the Church. There is no evidence that this was a widespread custom.[39]

The *Decretum* of Gratian also specified the services of a priest or the acts of religion for which no fee or offering was permitted. No fee was to be demanded for baptism; it was especially forbidden to place a coin in the shell which the priest had used for pouring the water at baptism. When one received a convert into the Church, it was also forbidden to demand a fee.[40] Also, no fee was to be demanded for administering Holy Communion or for performing any action which conferred grace, such as ordaining to Orders. If the recipient insisted on giving an offering upon his reception of a sacrament, the offering could be accepted.[41]

It is also apparent from this system of income from benefice that not every priest was to have a uniform income. Clerics were to be

---

[34] C. 24, 25, C. XXIII, q. 8.

[35] *Glossa* s.v. *mansus,* ad c. 24, C. XXIII, q. 8.

[36] C. 7, C. X, q. 1; c. 8, C. X, q. 1.

[37] *Glossa* s.v. *primitiae,* ad c. 1, C. XIII, q. 1.

[38] C. 9, C. XIII, q. 2; c. 11, C. XIII, q. 2.

[39] C. 8, C. XIII, q. 2.

[40] C. 99, C. I, q. 1; c. 1, C. I, q. 2.

[41] Cc. 100, 101, C. I, q. 1.

rewarded according to merit (of course within the possibility of human judgment, which could not attempt to estimate the interior spiritual life of the clerics).[42] Rufinus pointed out an apparent contradiction between this law which gaged the reward according to the merit and a canon which stated that all clerics were to receive equally in the distribution of tithes. The tithes derived from a spiritual right, so Rufinus explained, but the income from possessions derived, not from a divine command, but through merit, and thus a zealous cleric could be rewarded with more income from possessions than a less diligent cleric.[43] The glossators left room for a varied standard of living, adaptable according to the varied excellence and merit of the person, although they likewise insisted that all clerics were urged to be content with a frugal life.[44]

The great problem that beset the parochial clergy was not the slightness of the income but the vastness of the expenses. Each parish was obliged to contribute large sums for the support of the poor and the bishop.

Despite the confusion in the *Decretum* concerning the obligations on the part of pastors for the support of the bishop, there was clarity and unanimity on the central principles concerning the support of the clergy: the bishop was the supreme authority over ecclesiastical property in the diocese; only the clergy were to receive the income of the church, and they in turn were to support those who by ecclesiastical law depended on them; the clergy were to receive enough to enable them to discharge their obligations and to enjoy a decent sustenance which correspond to their dignity and personal accomplishments. It was left to the Decretals and the decretalists to resolve many of the conflicts in the *Decretum* concerning the income for and the support of the clergy.

SECTION 2. THE DECRETALS AND THE DECRETALISTS

Within a little more than a century after the publication of Gratian's *Decretum* many of the legal problems presented in Gratian's compilation were clarified through legislation, juris-

[42] C. 10, C. I, q. 2; c. 25, C. XII, q. 2.

[43] Rufinus, *Summa* (commenting on c. 10, C. 1, q. 2); p. 225.

[44] C. 3, C. X, q. 3; and *Glossa* s.v. *necessitate,* ad c. 1, C. XXI, q. 1.

prudence, and custom. Jurisprudence had been stimulated and sharpened by the diffusion of Roman Law as occasioned through the finding of the *Digest* in Pisa in the year 1070. The energetic and wise legislation of the great popes of the late twelfth and early thirteenth centuries, notably the jurists Alexander III (1159-1181) and Innocent III (1198-1216), culminated in the first authentic collections of canon law by Innocent III in 1210 and by Gregory IX (1227-1241) in 1234. Boniface VIII (1294-1303) added another volume of law in 1298 to the Decretals of Gregory IX. John XXII (1316-1334) promulgated in 1317 the *Libri Decretalium* which had been collected by his predecessor, Clement V (1305-1314), and the complexus of canon law, called the *Corpus Iuris Canonici*, became ultimately integrated through the minor additions which accrued during the fourteenth and fifteenth centuries.

The new legislation, promulgated when the feudal system was decaying, recognized the futility of trying to preserve the feudal system of a beneficed parish which could afford to divide its income into four portions, one portion being reserved for the support of the clergy and another portion being presented to the bishop. The changing conditions upset the controlled economic system which had ruled society, and with that change came a new approach to the determination of the income of the clergy.[45]

Of course the basic principle was maintained; the bishop was the supreme guardian and dispenser (under the Pope) of ecclesiastical property in his diocese; this right extended to all income, even to the tithes and offerings.[46]

But there was a great change in the concept of how much property was to be put at the disposal of a pastor for his use and how much income he needed. This change arose from the recognition that the primary purpose of the parish church was the spiritual care

---

[45] Abbas Panormitanus (Nicholaus de Tudeschis 1386-1453) stated that the old system of distribution of income was not widely practiced.—*Commentaria in Quinque Libros Decretalium* (5 vols. in 7, Venetiis, 1588), s.v. *ipse fructuarius,* ad c. 1, X, *de ecclesiis aedificandis et reparandis,* III, 48 (hereafter this work will be referred to as *Commentaria*).

[46] C. 7, X, *de constitutionibus,* I, 2; c. 2, X, *de consuetudine,* I, 4; c. 1, X, *de in integrum restitutione,* I, 41; c. un., *de rebus ecclesiae non alienandis,* III, 4, in Extravag com.

of the parishioners, and that in a case of necessity a parish could be established which would be able to support only the pastor and not the poor, nor be able to contribute to the support of the bishop. The innovation was reflected, not of course in the concept that a parish primarily served the spiritual good of the parishioners, but rather in the notion that an erected parish could abstract from the obligation of hospitality to the poor and the pilgrims, as also from the duty of support for the bishop.

This attitude was evident in the writings of the celebrated commentators Hostiensis (+1271) and Panormitanus (1386-1453), who differed with the glossator of the Decretals of Gregory IX on the amount of support necessary for the establishment of a new church or chapel. These commentators (who cited their opinion as the general one) contended that, since the bishop's primary duty was the care of souls, he could establish another church within the boundaries of a parish for the sake of making it convenient for the faithful to attend Mass, even if it meant the deprivation of part of the income of the parent parish. The bishop could compel either the parishioners to contribute to the support of the new parish, or the abbot, if the newly erected church was subject to his monastery. If adequate support was wanting under the circumstances, then the new church was to be supported by the bishop; if the bishop could not afford assistance to the church, then the pastor was obliged to help support himself by his own work or industry.[47]

It was specifically recognized therefore that there were circumstances in which the pastor of a poor parish was not required to contribute to the support of the bishop.[48] It was also recognized

---

[47] "Nam propter penuriam dotis non debet episcopus pati periculum animarum: puto, si propter longam distantiam saepe decederent homines sine sacris, et hoc dictum non singulariter."—Panormitanus (agreeing with Hostiensis), s.v. *pro facultate loci,* ad c. 3, X, *de ecclesiis aedificandis vel reparandis,* III, 48. Ioannes Andreae (1272-1348) agreed substantially with this opinion—*Commentaria Novella in Quinque Decretalium Libros* (6 vols. in 5, Venetiis, 1581), s.v. *et ibi tenetur,* ad c. 12, X, *de praebendis et dignitatibus,* III, 5 (this work will be referred to hereafter as *Novella*).

[48] Panormitanus, *Commentaria,* s.v. *nam et ipse fructuarius,* ad c. 1, X, *de ecclesiis aedificandis vel reparandis,* III, 48. Panormitanus in this passage noted that the bishop had no need of his share of the parish income, since he was no longer required to repair the church buildings, inasmuch as this duty had devolved on the pastor and his parishioners.

that the establishment of a hospice was not an integral part of the foundation of a new church.[49] But if the income of the parish increased, the pastor was obliged to establish a hospice and to pay his obligations to the bishop.[50] In view simply of the primary purpose of a church, it was even granted that a church could, in a case of necessity, be established without a dowry.[51]

This paring down to the element which was essential for the foundation of a church did not imply a relinquishment of the ideal which looked to the principal support of a church as flowing from an unencumbered estate, the *mansus integer.* The *mansus integer,* free of obligations to civil authority, was to be large enough to support the clergy and the dependents of the parish.[52]

The parochial clergy normally consisted of the pastor and at least one assistant cleric; it was universally recognized that the pastor was in need of another cleric who could assist him in the performance of the duties incidental to the parochial work.[53] Hence it was necessary to consider the needs of at least these two clerics when it was estimated how large the *mansus integer* should be. The minimum amount of land for a *mansus* came to be estimated at about twenty acres. Pope Alexander III permitted the Bishop of York to establish a new parish if it possessed twenty acres of arable and fertile land, and this extent of acreage seems to have

---

[49] "Nec est oppositum quod dos debetur a principio pro hospitalitate tenenda vel pro iuribus episcopalibus solvendis. Nam ecclesia impotens non tenetur ad ista."—Panormitanus, *Commentaria,* s.v. *recipere hospites,* ad c. 8, X, *de consecratione ecclesiae vel altaris,* III, 40. In fact, a parish was considered very wealthy if it could afford to receive all the poor or strangers who asked for hospitality.—Ioannes Andreae, *Novella,* s.v. *et ibi tenetur,* ad c. 12, X, *de praebendis et dignitatibus,* III, 5.

[50] Panormitanus, *Commentaria,* s.v. *recipere hospites,* ad c. 8, X, *de consecratione ecclesiae vel altaris,* III, 40.

[51] Panormitanus and Hostiensis, *Commentaria,* s.v. *pro facultate loci,* ad c. 3, *de ecclesiis aedificandis vel reparandis,* III, 48.

[52] C. 1, X, *de censibus, exactionibus, et procurationibus,* III, 39. Cf. Panormitanus and Hostiensis, *Commentaria,* s.v. *recipere hospites,* ad c. 8, X, *de consecratione ecclesiae vel altaris,* III, 40.

[53] C. 2, *de decimis, primitiis et oblationibus,* III, 13, in VI°; c. 30, X, *de praebendis et dignitatibus,* III, 5; Panormitanus, *Commentaria,* s.v. *secum cantent,* ad c. 3, X, *de vita et honestate clericorum,* III, 1; Ioannes Andreae, *Novella,* s.v. *sacerdotis,* ad c. 15, X, *de praebendis et dignitatibus,* III, 5.

been commonly accepted as the minimum throughout France, Spain and Italy.[54]

A *mansus* of twenty acres was considered the reasonable minimum for the support of a pastor and his cleric assistant, though the pastor was required also then to maintain his residence in a parish when disaster had robbed him of an income which would have represented the normal production value of the land. Thus, although a pastor was bound to maintain his residence even if the income fell to as little as twenty *solidi* a year, it cannot be argued that this represented in fact the minimum requisite income, for such a reduced income was the result of disaster, and not of design, and hence was considered insufficient. In fact, in such a case the pastor was entitled to assistance from the bishop, or to additional support as derived from another benefice.[55]

Furthermore, it was specifically forbidden to the bishop to reduce the size of the parishes, without a reason, to smaller proportions.[56] Likewise, the fact that a pastor was obliged to residence (as possessing a *beneficium curatum*) if he had ten serfs and their families (*mancipia*) together with five households (*mansionarii*) or families of freemen within his parish does not warrant the claim that this represented a true minimum. He was obliged to such residence when the formerly prosperous state of the parish had deteriorated

---

[54] C. 3, X, *de ecclesiis aedificandis vel reparandis,* III, 48. Hostiensis accepted twenty acres as a universal minimum: ". . . viginti acras . . . tum enim valet acra apud Anglicos quantum iornale apud nos, et quantum arpentum apud Gallicos, et quantum bubulcuta vel tabula apud Italicos et Lombardos."—*Commentaria,* s.v. *unus mansus,* ad c. 3, *de ecclesiis aedificandis vel reparandis,* III, 48. In another place Hostiensis defined a *mansus* as "*pecia terrae quae sufficit duobus bobus ad laborandum per totum annum.*"—s.v *xx acras,* ad c. 1, X, *de censibus, exactionibus et procurationibus,* III, 39. Since the writer has not been able to find how much land two oxen can till in a year, and since the farmers he has consulted have with their customary reticence refused to hazard a guess on the performance of a team of oxen, he cannot determine if this second definition of the extent of a *mansus* corresponds to the first.

[55] C. 6, X, *de clericis non residentibus in ecclesia vel praebenda,* III, 4; cf. Hostiensis on this canon; cf. also c. 4, *de praebendis et dignitatibus,* III, 2, in Extravag. com.

[56] C. 3, X, *de ecclesiis aedificandis vel reparandis,* III, 48; c. 10, X, *de praebendis et dignitatibus,* III, 5.

to such a condition; certainly a new parish would never have been started if so few parishioners were there, with no prospect of more parishioners arriving in the near future.[57]

In parishes that had become poor it was permitted to the clergy, for the purpose of supporting themselves, to engage in work that was not unbecoming to the priestly state. Such work precluded the holding of a public office, the functioning as an officer in a secular court or engaging in commerce; "becoming work" could be undertaken through the tilling of the soil or the plying of a manual trade. A cleric was allowed to engage in this "becoming work" solely with a view to supplying himself with the necessities of life, but not for the purpose of gaining wealth. The Church thus reluctantly allowed clerics to perform such work, but only under circumstances of necessity; it did not allow them to do so if the work interfered with their pastoral and priestly duties.[58]

The final indication that the Church did not approve of the practice whereby clerics would have sought support for themselves through such work is found in the law which forbade bishops to ordain clerics who apart from such work did not have a means of sufficient support (*titulus*).[59] In order to guarantee enough support for a pastor or a cleric, the bishop could effect the union of a prebend with a parish as well as the union of one parish with another.[60]

Although the decretalists had investigated the conditions under which a cleric was obliged to maintain residence at his benefice, and thus had determined the minimum support for a cleric, it was

---

[57] Hostiensis, *Commentaria,* s.v. *parochiales* (n. 5), ad c. 3, X, *de clericis non residentibus in ecclesia vel praebenda,* III, 4. Of course, when parishes lost a great part of their income or their parishioners, the pastors could petition for a union with nearby parishes, or this could be initiated by the bishop.

[58] Panormitanus, *Commentaria,* s.v. *pro facultate loci,* ad c. 3, X, *de ecclesiis aedificandis et reparandis,* III, 48; Hostiensis, *Commentaria,* s.v. *maxime* (n. 2), ad c. 15, X, *de vita et honestate clericorum,* III, 1.

[59] Cc. 1, 2, 4, *de temporibus ordinationum et qualitate ordinandorum,* I, 9, in VI°; cc. 13, 14, X, *de aetate et qualitate et ordine praeficiendorum,* I, 14.

[60] C. 33, X, *de praebendis et dignitatibus,* III, 5; c. 4, X, *de aetate et qualitate et ordine praeficiendorum,* I, 14; Letter of Alexander III to the Bishop of Canterbury.—JL, n. 8876.

still held that a "decent support" implied an income large enough not only to cover the living expenses of the clergy, but also to meet the obligations due to the bishop, to afford succor to the poor, and to extend hospitality to the guests.[61] It was also specifically implied that a cleric was to be accorded enough income to support any dependent members of his immediate family, including nephews and nieces.[62]

There was a further development of the demands of equity through a determining of the income of the clergy according to merit. Although all the clergy were to receive a decent income, those who deserved more because of eminence of learning or of other merits were to be fittingly compensated. Hostiensis rather saltily summed up the attitude of the Church when he stated that a better benefice was due to a good and noble cleric than to an ignoble, idiotic cleric, and that the accomplishments of the cleric as well as the circumstances of the church to which he was assigned were to be considered as determining the income of clerics.[63]

In line with this reasoning the income of clerics was to differ according to their rank and dignity; thus a priest was to receive more than a deacon, who in turn was to receive more than a subdeacon, etc.[64] The circumstances of the region constituted another factor in the determination of a proper income for clerics; thus clerics of equal merit, if they labored in regions which differed in

---

[61] *Glossa* s.v. *congrua,* ad c. 33, X, *de praebendis et dignitatibus,* III, 5; *casus* ad c. 12, X, *de praebendis et dignitatibus,* III, 5; Ioannes Andreae, *Novella,* s.v. *et ibi tenetur,* ad c. 12, X, *de praebendis et dignitatibus,* III, 5.

[62] Hostiensis summed up the argument on this point thus: "Et sic est hic argumentum quod sufficiens beneficium intelligitur quando tantum est, quod beneficiatus potest inde nedum se sed coniunctas personas substantare."—*Commentaria,* s.v. *sororem* (n. 4), and *subministrent* (n. 5), ad c. 1, X, *de cohabitatione clericorum,* III, 2; c. 8, X, *de praebendis et dignitatibus,* III, 5.

[63] "Nam nobili et bono clerico maius beneficium quam ignobili idiotae est merito assignandum. . . . Sed et facultates ipsius considerandae videntur—et potissime considerandae sunt ecclesiae quae providere coguntur facultates."—*Commentaria,* s.v. *secundum qualitatem personae,* ad c. 16, X, *de praebendis et dignitatibus,* III, 5.

[64] Panormitanus, *Commentaria,* s.v. *sine capella,* ad c. 3, X, *de vita et honestate clericorum,* III, 1.

wealth, could be expected to receive different incomes.[65] Of course the principle of interpreting a decent income according to the circumstances of rank, of accomplishments, and wealth of the region was never to be distorted to condone luxurious living by the clergy; luxury was always condemned. The type and amount of food and of clothing, and the character of the living quarters, would, however depend on the circumstances of the region.[66]

There was also a departure from the practice of the earlier centuries (the era of Chrodegang and Charlemagne) of having the cleric donate his private wealth to the Church before being considered worthy to receive support from the Church; the idea of enjoying income from private wealth and of also receiving the revenue from a benefice had been repugnant. This idea was completely abandoned. A cleric was acknowledged the right to support from a church benefice as long as he was serving the church, regardless of the amount of income accruing from his patrimony (even if he had been ordained with the *titulus patrimonii*). It was agreed that if a cleric enjoyed a sufficient income from his own patrimony he had no right to additional income from the "universal Church"—from the general funds or available wealth of a diocese; but if he served a church he had a right to income from such service.

This law applied not only to clerics engaged in parochial work (as understood today), but likewise to clerics who executed any work assigned to them by the bishop and which was compatible with the clerical state. The cleric who thus enjoyed income from two different sources was expected not to use the income from the benefice simply for the purpose of amassing wealth.[67] On the other

---

[65] "Secundum qualitatem personae et regionis, ut plus in Anglia quam in provincia assignetur etiam personis aequalibus, secundum Hostiensem."—Ioannes Andreae, *Novella*, s.v. *quantitatem*, ad c. 16, X, *de praebendis et dignitatibus*, III, 5.

[66] Ioannes Andreae, *Novella*, s.v. *vivere*, ad c. 16, X, *de praebendis et dignitatibus*, III, 5.

[67] Panormitanus, *Commentaria*, s.v. *tenent litteras*, ad c. 27, X, *de rescriptis*, I, 3. Panormitanus noted in his commentary the divergence between the former custom of sharing common goods and the system current in his day.—Cf. Hostiensis, *Commentaria*, s.v. *proventibus* (n. 3, 4, 5, 6), ad c. 27, X, *de rescriptis*, I, 3; Hostiensis, *Commentaria*, s.v. *de sua* (n. 3), ad c. 4, X, *de praebendis et dignitatibus*, III, 5.

hand, a cleric who had been ordained on his patrimony, without any benefice, had a right to support from his bishop if he lost his patrimony.[68] The minimum support due to a cleric from his bishop was adequate clothing, food and living accommodations in accordance with his state.[69]

It was also recognized that even clerics who for a cause had been removed from their office were nevertheless to receive enough for their sustenance.[70] This practice was a further evidence that the Church at that time did not conceive that the decent livelihood afforded to zealous clerics was to be so meager that it sufficed for the maintenance of only the most frugal life; if even unworthy or imprudent clerics were to be afforded sustenance, worthy and zealous clerics certainly had a right to much more.

It was stated that the Church still maintained the ideal of having the estate, the *mansus integer,* as the principal source of income for the support of the clergy. This does not mean that the Decretals and the decretalists did not insist on the other sources of income recognized in the former ages. Hostiensis enumerated the different sources (other than the income from lands owned by the church) as, tithes, first-fruits, offerings made at the conferral of the sacraments, all other offerings, including offerings made at Mass and bequests left at the time of death.[71] Mention was likewise made of the double-tithes, but probably not so much stress was laid on it as in past centuries.[72]

The obligation to pay tithes was urged as rigorously as in other centuries; they were to be collected from all classes of society, even from the monks who owned land or resided in a parish and attended its church or were ministered to by the parish priest. There

---

[68] Panormitanus, *Commentaria,* s.v. *iudicium sibi manducavit,* ad c. 23, X, *de praebendis et dignitatibus,* III, 5.

[69] Ioannes Andreae, *Novella,* s.v. *necessaria,* ad c. 16, X, *de praebendis et dignitatibus,* III,.5.

[70] Letter 39 of Alexander III to King Louis VII (uncertain date)—JL, n. 10745.

[71] Hostiensis, *Commentaria,* on the Rubr. (n. 1, 2), ad c. 1, *de parochiis, et alienis parochianis,* III, 29.

[72] Cc. 12, 13, 27, X, *de decimis, primitiis et oblationibus,* III, 30.

were some exemptions to this, as in the case of the Cistercians, who by privilege were exempted from the payment of the tithes.[73]

The tithes apparently constituted a very considerable portion of the income of the Church, and there arose the tradition of supporting the poor and of repairing the church buildings from the tithes.[74] In line with this tradition Ioannes Andreae (1272-1348) stated that tithes usually were given back to the poor (which thus preserved the universal observance of the law of tithes.)[75] Together with the tithes there was the donation of the first-fruits. These amounted, as in other centuries, to from 1/40 to 1/60 of the produce of grain and wine; the first-fruits of livestock were offered in the ratio of one for every two hundred head.[76]

The clergy's support also depended largely on the amount of the *portio canonica* contributed from the estate of the deceased at the time of the burial. The amount of the contribution was not fixed by law, but it was a considerable amount.[77]

It must be remembered, however, that none of the foregoing rules on the sources of income for the Church were accepted with the rigidity that marked the earlier centuries of the Church's history. Ioannes Andreae, after enumerating the sources of church income, distinguished between those that were voluntary and of undetermined amount and those that were of a fixed amount.[78] There was a marked increase in the prominence of voluntary contribu-

---

[73] C. 4, X, *de decimis, primitiis et oblationibus,* III, 30.

[74] Hostiensis, *Commentaria,* Rubric preceding c. 1, X, *de decimis, primitiis et oblationibus,* III, 30.

[75] Ioannes Andreae, *Novella,* s.v. *decimas,* ad c. 2, X, *de immunitate ecclesiarum coemiterii, et rerum ad eas pertinentium,* III, 49.

[76] Hostiensis, *Commentaria,* s.v. *primitiae* (n. 9), ad c. 1, X, *de decimis, primitiis et oblationibus,* III, 30.

[77] Hostiensis (*Commentaria,* s.v. *salva iustitia* [n. a], ad c. 9, X, *de sepulturis,* III, 28), stated that the amount was uncertain, but that it was unreasonable to ask nothing or very little at the time of burial. Cf. c. 2, *de sepulturis,* III, 7, in Clem.

[78] Ioannes Andreae, *Novella,* Rubric of c. 1, X, *de parochiis, et alienis parochianis,* III, 29. According to Ioannes Andreae, the offerings at church on feast days and at times when the needs of the clergy made it imperative to collect offerings were voluntary "quoad quantitatem et speciem." This also is evidence that the use of money for offerings to the church was very common at that time, in contrast with the usage of the earlier centuries when goods and animals were offered.

tions as part of the income of the Church, yet Ioannes Andreae concluded wearily that despite the laws the priests tried to collect as much as possible from both strangers and their own parishioners.[79]

Naturally, wherever the income of the parish was normal, the pastor was bound to fulfill all the obligations towards the bishop and the poor as in the previous centuries. The law of Christian charity was still upheld and extolled to the extent that it contained the magnificent charge on the clergy, *"Quidquid habeant clerici, est pauperum."*[80] In fact, so normal and constant was the practice of the clergy in receiving strangers and guests in a special guest house, and even in their homes, that a specific canon was promulgated for the purpose of refuting the presumption that a pastor was obliged to receive any public officials or persons in his home.[81]

Furthermore, pastors who enjoyed normal incomes were obliged to pay their obligations to the bishop. As was indicated above, the blanket rule of contributing one-fourth or one-third of the income to the bishop was abandoned, and the paying of the *census* and the *cathedraticum* along with the tendering of hospitality at the time of the visitation became the accepted contributions.[82]

There was an awareness of the demands of equity in the levying of these obligations, since the general rule was accommodated to the particular circumstances. Hostiensis stated that in collecting the *cathedraticum* the bishop was permitted to collect what was allowed by law (which was two *solidi*), but in a case of doubt about the legal prescriptions for that region he could follow the regional custom (*consuetudo*).[83] Likewise, a *census* could not be levied unless the proper authority stated the cause,[84] nor could an estab-

---

[79] "Quidquid tamen scribatur, clerici semper recurrunt ad eleemosynas et parochianos tam proprios quam alienos excutientes quantum possunt humeros suos."—*Novella,* s.v. *et in fine,* ad c. 1, X, *de ecclesiis aedificandis vel reparandis,* III, 48.

[80] Panormitanus, *Commentaria,* Introductio ad c. 4, X, *de ecclesiis aedificandis vel reparandis,* III, 48.

[81] Panormitanus, *Commentaria,* Introductio ad c. 1, X, *de immunitate ecclesiarum coemiterii, et rerum ad eas pertinentium,* III, 49.

[82] C. 9, 20, X, *de censibus, exactionibus et procurationibus,* III, 39.

[83] Hostiensis, *Commentaria,* s.v. *imponuntur* (n. 3), ad c. 9, X, *de censibus, exactionibus et procurationibus,* III, 39.

[84] Panormitanus, *Commentaria,* s.v. *non debetur census,* ad c. 5, X, *de censibus, exactionibus et procurationibus,* III, 39.

lished *census* be increased without reason.[85] To obviate completely any misunderstanding or avarice in the levying of the *census,* it was also decided that a new *census* (which was ordinarily forbidden) was any *census* levied after the past general council, the IV General Council of the Lateran (1215).[86]

Possibly the best comprehensive statement of the attitude of the Church towards the support of the clergy was made by Panormitanus. He stated that one who established a church had to endow it according to its purpose: if its purpose served the contemplative life, then it had to be sufficiently endowed for the support of the persons in the number as required—as was illustrated by the Pope when he obliged the Queen of Hungary to increase the dowry for such a church; if its purpose was that of a parish church, it had to be sufficiently endowed for the support of two clerics, but not necessarily for the maintenance of a hospice, for the hospice could be added later when the church could afford to maintain one. A parish was also to have a sufficient endowment which would enable it to pay its obligations to the bishop.[87] In his summation Panormitanus did not specifically state (though perhaps he adumbrated it) that a parish could be erected without any dowry if the bishop deemed that the welfare of souls so demanded.

In the Decretals and by the decretalists the decent livelihood due to the clergy was appraised with reference particularly to two factors: the welfare of souls and the claim of equity. The welfare of souls, the highest end of the Church, demanded that churches and priests be afforded to Christians even when the circumstances permitted only a meager sustenance. Equity demanded that a cleric be supported not only according to his rank and dignity, but also according to his accomplishments. Since the support of clerics as well as that of the prominent persons of a region found its measure in the wealth of that region, the support of clerics differed according as the wealth and material assets of the region differed. Luxury, however, was never permitted.

---

[85] C. 7, X, *de censibus, exactionibus et procurationibus,* III, 39.

[86] Hostiensis, *Commentaria,* s.v. *de novo* (n. 7), ad c. 13, X, *de censibus, exactionibus et procurationibus,* III, 39.

[87] Panormitanus, *Commentaria,* s.v. *recipere hospites,* ad c. 8, X, *de consecratione ecclesiae vel altaris,* III, 40.

CHAPTER V

Council of Trent and the Sixteenth Century

Section 1. Support by Benefice, Pension or Patrimony

The Council of Trent (1545-1563) reiterated and reorganized the currently accepted regulations on the support of the clergy. In doing so it relied to some extent on the decrees which more than two hundred years earlier had been promulgated in the Council of Vienne (1311-1312).[1] The Council of Trent decreed that a cleric could not receive ordination without a *titulus ordinationis,* which furnished guarantee of a sufficient support for the rest of his life. The elements of this title of ordination were sufficiency and perpetuity of the guaranteed support. The only titles of ordination which the Council approved were those of a benefice, a pension, or a patrimony.[2]

Very shortly after the close of the great Council, the reigning Pontiff, St. Pius V (1566-1572), repeated and clarified the decrees on the necessity of providing a cleric with the guarantee of a sufficient support before he received ordination. St. Pius V declared that even if a candidate were otherwise acceptable because of his moral conduct, knowledge, and age, he could not receive ordination unless he had the guarantee of a sufficient means of support—a strong statement from the saintly Pope who had vigorously championed the spiritual reform of the Church.[3] A decision shortly

[1] Conc. Trident., sess. XXV, *de ref.,* c. 8; sess. VII, *de ref.,* c. 15.

[2] Conc. Trident., sess. XXI, *de ref.,* c. 2; St. Pius V, const. *Ad exequendum,* 1567—*Magnum Bullarium Romanum, Leo Magnus ad Benedictum XIII* (opus Laertii Cherubini, auctum a D. Angelo M. Cherubino, deinde a R.R.P.P. Angelo a Lantusca et Joanne Paulo a Roma, 19 vols., Luxemburgi, 1727), II, 259.

[3] St. Pius V, const., *Romanus Pontifex,* 14 oct. 1568, § 1—*Codicis Iuris Canonici Fontes,* cura Emi Petri Card. Gasparri editi (9 vols., Romae: Typis Polyglottis Vaticanis, 1923-1939. Vols. VII, VIII et IX ed. cura et studio Emi Iustinani Card. Serédi), n. 129 (hereafter referred to as *Fontes*).

thereafter by the Sacred Congregation of the Council extended the legislation of the Church on the means of support necessary for the ordination of a cleric. A donation sufficiently large for the lifelong support of a cleric could be accepted in place of a benefice, pension or patrimony.[4]

On the other hand, the Church insisted that the cleric possess a benefice or an actual means of support before he receive ordination. Hence it was not permitted to ordain to sacred Orders a cleric who was either an artist, a musician, or a teacher, capable of supporting himself by these or other professions; no cleric in major Orders was permitted to undertake such work.[5] The Church likewise ruled that the possession of a doctorate in theology or in canon law was not a sufficient guarantee of support for the ordination of a cleric to sacred Orders. The doctor needed also a benefice, a pension, or a patrimony before he could be ordained.[6]

Since no cleric was to be ordained to sacred Orders until he had secured the guarantee of a sufficient means of support, a cleric was not permitted to work at or to engage in a trade except in certain cases of necessity, such as his unforeseen impoverishment, or that of his near-relatives and dependents. He was obliged to secure permission from his ordinary or from the Apostolic See before he was permitted to engage in a craft or a trade, even if the nature of these was not inherently foreign to his sacred profession.[7]

Inasmuch as any single benefice was supposed to provide a sufficient support for a cleric, the Council of Trent repeated the prohibition against the possession of a plurality of benefices, which prohibition was sanctioned under the penalty of deprivation of both or all benefices.[8] The exception to this rule occurred when the

---

[4] S.C.C., *Feretrana,* a. 1573, ad 3—*Fontes,* n. 2120; S.C.C.,*Cortonen.,* mense maio 1589—*Fontes,* n. 2207.

[5] S.C.C., *Seguntina,* mense oct. 1589, ad 4—*Fontes,* n. 2218; Conc. Trident., sess. XXII, *de ref.,* c. 1.

[6] S.C.C., *Pacen.,* 23 maii 1609—*Fontes,* n. 2377.

[7] Pius IV, const. *Decens esse,* 5 nov. 1560—*Bullarum Diplomatum et Privilegiorum Sanctorum Pontificum Taurinensis Editio* (24 vols. in 25, Augustae Taurinorum, 1857-1872), IV, pars II, 58 (hereafter referred to as *Bull. Rom.*).

[8] Conc. Trident., sess. VII, *de ref.,* c. 4.

returns from one benefice were insufficient for the decent support of a cleric; in such an event the incumbent could secure a dispensation to hold two benefices to both of which was attached the care of souls (*beneficia curata*) along with the obligation of residence.[9] If the cathedral or collegiate prebends were too small for the support of the canons, simple benefices could be added to the prebends for the increase of the income to a proper amount.[10]

Once the Council had decreed that every cleric in major Orders was to have the guarantee of a sufficient income for his support, it obviously became necessary to define which financial obligations were incumbent on a cleric. Besides the demands made by his physical needs, which further duties entailing financial obligations were imposed on a cleric?

The income for a cleric was to be large enough to enable him to discharge his duties to the bishop, to repair and to maintain the church, and to extend hospitality and succor to those who deserved it.[11] Further, it was the accepted doctrine that any cleric who held a parochial benefice required the assistance of a cleric or of a vicar; consequently he was charged with paying to this assistant cleric or vicar an income sufficient for his decent support.[12]

Moreover, the income of a cleric was to be influenced by an appraisal of the accomplishments of the cleric as well as to the circumstances of the region. Everything that enhanced the worth of a cleric—his zeal, nobility, knowledge—was a contributing factor in the determining of a fitting income for him.[13]

The Council did more than simply lay down general principles for governing the determination of the support due to the clergy—it specified a definite minimum income. Cathedral churches were to have an income of at least one thousand ducats, and parish churches an income of at least one hundred ducats; cathedrals and

---

[9] Conc. Trident., sess. XXIV, *de ref.*, c. 17.

[10] Conc. Trident., sess. XXIV, *de ref.*, c. 15.

[11] Conc. Trident., sess. XXV, *de ref.*, c. 8; sess. XXI, *de ref.*, c. 7; sess. VII, *de ref.*, c. 8.

[12] Conc. Trident., sess. VII, *de ref.*, c. 5.

[13] ". . . decenti canonicorum gradui pro loci et personarum qualitate. . . ."—Conc. Trident., sess. XXIV, *de ref.*, c. 15.

parish churches were not to be taxed for pensions or other financial obligations unless they received at least these amounts.[14]

Besides the fixing of these incomes for the rectors and clerics of a cathedral and for the pastors of parish churches, it was the conviction in Rome at the time of St. Pius V (1566-1572) that thirty gold ducats a year was the minimum income for the fitting support of any cleric. The *Collectores Camerae Apostolicae* (the Collectors of the Apostolic Household or Camera were entrusted with the duty of collecting the possessions of deceased clerics which were considered due to the Church) were not allowed to touch the effects of a deceased cleric who had not enjoyed an income of more than thirty ducats a year. Anything that such a cleric managed to save was eked out of what was due him for his support, and therefore belonged to him personally.[15]

Since the income from the benefice or pension was intended only to supply a cleric with his legitimate needs, and not to serve for his enrichment or aggrandizement, the cleric was bound to devote the surplus income from his benefice or pension to the cause of the poor or to pious works. The legitimate needs of a cleric were interpreted in a broad and humane way, so that it included the support of his dependents and some reserve for possible unusual expenses.[16] The discussion on the disposition of surplus income from a benefice or pension naturally involved the question about the amount needed by clerics in the various ranks and dignities of the Church. The Church always maintained that a difference in personal dignity and in rank of authority implied also a different in the allowance for support, even in regard to food; this accepted rule held true for the clergy and the laity alike.[17]

---

[14] Conc. Trident., sess. XXIV, *de ref.*, c. 13; St. Pius V decreed that the income of a vicar should not be less than 50 ducats a year—St. Pius V, const. *Ad exequendum*, 1567—*Magnum Bullarium Romanum, Leo Magnus ad Benedictum* XIII, II, 259.

[15] St. Pius V, const. *Romani Pontificis*, 30 aug. 1567, § 6—*Fontes*, n. 123.

[16] Conc. Trident., sess. XXV, *de ref.*, c. 1.

[17] S.R.R., Dec. XXXI, 22 mai 1593—*Decisiones Recentiores Sacrae Romanae Rotae* (19 vols. in 24, citing decisions from 1558 to 1684, published 1623-1703), pars I (ed. Prosper Farinacius, Francofurti, 1623), p. 30 (hereafter referred to as *Decisiones Recentiores;* Ferraris, *Prompta Bibliotheca Canonica, Juridica, Moralis, Theologica, necnon Ascetica, Polemica, Rubricistica, Historica* (9 vols., Romae, 1885-1899), II, s.v. *Congrua* (hereafter referred to as *Bibliotheca*).

Added to the vexing question of the amount due to a cleric for his support was the related question of the nature of a cleric's duty to devote his surplus income to charitable causes. Was it an obligation of strict justice, or was it rather an obligation of pressing charity? This question was not settled by the Council of Trent. A great deal of controversy arose about it in the ensuing centuries.

Contemporary with the deliberations of the Council of Trent there was lengthy consideration by canonists and theologians on the question of the decent support for the clergy. The outstanding writer of this period on the subject was Petrus Rebuffus (1487-1557), professor at the University of Paris, who wrote a special tract on the amount of income due to vicars. His writings, as well as the decisions of the Roman Congregations at the time, provide a clarification of some of the principles enunciated at the Council. It is amazing how closely his writings and commentary(all of them written before the end of the Council) concur with and illustrate the decisions of the Council of Trent and those of the Sacred Congregations.[18]

In indicating the nature of the support of the clergy, Rebuffus insisted that the income had to be secure, that is, derived from an unfailing source. Such an unfailing source was constituted by the returns from lands owned by the church, even though the amount of income could be variable; other such sources were the contributions regularly made by the parishioners.[19] The cleric should not be assigned the income from a particular field or vineyard lest the crop failure in that field rob him of his support.[20]

Although generally a cleric was forbidden to engage in non-avocational work (since his income was supposed to be sufficient for his support), Rebuffus easily admitted that a cleric could per-

[18] The lengthy and descriptive title of his work illustrates its scope—*Tractatus Congruae Portionis Beneficiorum Vicariis maxime Debitae, brevis et admodum utilis ac in forensi iudicio usu veniens* (Coloniae Agrippinae, 1572). Hereafter the work will be referred to as *Tractatus.*

[19] With reference to the practice current at that time, Rebuffus related that each parishioner gave annually three or four measures of wine, a donation of wheat and oil, besides a contribution of money—Rebuffus, *Tractatus,* n. 81, pp. 386-389; S.R.R., *Pacen.,* Dec. CCCCXX, nn. 2, 3, 8 iun. 1612—*Decisiones Recentiores,* pars I, 482.

[20] Rebuffus, *Tractatus,* n. 84, p. 390.

form such work for his support if he had willingly accepted a benefice or an office that yielded only a very small income. Of course the type of work permitted was that performed by his own labor, *ex industria sua,* not by his engaging in commerce.[21]

The determined guarantee income due to the cleric depended upon the obligations and duties of the cleric. Rebuffus was specific in enumerating the various duties and expenses of a cleric. The obligations entailing financial expenditures were numerous, foremost of which was the duty of a parish priest to have at least one assistant cleric for help at the solemn celebration of Mass and of the divine offices. Rebuffus looked askance at the custom, prevalent in certain sections of Italy, which allowed priests to celebrate Mass without an assistant cleric; specifically he condemned the custom which allowed the celebrant to sing the Epistle (*lectio.*)[22]

If there were several chapels in the parish, the pastor or the vicar was to have an assistant cleric for each chapel.[23] Naturally the pastor was to have enough to discharge his obligations to the bishop (the *cathedraticum*), including the contribution called the "*synodaticum,*" and the offering made at the time of the episcopal visitation.[24] Likewise, the pastor was to have an adequate income which would enable him to make the contribution to the Pope,[25] and to take care of the repairs necessary for the proper maintenance of the church buildings, although it was conceded that often the pastor or the vicar needed contributions from the parishioners to help defray the expense of church repairs.[26]

The pastors were reminded also that they were bound to give their servants decent food and lodging along with a support which was commensurate with the dignity and the income of the cleric.[27] Rubuffus also repeated the old admonition that the pastor was obliged to support the poor, which duty according to Rebuffus

[21] Rebuffus, *Tractatus,* n. 92, p. 394.

[22] Rebuffus, *Tractatus,* n. 65, p: 373; S.R.R., *Pacen.,* Dec. CCCCXX, n. 10, 8 iun. 1612—*Decisiones Recentiores,* pars I, 482.

[23] Rebuffus, *Tractatus,* n. 68, pp. 376-377.

[24] Rebuffus, *Tractatus,* n. 69 (mistakenly printed "73" in the text of the book), p. 377; n. 74, p. 381.

[25] Rebuffus, *Tractatus,* n. 75, p. 381.

[26] Rebuffus, *Tractatus,* n. 72, p. 379.

[27] Rebuffus, *Tractatus,* n. 63, p. 372.

postulated the maintaining of a separate hospice (*hameau* or *secours*) for each chapel.[28] Rebuffus admitted that a pastor or a vicar was not bound to receive so many poor that he could not decently pay his servants or support himself,[29] but the obligation of charity was urgent enough to warrant, in the event of a famine, the foregoing of repairs on the church in order to feed the poor.[30]

In determining how much constituted a decent living for a cleric, Rebuffus also pointed out that it was necessary to consider the qualifications of the cleric—his knowledge, rank, nobility. A cleric of superior accomplishments and of a higher ecclesiastical dignity was acknowledged to have more obligations than a simple cleric.[31] Rebuffus further contended that an older cleric should receive more than a younger one, since the older cleric generally needed more help.[32] The customs and circumstances of the region were also a factor in determining the amount which sufficed to constitute a decent livelihood for a cleric.[33]

After explaining the duties and the needs of a cleric, Rebuffus proved himself a very practical professor by estimating the amount needed by a cleric for meeting these needs. A decent livelihood to Rebuffus meant an adequate income which enabled a cleric to live conveniently, and not simply without penury; a decent livelihood connoted more than just the absence of pressing want. He estimated that a cleric could live without penury on 20 gold pieces a year (*pro viginti aureis*), but a cleric could not live comfortably without an income of one hundred gold pieces.[34]

It is obvious, however, from the title and tenor of Rebuffus'

---

[28] Rebuffus, *Tractatus*, n. 68, p. 376; n. 71, p. 379.

[29] Rebuffus, *Tractatus*, n. 71, pp. 378-379.

[30] Rebuffus, *Tractatus*, n. 72, pp. 379-380.

[31] Rebuffus, *Tractatus*, n. 63, p. 372; Ferraris, *Bibliotheca*, s.v. *Congrua*, art. II, n. 7, 35.

[32] Rebuffus, *Tractatus*, n. 76, p. 382.

[33] Rebuffus, *Tractatus*, n. 76, p. 328; Ferraris, *Bibliotheca*, s.v. *Congrua*, art. II, n. 7; S.R.R., *Mediolanen.*, 18 dec. 1617, Dec. DXCV, n. 1—*Decisiones Recentiores*, pars 4, tom. 1, 460.

[34] ". . . quia sine penuria quis vivere potest pro viginti aureis, et tamen commode non poterit nisi habeat centum vel aliam similem summam."—Rebuffus, *Tractatus*, n. 78, p. 382; S.R.R., *Pacen.*, 8 iun. 1612, Dec. CCCCXX, n. 3—*Decisiones Recentiores*, pars I, 372.

work, as well as from the decisions of the Roman Rota, that no specific sum could be arbitrarily assigned as a sufficient income for clerics. The ordinary was the authority who determined this for his territory.[35] Of course, a decision could be appealed.[36]

The obligations of a cleric were to be met from the income of his benefice, his pension, or his patrimony. Any returns he received from his own labors, or from any source not identified as part of his regular income, the cleric could keep or disburse as he wished. For instance, any payment for teaching was apart from the normal income of his benefice or pension, and thus could be freely disbursed by the cleric. The cleric was however bound to devote any excess or surplus income from his benefice or pension to some charitable cause.[37] Hence, any income granted to a cleric by his family, as well as a bequest or a gift on an anniversary, could be kept by him as separate from the regular income due from his office.[38]

Rebuffus also considered the daily distributions made to canons as apart from their income from the benefice, and hence as funds that could be kept or disbursed at will. He reasoned that the income of a benefice was supposed to support a cleric regardless of the state of his health. But, since the canon would lose the daily distribution in the event of sickness and consequent absence from the celebration of the divine office, the daily distribution was rather to be regarded as not constituting part of the regular income of the benefice.[39] This doctrine showed how thoroughly Rebuffus was persuaded that the income from a benefice was to furnish a complete support for the cleric who held the office, and that holding that office did not mean that the cleric was to go unrewarded for all the religious services he performed, whether proximately or remotely connected with his office.

---

[35] Rebuffus, *Tractatus,* n. 52, p. 364; n. 54, p. 365; n. 86, p. 392; cf. Ferraris, *Bibliotheca,* s.v. *Congrua,* art. II, n. 1.

[36] Rebuffus, *Tractatus,* n. 55, p. 366; Ferraris, *Bibliotheca,* s.v. *Congrua,* art. II, n. 5; S.R.R., *Pacen.,* 8 iun. 1612, Dec. CCCCXX, n. 1—*Decisiones Recentiores,* pars I, 372; S.R.R., *Atrien.,* 27 iun. 1674, Dec. CCCLI, n. 3—*Decisiones Recentiores,* pars 18, tom. 1, 654.

[37] Rebuffus, *Tractatus,* n. 89, p. 393.

[38] Rebuffus, *Tractatus,* n. 88, p. 393; n. 82, p. 378; n. 86, p. 391.

[39] Rebuffus, *Tractatus,* n. 86, p. 391.

Rebuffus devoted special attention to the rights of vicars. The vicar of a church, if appointed by a monastery, had a right not only to a lodging outside the monastery, but also to the maintenance of a separate table.[40] The quality of the food was to be in accordance with the dignity and the rank of the cleric, who never was to be forced to accept the cheapest or poorest kind of food.[41]

The swiftly changing economic conditions, coupled with the failings to which human nature is prone, necessitated the very specific determinations of writers like Rebuffus regarding the rights of clerics to a decent support. The fixing of a definite sum as a proper income for a cleric could not be maintained, for the flood of money entering Europe from the New World and the Orient caused a very sharp inflation in prices. Prices sky-rocketed especially in the Iberian Peninsula, which had profited most from the new discoveries.[42]

The Council of Trent and the Church authorities could hardly have encountered a more difficult time than the sixteenth century in fixing the amount, even in a general way, for the decent support of the clergy. The principles governing the decent support of the clergy could be enunciated, as indeed they were, but the interpretation of how much was due to the clergy in the various regions, in terms of a fixed income, was difficult.

SECTION 2. SUPPORT BY TITULI MISSIONIS, SERVITII ECCLESIAE, MENSAE

While the wealth of the Americas and the East Indies was enriching Catholic countries during the sixteenth century, the Protestant Reformation was despoiling and pauperizing the Church in the Germanic, Anglo-Saxon, and Scandinavian countries. In the coun-

---

[40] Rebuffus, *Tractatus,* n. 96, p. 398.

[41] Rebuffus, *Tractatus,* n. 64, p. 373. Beans and "other vile foods" were considered too common for a cleric!

[42] John M. Ferguson, in his book, *Landmarks of Economic Thought* (New York: Longmans, Green and Co., 1938), p. 28, notes: "The yearly output of the precious metals soared to unheard-of heights. European coinage increased at least tenfold during the sixteenth century, and from 1550 to 1650 the general price level in Europe rose by 300 per cent, giving rise to the famous 'Revolution of Prices'."

tries affected by the Protestant Revolt, conditions made it impossible to ordain many clerics according to the statutes of the Council of Trent, which had demanded that clerics in major Orders have the guarantee of a sufficient income by means of a *titulus beneficii, pensionis,* or *patrimonii.* Obviously it was necessary to find new means of support for the clergy, new titles of ordination, to enable the Church to work in non-Catholic territory.

Article 1. Support by titulus missionis

The concept of economic security for clerics, as ordained by the Council of Trent, stood in conflict with the concept of the missionary activity of the Church (also a project of the Council of Trent) in non-Catholic regions. Obviously there were few if any benefices, pensions, or patrimonies available for missionaries. Patently the Holy Father was obliged to grant a new title of ordination to clerics ordained for, or engaging in, missionary activity.

Pope Gregory XIII (1572-1585), in the year 1578, permitted seminarians at the English College in Rome to receive ordination with a *"titulus missionis."*[43] This new title permitted tested and gifted candidates to be ordained for missionary activity in lands where they could be supported by a group of loyal Catholics amid hazardous and unpredictable circumstances. It must be noted, however, that in granting such a title the Church did not derogate in any way from its doctrine on the decent support due to the clergy; as far as possible, the Church applied to the priests in missionary activity as much of the doctrine on sufficient support as the circumstances permitted. For the good of souls the Pope permitted an unusual title of ordination, which however preserved the substance of the provisions inherent in the other recognized titles of ordination.[44]

---

[43] Cf. F. X. Wernz, *Ius Decretalium,* II, n. 91. Gregorius XIII, Bulla *Quoniam divinae bonitati,* 23 apr. 1578, § 12—*Bull. Rom.,* Vol. VIII (cura et studio collegii adlecti Romae Virorum S. Theologiae et SS. Canonum Peritorum, Neapoli, 1883), p. 212.

[44] This is evident also from the later documents of the Church, notably the lengthy Instruction of the Sacred Congregation for the Propagation of the Faith, 27 apr. 1871, §§ 6, 7—*Fontes,* n. 4878.

As intended, the Holy See later extended the use of the *titulus missionis* to other groups. In 1584, the seminarians of the German and Hungarian College were permitted to receive ordination under this title.[45]

Article 2. Support by titulus servitii ecclesiae (dioecesis, administrationis)

At the same time that the Council of Trent was determining the approved titles of ordination for clerics in major Orders, another system of supporting the clergy (or another title of ordination) became prevalent in Italy. Pope Sixtus V (1585-1590) granted permission to the Church in Venice to ordain clerics who had no benefice, pension or patrimony, but who could be supported fittingly from the income of the church to which they were to be assigned; this was called the *titulus servitii ecclesiae.*[46] Later, under different circumstances, this title of ordination was called the *titulus servitii dioecesis* and the *titulus administrationis.*[47]

It is evident from the practice as followed both in Venice and in Mexico that the substance of the doctrine of the Church on decent support of the clergy was maintained. In both regions no cleric was to be ordained to major Orders unless there was the guarantee of a secure and sufficient source of income for life.

---

[45] Wernz, *Ius Decretalium,* II, n. 91; Gregorius XIII, Bulla *Ex collegio Germanico,* 1 apr. 1584, n. 12—*Bull. Rom.,* VIII, 451.

[46] Garcia, *De Beneficiis Ecclesiasticis* (Venetiis, 1618), part. 2, c. V, n. 96, 97; Wernz, *Ius Decretalium,* II, n. 92, p. 135.

[47] The description of the *titulus servitii ecclesiae* makes it clear that substantially this *titulus* was the basis for the development of the *titulus servitii dioecesis* and *administrationis.*—". . . qui, cum beneficio ecclesiastico vel pensione careant, aut patrimonialia aliaque bona non possideant, ea lege ordinantur, ut alicui Ecclesiae sint mancipati, ex cuius servitio et eleemosynis a piis christifidelibus elargiendis substentari possint, et ab eadem Ecclesia nulla umquam tempore amoveri, vel ipsi recedere nequeant, nisi aliter eis provisum fuerit."—S.C. de Prop. Fide., instr. 27 apr. 1871—*Collectanea Sacrae Congregationis de Propaganda Fide* (2 vols., Romae, 1907), n. 1369; *Fontes,* n. 4878. When the cleric was ordained for the service of the diocese. the title became *titulus servitii dioecesis.* This development will be treated more fully in the next chapter.

Article 3. Support by titulus mensae

Another title of ordination was widely in use, though not approved by the Holy See, from the time of the sixteenth century—the granting of an annual income for a cleric by municipal or national authorities. In the absence of sufficient benefices, pensions, and patrimonies for the support of the clerics as needed in a certain community or region, the civil authorities granted a sufficient annual income to clerics ordained to major Orders for the care of souls in that section.[48]

This system of support was not approved at the Council of Trent. In fact, although it continued in use it was disapproved by the Roman Curia as late as 1704.[49] The practice of ordaining under this *titulus mensae* must have been fairly widespread and well known, for it was later adopted by religious congregations and societies.[50]

---

[48] Wernz, *Ius Decretalium,* II, n. 91.

[49] S.C.C., *Florentina,* 28 iun. 1704—*Fontes,* n. 3023.

[50] S.C. Ep. de Reg., *Novarien.,* 20 dec. 1838—*Fontes,* n. 1919.

CHAPTER VI

Seventeenth Century to the Present

SECTION 1. SUPPORT BY BENEFICE, PENSION OR PATRIMONY

In the century following the Council of Trent and the Constitution *Ad exequendum* of Pius V, the canonists commented and interpreted the still undetermined and flexible provisions of these two bodies of law on the decent support of the clergy. The points most controverted were:

1) the constituent elements of the *congrua portio* or the *sustentatio* as derivable from a benefice, a pension or a patrimony, that is, which sources of income were considered the essential part of a benefice, pension, or patrimony, and which elements were extraneous or subsidiary;
2) the factors determining the amount of a cleric's *congrua portio;*
3) the actual amount specified as the *congrua portio;*
4) the nature and the gravity of the obligation to devote the excess income of a benefice or a pension to pious causes.

Article 1. Constituent Elements of the Congrua Portio[1]

In the light of the unequivocal words of the Council of Trent and the Constitution of Pius V, it could not be denied that a cleric was to receive a perpetual, sufficient, and assured support which was in keeping with his sacred calling, so that the dignity of his

[1] It was considered advisable to retain in the heading of the Article and in the introduction to it the Latin phrase *"congrua portio,"* which is the equivalent of *congrua* or *honesta sustentatio.* The phrases in English, "decent livelihood," "decent support," "fitting allowance," will be used interchangeably with the Latin phrases in the text to avoid excessive repetition of the Latin phrase.

calling would not be marred by the compulsion to beg or to engage in secular commerce or work. All the canonists agreed that these declarations were to be accepted in the clear and obvious sense of the terms. There will now be considered the elements of the *congrua portio* in the three titles of support recognized at the Council of Trent—benefice, pension, patrimony.

1. Support by benefice

Before consideration is given to the returns of the benefice which constituted the *portio congrua* of a benefice, it is necessary to note the discussion which had arisen concerning the perpetuity of a benefice. The concept of a benefice and of its essential elements had not changed, but there was, in some respects, a new acceptation relative to the meaning of these elements, notably that of perpetuity. The perpetuity was considered from the viewpoint of the beneficiary as well as from the viewpoint of the funds or lands constituting the resources of the benefice.

From the viewpoint of the beneficiary, the perpetuity of a benefice was interpreted to mean that a beneficed cleric was not to be deprived of his office and benefice because of any infirmity, even if it was incurable. To deprive an incapacitated cleric of his benefice was considered so cruel that, if permitted, it would injure the morale of the clergy and deter worthy men from aspiring to the priesthood.[2] However, a cleric so incapacitated was obliged to

[2] Garcia, *De Beneficiis Ecclesiasticis,* Tom. I, pars I, cap. 2, n. 70; Augustinus Barbosa, *Collectanea Doctorum in Ius Pontificium Universum* (6 vols., Lugduni, 1659), lib. III, tit. 5, c. 12, n. 5 (hereafter referred to as *Collectanea*); Prosper Fagnanus, *Ius Canonicum seu Commentaria Absolutissima in Quinque Libros Decretalium* (4 vols., Venetiis, 1696), lib. III, tit. 25, c. 5, n. 1 (hereafter referred to as *Commentaria*). The opinion of Fagnanus (1598-1678) is of singular importance, since in virtue of his position as secretary of the Sacred Congregation of the Council it is presumed that his views are those of the Congregation. Fagnanus' view is important also as representative of the more rigorous and stringent interpretation, "*magnus princeps rigoristarum*" (Van Hove, *Commentarium Lovaniense in Codicem Iuris Canonici Prolegomena ad Codicem Iuris Canonici* (2. ed., Mechliniae et Romae: H. Dessain, 1945), p. 537. Joannes Cardinalis Baptista de Luca, *Theatrum Veritatis et Justitiae* (15 vols. in 9, Coloniae Agrippinae, 1706), Tom. XI, *De Donatione,* Disc. XI, n. 8 (hereafter referred to as

secure a coadjutor to perform all the pastoral duties.[3]

There was in use however a type of benefice which in its intrinsic character was not perpetual. This was the *beneficium manuale,* an income that was given to a cleric, generally by a religious house, from the returns of a bequest or grant donated for that purpose. In the granting of the *beneficium manuale* there were not employed the formalities that attended the granting of a benefice, and the cleric was removable *ad nutum superioris.*[4]

The main point of discussion was the determination of which elements or sources of income constituted the *congrua portio* of the benefice. The importance of the discussion is obvious, since whatever did not constitute the essential parts of the benefice could be freely expended by the beneficiary. It was generally agreed that whatever constituted the certain and unfailing returns of a benefice was the constituent part of the *portio congrua* which was due to a cleric, the beneficiary; this interpretation rested on a phrase from the Council of Trent, *"portione assignanda, etiam super re certa,"*

Theatrum), Emmanuel Gonzalez-Tellez, *Commentaria,* s.v. *competens,* lib. III, tit. 5, c. 16; Schmalzgrueber, *Ius Ecclesiasticum Universum* (5 vols. in 12, Romae, 1843-1845), lib. III, tit. 25, n. 20 (hereafter referred to as *Ius Ecclesiasticum*). The views of the canonists were confirmed by a Constitution of Innocent XIII and by decisions of the Rota; cf. Innocent XIII (1721-1724), const. *Apostolici ministerii,* 23 maii 1723, § 7—*Fontes,* n. 280; S.R.R., *Ianuen.* (Parochialis), 1 iul. 1633, Dec. CCXXX, n. 6—*Decisiones Recentiores,* pars VI, 432. ". . . si enim clerici aegrotantes tam inhumaniter tractarentur, caeteri deterrerentur a clericatu."—Reiffenstuel, *Ius Canonicum Universum* (5 vols. in 7, Parisiis, 1864-1870), lib. III, tit. 6, n. 3 (hereafter referred to as *Ius Canonicum*).

[3] Benedictus XIV, const. *Ad militantis,* 30 mart. 1742, § 12—*Fontes,* n. 326; ep., *Ex quo,* 14 ian. 1747, § 18—*Fontes,* n. 374.

[4] De Luca, *Theatrum,* Tom. XI, *De Donatione,* Disc. XI, n. 8; Tom. II, *De Jure Patronatus,* Disc. XV, n. 3; Garcia, *De Beneficiis Ecclesiasticis,* Tom. I, pars I, cap. 2, n. 70. Garcia (+1613) attempted to reconcile the perpetuity of the income of a benefice and the temporary provision of the *beneficium manuale* by contending that the *manuale* is perpetual *"aptitudine";* Reiffenstuel (+1703) stated that it was better to have manual benefices than permanent chaplains, since the fear of removal could serve as a great incentive to the clerics to fulfill well their duties and to lead a pious life.—*Ius Canonicum,* lib. III, tit. 5, n. 44.

and the controversial phrase of St. Pius V, *"computatis omnibus etiam incertis emolumentis communiter percipi solitis."*[5] As the certain ("certain" here means "fixed") income of the benefice, therefore as the *portio congrua,* were considered the tithes of grain, oil, and wine, or the definite amount of money that came from a fund, or the certain monetary contributions of the people. Even if the tithes of a crop fluctuated with the yield of the crop, they were considered an assured or certain income.[6] The uncertain ("uncertain" here means "contingent") part of a cleric's income—and therefore not computed in the *congrua portio* owed for his support—included the offerings at funerals and weddings, Mass stipends, gifts, offerings and blessings.[7] There was not, apparently, a strict demarcation in all cases, between what were considered the certain and uncertain returns of a benefice. The Rota, in one instance, enumerated the usual types of income which were considered as uncertain, but appended the clause "unless local custom holds otherwise."[8] In other circumstances, when it was definitely felt that the certain income granted to a vicar was insufficient, it was stated that the same sources of income were to be considered uncertain and not a part of the *congrua portio.*[9]

[5] Conc. Trident., sess. VII, *de ref.,* c. 7; St. Pius V, const. *Ad exequendum,* 1567—*Magnum Bullarium Romanum, Leo Magnus ad Benedictum XIII,* Tom. II, 259.

[6] S.R.R., *Vallisoletana* (Congruae), 11 ian. 1677, Dec. I, n. 2—*Decisiones Recentiores,* pars XIX, tom. I, 1; S.R.R., *Murana* (Congruae), 15 iun. 1661, Dec. CCCXLVII, n. 8—*Decisiones Recentiores,* pars XIII, tom. 1, 612; S.C.C., *Papien.,* 2 maii 1722—*Thesaurus,* II, 164; Fagnanus, *Commentaria,* lib. III, tit. 25, c. 5, n. 1 sq.; Reiffenstuel, *Ius Canonicum,* lib. III, tit. 25, n. 1, 5.

[7] S.C.C., *Papien.,* 2 maii 1722—*Thesaurus,* II, 164; ". . . eleemosyna altaris, funeralium et similium, quia ista non computantur in congruam."—S.R.R., *Ianuen.* (Parochialis), 1 iul. 1633, Dec. CCXXX, n. 4—*Decisiones Recentiores,* pars VI, 432; S.R.R., *Murana* (Congruae), 15 iun. 1661, Dec. CCCXLVII, n. 8—*Decisiones Recentiores,* pars XIII, 612.

[8] ". . . incerta . . . funeralibus, oblationibus, nuptialibus, eleemosynis, aliisque similibus, nisi de consuetudine loci aliter introductum doceatur."—S.R.R., *Vallisoletana* (Congruae), 11 ian. 1677, Dec. I, n. 9—*Decisiones Recentiores,* pars XIX, tom. I, 1.

[9] The Dominican convent of St. Peter the Martyr in Pavia, which gave to the vicar of a church under its jurisdiction an income of 26 *scudi,* 6 *julii* (200 imperial pounds), contended that this sum was sufficient, since the vicar also

It seems that the Roman Curia felt that the distinction between the uncertain and certain elements of the income depended to a great extent upon the amount of the principal source of income of the benefice. The uncertain emoluments were certainly to augment this principal source; if the principal source was of itself large enough to support conveniently a cleric, there was no great need for subsidiary income. If, however, the principal source was scanty or insufficient, the tendency was not to include the uncertain elements as a part of the *portio congrua*. The ecclesiastical authorities maintained this attitude apparently to force the person furnishing the support to be more liberal, and to enable the beneficiary to enjoy an extra subsidy from the uncertain emoluments. It is also obvious that the amount of the uncertain income was a factor which helped to determine whether it was to be included in the *portio congrua*.[10]

The flexibility of the concept of the certain and uncertain elements of a cleric's income led to a great deal of discussion by the canonists. Barbosa (1589-1649) held that all the uncertain emoluments, such as stole fees and offerings, were not to be included in the *congrua portio*.[11] Garcia (+1613), who ordinarily was rather strict in his interpretation, granted that even the daily distributions made to canons were not to be included in the *congrua portio*, and therefore were to be regarded as a part of the uncertain or subsidiary emoluments.[12] Cardinal De Luca (1614-1683) made sharp and clear distinctions between the elements of the income. Whatever a cleric gained by his labors for anything which was not demanded by or intimately connected with the duties of his benefice (or pension or patrimony) was not part of the *congrua portio*—and he included

received the normal "uncertain" income which always amounted to a certain sum; it contended that the uncertain emoluments which always amounted to a certain sum should be computed, "according to the teaching of the doctors," as part of the *portio congrua*. The Sacred Congregation of the Council upheld the decision of the bishop, who had ordered the Convent to pa
vicar a greater sum as his *congrua portio*, although he also received the uncertain emoluments.—S.C.C., *Papien.*, 2 maii 1722, 20 febr. 1723—*Thesaurus*, II, 164, 282.

[10] Barbosa, *Collectanea*, lib. III, tit. 5, c. 12, n. 5.

[11] Barbosa, *Collectanea*, lib. III, tit. 5, c. 12, n. 5.

[12] Garcia, *De Beneficiis Ecclesiasticis*, pars II, cap. 5, n. 321.

the daily distributions to the canons for their participation in the divine office as part of this *fructus laboris personalis.*[13] However, De Luca considered the stole fees and offerings received by the cleric on the regularly occurring occasion of his spiritual services as part of the *congrua portio.* He contended that such offerings and stole fees constituted a certain income, since it was not possible for people "not to die, not to be born, not to be baptized and not to marry."[14] Certainly no one will deny the cogency of the Cardinal's argument.

The later commentators, for example, Leurenius (1646-1723) and Reiffenstuel (1642-1703), made a more specific distinction concerning the various elements of a cleric's income. Reiffenstuel divided the sources of income of the clergy into patrimonial, quasi-patrimonial, parsimonial, and ecclesiastical funds (*bona ecclesiastica*). The quasi-patrimonial funds included not only whatever the cleric received in consequence of his own industry, but also the stole fees and what were considered the uncertain emoluments of a cleric. The ecclesiastical fund (*bona ecclesiastica*), which constituted the *portio congrua,* were the certain returns from the benefice. Leurenius concurred in this opinion, although he used a different terminology.[15] Reiffenstuel referred to this doctrine as the common one, and it seems that the outstanding writers of that era subscribed to that opinion.[16]

In the succeeding century the opinion changed. Schmalzgrueber (1663-1735) restated the opinion of Cardinal De Luca. The stole fees and offerings which derived from such services that occurred regularly were to be considered as certain income, and therefore as part of the *portio congrua* that was due to the cleric. His opinion

---

[13] De Luca, *Theatrum,* Tom. I, *De Parochis,* Disc. XI, n. 5.

[14] ". . . cum non possit populus non mori, non nasci, et non baptizari atque non contrahere matrimonia."—De Luca, *Theatrum,* Tom. I, *De Parochis,* Disc. XVIII, n. 11; cf. also nn. 8 and 9 of the same *Discussio.*

[15] Reiffenstuel, *Ius Canonicum,* lib. III, tit. 25, n. 3, 5, 6, 7; Leurenius, *Forum Ecclesiasticum in quo Ius Canonicum Universum Librorum ac Titulorum Ordine explanatur* (5 vols. in 4, Venetiis, 1729), lib. III, tit. 25, qu. 582, nn. 1, 2 (hereafter referred to as *Forum Ecclesiasticum*).

[16] Pirhing, *Ius Canonicum Universum secundum Titulos Decretalium Distributum Nova Methodo Explicatum* (5 vols. in 4, Dilingae, 1674-1678), lib. III, tit. 25, n. 2 (hereafter referred to as *Ius Canonicum*).

rested on the supposition that from year to year the stole fees and offerings in a given parish approximated the same amount; if there was a wide divergence, then they were not to be considered as part of the "certain income."[17]

Inasmuch as the *portio congrua* was due to the cleric in virtue of his spiritual office (if he held a benefice), it was accepted by the Roman Curia and the canonists that this support was due to the cleric independently of any other income enjoyed by him. The Rota issued a decision which recognized this rule under circumstances that sharply emphasized its acceptance. Clerics of the diocese of Atri demanded an increase in the pension they received on the grounds that it was not sufficient in view of the excessive income of the bishop, who received seven hundred scudi. The protesting clerics strengthened their demand by stating that the bishop also enjoyed a private income independent from that of his ecclesiastical benefice. The contention was that the bishop should reduce his income from his benefice and distribute these funds to the clerical pensioners.

The Rota decreed that, since the income of the bishop was not excessive (according to the standard of the Council of Trent and the standards then enforced in Italy), he was not obliged to reduce it, for he was owed support because of his office regardless of any other income enjoyed by him. The penury of the diocese, accountable for the small pensions of the complaining clerics, was to be borne by the clerics of the diocese (the bishop was considered to be bearing a share of this since his income was smaller than that enjoyed by neighboring bishops). The decision also recognized the principle that the beneficiary was to enjoy priority on the returns of the benefices, so that the pensioners were to be compensated simply with the surplus returns.[18]

The canonists, adverting to this decision of the Rota, subscribed

---

[17] Schmalzgrueber, *Ius Ecclesiasticum,* lib. III, tit. 39, n. 136.

[18] ". . . ideo etiam si habeat aliunde, tamen debet illam consequi ex fructibus Ecclesiae, quia congrua datur in remunerationem diei, et aestus quod suffert Episcopus aut Rector in regimine animarum."—S.R.R., *Atrien.* (Congruae), 1 febr. 1673, Dec. XXIII, n. 5—*Decisiones Recentiores,* pars XVIII, tom. I, 42. N. 4 of the same Decision stated specifically that a bishop or a cleric need not contribute part of his patrimony as a share of his *congrua portio.*

to the doctrine it implied. Reiffenstuel quoted this as the common teaching of the canonists and the doctors.[19] Even the rigorist Fagnanus (1898-1678) had stated absolutely that clerics enjoying a patrimony could be supported from the income of their benefices, thus leaving them free to dispose of the income from their patrimony as they wished. Further, the cleric could live from the returns of his benefice in a way becoming his condition and dignity.[20]

In the discussion regarding the elements that constituted a part of the cleric's *portio congrua,* it must be remembered that stipends for the celebration of Mass constituted a special category of income. The support due for the celebration of "founded Masses" (Masses celebrated by a priest for the intention of the donor of a fund the returns from which supported or helped to support the cleric) differed from the income received for "manual Masses" (Masses celebrated for the intention of a person who handed an offering to a priest for that purpose). The income from "founded Masses" constituted a part, or perhaps even all, of the *portio congrua* of a cleric; the income from the "manual Masses" was not a part of the *portio congrua,* but belonged to the "uncertain income" of the cleric.[21]

2. Support by pension

Besides support from a benefice, the Church permitted support of the clergy by a pension. The pension was to consist of a certain, unfailing sum that was sufficient for the decent support of the cleric.[22] Conflicts arose however over the precedence of the support due the beneficiary and the support due to the pensioner when the same benefice was the source of the support for both.

It was agreed that the incumbent of the benefice was to have

[19] Reiffenstuel, *Ius Canonicum,* lib. III, tit. 5, n. 227; Leurenius, *Forum Ecclesiasticum,* lib. III, tit. 25, qu. 582, n. 1; *ibid.,* qu. 83, n. 1, 2.

[20] ". . . statuenda est pro indubitata praesens conclusio."—Fagnanus, *Commentaria,* lib. III, tit. 25, c. 5, n. 6.

[21] S.C.C., *Cremonen.,* 8 febr. 1738—*Fontes,* n. 3481; S.C.C., *Ariminen.,* 8 et 29 aug. 1722, 15 maii 1723—*Fontes,* nn. 3245, 3261.

[22] Fagnanus, *op. cit.,* lib. III, tit. 5, c. 30, n. 18, 19; Gonzalez-Tellez, *Commentaria,* lib. III, tit. 5, c. 21, n. 1, 7; Garcia, *De Beneficiis Ecclesiasticis,* Tom. I, pars I, cap. 5, § 3, nn. 362, 379.

priority over the pensioner in the income of the benefice.[23] Pensions were not to become so burdensome that they would detract seriously from the income due to the incumbent of the benefice. The Council of Trent had decided that a parish was not bound to pay any obligations, including pensions, unless it had an income of at least 100 ducats, and a cathedral enjoyed the same exemption unless it had an unencumbered income of at least 1,000 ducats.[24] Commenting on this provision of the Council of Trent, Gonzalez-Tellez (+ after 1673) thought that the pension should not comprise more than one-third of the income of the benefice.[25] A definite amount, however, was to be determined for the pension, and not simply a quota or a percentage of the returns of the benefice.[26]

3. Support by patrimony

The elements of sufficiency, of certainty and of permanence that applied to incomes which derived from benefices and pensions also applied to the income which derived from patrimony. No patrimony could be assigned on movable (in this case, mobile) goods such as animals, since such goods lacked permanency.[27] But a patrimony could be founded on the certain returns of investments, as long as the investments were made in immovable or landed goods.[28]

Once a cleric was ordained on the title of patrimony, any alienation of that patrimony was invalid, unless it was permitted by the bishop, and provided also that the cleric was assured of another source of permanent support.[29] Even if the goods which constituted the patrimony were to be exchanged for other goods that would bring equal or even greater returns, the bishop was nevertheless to be notified, and his permission was required before the transaction could be completed; in fact, the bishop had to declare

---

[23] S.R.R., *Atrien.* (Congruae), 1 febr. 1673, Dec. XXIII, nn. 10-45—*Decisiones Recentiores,* pars XVIII, tom. I, 421.

[24] Conc. Trident., sess. XXIV, *de ref.,* c. 13; cf. Fagnanus, *Commentaria,* lib. III, tit. 5, c. 30, n. 18.

[25] Gonzalez-Tellez, *Commentaria,* lib. III, tit. 5, c. 21, n. 7.

[26] Garcia, *De Beneficiis Ecclesiasticis,* Tom. I, pars I, cap. 5, § 3, n. 362.

[27] S.C.C., *Sypontina,* 29 nov. 1670—*Fontes,* n. 2819.

[28] S.C.C., *Terracinen.,* 20 iul. 1629—*Fontes,* n. 2512.

[29] S.C.C., *Caiacen.,* 6 mart. 1638—*Fontes,* n. 2591.

specifically which goods had been subrogated in place of the former.[30]

Inasmuch as the income from the benefice, pension or patrimony was required to be sufficient for the support of the cleric in accordance with his position, it was natural that a cleric should not be obliged to engage in work which was extraneous to his office. Moreover, it was forbidden for a cleric to engage in secular commerce or trade—of which the sole or principal end was financial gain—since that detracted from the dignity of the clerical state; forbidden occupations were such, for example, as trading for profits, speculation on the financial market or in stocks and bonds, or conducting a tavern.[31] Whenever it was necessary, it was permitted to clerics to engage in an occupation which was consonant with the clerical dignity, as long as the occupation was undertaken for the purpose of securing the necessities of life for oneself and one's dependents. Such an occupation could be agriculture or a craft.[32] The performance of this kind of work by clerics was permitted only for the good of souls (usually because the small or poor parish did not offer sufficient support), and hence it was forbidden if it prevented the cleric from attending to his clerical duties.[33]

---

[30] S.C.C., *Terracinen.*, 20 iul. 1619—*Fontes,* n. 2416.

[31] Urbanus VIII, litt. ap. *Ex debito,* 22 febr. 1633, § 8—*Fontes,* n. 211; Clemens IX, const. *Sollicitudo,* 17 iun. 1669, § 1—*Fontes,* n. 243; Benedictus XIV, const. *Apostolicae servitutis,* 25 febr. 1741—*Fontes,* n. 306; Barbosa, *Collectanea,* lib. III, tit. 1, c. 16, n. 3; Gonzalez-Tellez, *Commentaria,* lib. III, tit. 5, c. 4, n. 5; Reiffenstuel, *Ius Canonicum,* lib. III, tit. 1, n. 126; cf. Ferraris, *Bibliotheca,* s.v. *clericus,* art. III, nn. 48-55.

[32] Reiffenstuel defines a permissible craft thus: ". . . quando quis emit aliquam materiam, quae postea per artem reducitur ad aliam formam, ut si quis emat vimina et faciat canistra."—*Ius Canonicum,* lib. III, tit. 1, n. 132; he approved of agriculture also—*loc. cit.;* Gonzalez-Tellez, *Commentaria,* lib. III, tit. 5, c. 4, n. 5; Fagnanus, *Commentaria,* lib. III, tit. 42, c. 3, n. 7; Schmalzgrueber, *Ius Ecclesiasticum,* lib. III, tit. 50, n. 10. Barbosa cited the case of missionaries in Brazil, who were permitted to trade the goods which had been produced there for church furniture and other products in Spain—*op. cit.,* lib. III, tit. 1, c. 16, n. 3. Clement XIII, in his Encyclical Letter *Cum primum,* 17 sept. 1759, § 10, stated that clerics had to secure permission from their ordinary to engage in work, and that this work had to be "honestioribus artibus suaeque professioni conforme."—*Fontes,* n. 452.

[33] Fagnanus, *Commentaria,* lib. III, tit. 48, c. 3, n. 5; Reiffenstuel, *Ius Canonicum,* lib. III, tit. 1, n. 132; Barbosa, *Collectanea,* lib. III, tit. 1, c. 16.

Lest it be forgotten that a zealous priest who had accepted a parish with a very small income was always owed a decent support, it was reiterated that his income was to be increased if that was possible.[34] The bishop, the patron of the church and the parishioners were obliged, according to their resources, to assist the indigent pastor or vicar of such a parish.[35] The bishop could also alleviate the poverty of a church through the union of a benefice with the church, or through the conferring of two benefices on the same cleric (which normally was forbidden). If two benefices were conferred, they could not both entail the care of souls and the duty of residence.[36]

Article 2. Factors Determining the Amount of the Portio Congrua

The amount necessary for the decent support of a cleric depended upon the number of factors that were to be considered as included in that support. It was agreed that the amount of a cleric's decent support depended on these factors:

1) the dignity or rank of his office;
2) his personal accomplishments, which included his learning and sanctity;
3) his state in life—whether of the nobility or of the untitled gentry;
4) his ecclesiastical duties, spiritual and material (payment of the obligations due to the bishop and to the Holy Father, support of assistant clerics, repair and maintenance of the church buildings);
5) the duties of hospitality to dependent relatives and to the poor of the parish; and
6) the customs and the wealth of the region.

---

[34] S.R.R., *Ianuen.* (Parochialis), 1 iul. 1633, Dec. CCXXX—*Decisiones Recentiores,* pars VI, 432.

[35] Fagnanus, *Commentaria,* lib. III, tit. 48, c. 3, n. 6; De Luca, *Theatrum,* Tom. I, *De Parochis,* Disc. XVIII, n. 11.

[36] S.R.R., *Narnien.* (Unionis), 1 iul. 1643, Dec. CCXXII, n. 16—*Decisiones Recentiores,* pars IX, 631; Reiffenstuel, *Ius Canonicum,* lib. III, tit. 5, nn. 265, 272; *ibid.,* nn. 203-204.

1. Dignity or rank of office

The dignity of the office was a factor in determining the amount of support due to a cleric, for a bishop was understood to have a higher standing in the community than a pastor; likewise, a pastor enjoyed a higher position than a vicar or an assistant cleric. Consequently an ecclesiastic required support according to this difference in his standing.[37]

2. Personal accomplishments

The personal accomplishments of a cleric were also to determine how much his support was to be. Learning and sanctity were recognized as worthy of reward even in a material way. The Church definitely allowed a difference in income according to merit.[38]

The canonists, complying with the letter and spirit of the decrees of the Council of Trent, stressed the fact that learning should be rewarded with an increase in the allowance due to the cleric. The stress on the importance of learning did not deprecate the necessity for sanctity, but it was easier to judge, in the external forum, the degree of learning than the degree of sanctity.[39] Barbosa considered

---

[37] S.R.R., *Atrien.* (Congruae), 1 febr. 1673, Dec. XXIII, nn. 5, 10—*Decisiones Recentiores,* pars XVIII, tom. I, 42; S.R.R., *Narnien.* (Unionis), 1 iul. 1643, Dec. CCXXII, n. 15—*Decisiones Recentiores,* pars IX, 631; Fagnanus, *Commentaria,* lib. III, tit. 25, c. 5, n. 22. Fagnanus pointed out that the Church had allowed the concept of a higher income due to a cleric in proportion to his rank to develop more sharply in his own era.—*ibid.,* n. 7. Cf. De Luca, *Theatrum,* Tom. I, *De Beneficio,* Disc. XC, n. 60; Tom. II, *De Pensionibus,* Disc. XVI, n. 4; Gonzalez-Tellez, *Commentaria,* s.v. *competens,* lib. III, tit. 5, c. 16, n. *h;* Leurenius, *Forum Ecclesiasticum,* lib. XII, tit. 25, qu. 83, n. 3; Reiffenstuel, *Ius Canonicum,* lib. III, tit. 25, n. 76.

[38] S.R.R., *Murana* (Congruae), 15 iun. 1661, Dec. CCCXLVII, n. 7—*Decisiones Recentiores,* pars XIII, 612; ". . . sed etiam qualitates personae, ejusque meritorum ac viae per quam ad illam dignitatem evectus est."—De Luca, *Theatrum,* Tom. II, pars II, *De Pensionibus,* Disc. XVI, n. 4; Fagnanus, *Commentaria,* lib. III, tit. 25, c. 5, n. 17; Leurenius, *Forum Ecclesiasticum,* lib. III, tit. 25, qu. 583, n. 3; Schmalzgrueber, *Ius Ecclesiasticum,* lib. III, tit. 39, n. 137.

[39] Conc. Trident., sess. XXI, *de ref.,* c. 2, 6. The latter of these two chapters stated that the unlearned and illiterate pastors or rectors were to be replaced with vicars who were to receive support according to their worth. Cf.

a cleric who was eminent in learning to be equal to the most noble lord in the land—and to deserve support accordingly.[40]

3. State in life

The words of the canonists concerning the proportionate support for learning and merit illustrated also their attitude towards the recompense due to a cleric for his status of nobility. It was accepted that a member of the nobility had more obligations to meet and a higher status to maintain than a cleric who was not titled. The canonists generally adequated nobility and learning.[41]

This attitude of the canonists represented the general attitude of society towards learning and nobility.

There was, however, one discordant voice in this general choir of agreement; Garcia denied that allowance had to be made in incomes in consideration of the degree of nobility and learning of a cleric. He contended that the income should be enough merely to allow the cleric to live in that particular benefice according to its native circumstances. Of course he held that a cleric should not be obliged to beg or to be in want. But he flatly rejected Rebuffus' distinction between a "convenient or commodious living" and a "plain living"; he considered any living which guaranteed the essentials of life as adequate for a cleric.[42] In the light of all the decisions of the Roman Curia, as well as of the statements of the Pontiffs, which recognized the justice of a difference in income

---

Clemens XIII, ep. encycl., *Cum primum,* 17 sept. 1759, § 18—*Fontes,* n. 452; Schmalzgrueber, *Ius Ecclesiasticum,* lib. III, tit. 39, n. 137.

[40] "Scientia nobilitat hominem . . . nam literatae personae aequiparantur nobilibus et sublimibus."—*Collectanea,* lib. III, tit. 5, c. 28, n. 21; Reiffenstuel, *Ius Canonicum,* lib. III, tit. 5, n. 223; Schmalzgrueber, *Ius Ecclesiasticum,* lib. III, tit. 39, n. 137; lib. III, tit. 25, n. 21.

[41] Barbosa, *loc. cit.* "Plura in hac sufficientia considerantur: puta, nobilitas et scientia personae, quia tales personae majoribus redditibus sunt honorandae."—Reiffenstuel, *Ius Canonicum,* lib. III, tit. 5, n. 223; Schmalzgrueber, *Ius Ecclesiasticum,* lib. III, tit. 39, n. 137; lib. III, tit. 25, n. 21; De Luca, *Theatrum,* Tom. I, *De Parochis,* Disc. XI, n. 9; Leurenius, *Forum Ecclesiasticum,* lib. III, tit. 25, qu. 83, n. 3; Fagnanus, *Commentaria,* lib. III, tit. 25, c. 5, n. 22.

[42] Garcia, *De Beneficiis Ecclesiasticis,* pars II, c. 5, n. 115-118; Corradus Pyrrhus, *Praxis Beneficiaria* (Venetiis, 1735), lib. V, c. 1, s.v. *commode sustentari.*

because of a difference in knowledge and nobility, it is submitted that the position of Garcia was untenable.

4. Ecclesiastical duties

Possibly the most important factor in determining the amount of income for a cleric was the extent of his ecclesiastical obligations, spiritual and material.

The Church showed its regard for the added responsibility entailed in the care of large numbers of souls by approving an increase in support according to the number of souls cared for in a parish. Added spiritual duties meant added income.[43] The Church approved a statute in the Kingdom of the Sicilies which graduated the salaries paid to vicars according to the number of souls in the parish. The vicar of a church was to receive 60 ducats for a parish of not more than 2,000 souls, 80 ducats for a parish of not more than 5,000 souls, and 100 ducats if the parish exceeded 5,000 souls in number.[44]

The support due to an assistant cleric was also to be reckoned among the obligations of the pastor or the rector. There was a very strict obligation for every cleric in charge of a parish church to have an assistant cleric, for it was held that the normal pastoral duties, such as the proper celebration of the divine offices and the catechizing of the parishioners, required the assistance of at least one cleric. Barbosa held that it was a mortal sin for a priest to celebrate Mass without an assistant cleric.[45]

Foremost among the material obligations of a cleric was the providing of daily sustenance for the cleric and the members of his household. This included adequate food, comfortable housing, and suitable clothing; of course it also included the other necessaries of a cleric's life, such as medical care and necessary books.[46]

---

[43] "... congrua ... proportionata oneribus in curae exercitio obeundis. . . ."—S.R.R., *Murana* (Congruae), 15 iun. 1661, Dec. CCCXLVII, n. 7—*Decisiones Recentiores,* pars XIII, 649.

[44] Ferraris, *Bibliotheca,* s.v. *congrua,* art. II, n. 53; also cf. Clemens XIII, ep. encycl. *Cum primum,* 17 sept. 1759, § 18—*Fontes,* n. 452.

[45] Barbosa, *Collectanea,* lib. III, tit. 1, c. 3, n. 3.

[46] Reiffenstuel, *Ius Canonicum,* lib. III, tit. 25, n. 76; Leurenius, *Forum Ecclesiasticum,* lib. III, tit. 25, qu. 83, n. 3; Schmalzgrueber, *Ius Ecclesiasticum,* lib. III, tit. 39, n. 118.

Other material or financial obligations (apart from the support due to the assistant cleric (were the contributions due to the Holy Father and the ordinary, as well as the maintenance of the church buildings. The nature of these duties had not changed greatly, except for the mitigation of the obligation of the bishop (with his chapter) and the pastor to maintain the cathedral and parish churches. The practice of permitting or even of urging the parishioners (if the patron was not sufficiently affluent) and diocesans to contribute to the maintenance of the cathedral and parish churches had developed considerably.[47]

The sum available for the support which was due to the cleric consisted of the amount which was in excess of all the aforementioned obligations. The cleric's income was supposed to be sufficiently large to enable him to discharge all these obligations and still to be able to support himself decently. Pope Innocent XIII (1721-1724) in his Constitution *Apostolici ministerii*, of May 23, 1723, stated specifically that the *congrua portio* due to the clergy was to be in excess of all obligations—*"detractis oneribus."*[48]

5. Duties of hospitality

The most discussed and indeterminate duties of the clerics were those of hospitality or of charity towards dependent relatives and to the poor of the parish. Despite the complaint of Fagnanus that in his day there was a great change from the previous ages in the attitude towards these obligations of hospitality and of charity, the law of the Church was still very urgent in regard to this form of charity. Fagnanus stated that whereas in former centuries these duties of charity and hospitality had been of the same importance as the demands of the cleric for support, the income of the benefice in his time was devoted primarily to the support of the cleric, and only secondarily to the cause of charity and hospitality.[49]

---

[47] De Luca, *Theatrum*, Tom. III, *Miscellanea*, Disc. XXIX, n. 2-5.

[48] § 7—*Fontes*, n. 280.

[49] Fagnanus, *Commentaria*, lib. III, tit. 25, c. 5, nn. 15-22. The term hospitality in those days included our modern acceptance of charity as something distinct from hospitality; often, today, charity means help extended to the

There was, however, a clearly defined duty to extend charity and hospitality to all who had a claim to it. Furthermore, this duty of charity and hospitality obliged under pain of grave sin.[50] There is no doubt that hospitals and hospices were erected and supported for the needy. The poor were certainly not neglected, even if the magnificent phrase of earlier centuries was no longer frequently quoted, "*quidquid clerici est, pauperum est.*"[51]

Special emphasis was laid on the duty to support one's dependent relatives, and this duty gave the cleric a claim to greater income if he had dependent relatives. Furthermore, the cleric was obliged to support his dependent relatives—which included his parents, brothers, sisters, and legitimate children—according to their proper state in life. He was, of course, forbidden to aggrandize the family's fortune at the expense of the ecclesiastical funds.[52]

Because of the greater demand of charity arising from the close bond of consanguinity, it was definitely permitted to give more to one's needy relatives than to other indigent or dependent persons.[53] In fact, a cleric was considered obliged, or at least permitted, to pay the dowry of a sister according to her position in society (even the rigorist Fagnanus granted this). Schmalzgrueber stated that a cleric could pay, out of the income derived from his benefice, the expenses of a brother or of a close relative for learning an art or a trade.[54]

On the perimeter of the family circle, and therefore enjoying prior rights of charity, were the servants of the clerical household.

---

poor, while hospitality means the reception of those who are our social equals or superiors. Formerly, hospitality included our modern concepts of charity and hospitality alike.

[50] Fagnanus, *Commentaria,* lib. III, tit. 25, c. 5, n. 5; Barbosa *Collectanea,* lib. III, tit. 5, c. 5, n. 2.

[51] Fagnanus, *Commentaria,* lib. III, tit. 25, c. 5, n. 22; Reiffenstuel, *Ius Canonicum,* lib. III, tit. 6, n. 15.

[52] "Quod tamen secundum eum limitatur et intelligitur si indigeant, non autem ad pompam vel alium statum."—Fagnanus, *Commentaria,* lib. III, tit. 25, c. 5, n. 19; Reiffenstuel, *Ius Canonicum,* lib. III, tit. 25, n. 82; Leurenius, *Forum Ecclesiasticum,* lib. III, tit. 25, q. 83, n. 3; Schmalzgrueber, *Ius Ecclesiasticum,* lib. III, tit. 39, n. 118; Wernz, *Ius Decretalium,* III, 177.

[53] Reiffenstuel, *Ius Canonicum,* lib. III, tit. 5, n. 222.

[54] Fagnanus, *Commentaria,* lib. III, tit. 25, c. 5, n. 19; Schmalzgrueber, *Ius Ecclesiasticum,* lib. III, tit. 25, n. 25.

They were to receive preferential treatment in the distribution of charity.[55] Reiffenstuel held, though he admitted that it was a disputed question, that a cleric or a master should pay wages (especially if there was not a hospital nearby) also to a sick employee. The duty was more grave if the employee was penniless and the master was affluent; in such a case there was cause for action by the sick servant against the master in an ecclesiastical court. If the master was not obliged to pay the heavy expense of a sick employee, he was bound at least to give him enough for food and small expenses.[56]

Among those outside the family circle to whom charitable support was due, once the neediest poor had been assisted, more was due to those who occupied a higher station in life. A cleric could give to the indigent nobility more than simply what was necessary to sustain life, and enough to support them according to their state.[57]

A cleric could use the funds destined for hospitality and charity to give moderate donations not only in token of gratitude but also in consideration of friendship and liberality. He could also use the funds of his office to entertain and accommodate guests.[58]

It was also readily granted that a cleric was entitled to a moderate amount of recreation, and hence provision for this was also to be made in his allowance. Of course, all pomp, vulgarity, and unseemliness was to be avoided. The recreation could be either mental or physical (sports).[59]

---

[55] Fagnanus, *Commentaria,* lib. III, tit. 25, c. 5, n. 19; Reiffenstuel, *Ius Canonicum,* lib. III, tit. 6, nn. 10-15; De Rosa, *De Recta Distributione Redituum Beneficiorum Ecclesiasticorum Saecularium* (Neapoli, 1682), c. 1, n. 46 (hereafter referred to as *De Recta Distributione*).

[56] Reiffenstuel, *Ius Canonicum,* lib. III, tit. 6, nn. 10, 15, 16. Lanfrancus Zacchia, *De Salario* (Romae, 1666), Qu. 18, n. 12.

[57] Fagnanus, *Commentaria,* lib. III, tit. 25, c. 5, n. 18, 22; Schmalzgrueber, *Ius Ecclesiasticum,* lib. III, tit. 39, n. 119.

[58] Leurenius, *Forum Ecclesiasticum,* lib. III, tit. 25, qu. 583, n. 3; Reiffenstuel, *Ius Canonicum,* lib. III, tit. 25, n. 82.

[59] Reiffenstuel, *Ius Canonicum,* lib. III, tit. 25, nn. 82, 83; De Rosa, *De Recta Distributione,* c. 1, n. 42; Leurenius, *Forum Ecclesiasticum,* lib. III, tit. 25, qu. 583, n. 3; Schmalzgrueber, *Ius Ecclesiasticum,* lib. III, tit. 39, n. 121.

6. Local circumstances

The amount that could rightfully be devoted to all these factors involved in the decent support of a cleric—which included the consideration of the dignity of the cleric's position, of the cleric's degree of learning, his title of nobility, the extent of his burden in the care of souls, relaxation and recreation besides his claim to food, shelter and clothing—depended on the circumstances and customs of the region. The wealth of the region and the customs of the country determined what was a fitting allowance for these factors. An amount that allowed for an almost luxurious living in one country could in another country be hardly more than enough for a bare subsistence.[60] Hence a cleric of the same dignity and learning in one country could not rightfully hope to receive the same amount of sustenance, or be entitled to live in the same comfort, as a like cleric in a wealthy country.

Article 3. Amounts Specified for the Portio Congrua

Obviously it was not possible to establish a uniform, world-wide minimum and maximum rate for the amount due to the clergy, nor was it possible to maintain as a norm the provision of the Council of Trent and of Pius V that pastors were to receive 100 ducats, the bishops 1,000, and that any cleric should have at least an income of 50 ducats a year. There are ample records to show that the income differed widely between regions.

The amounts established at the Council of Trent and by Pius V were accepted as amenable to change according to circumstances; the figures there employed were to be accepted *"demonstrative"* not

---

[60] Clemens XIII, ep. encycl., *Cum primum,* 17 sept. 1759, § 18—*Fontes,* n. 452; Benedictus XIII, const. *In supremo,* 23 sept. 1724, § 5—*Fontes,* n. 283; S.R.R., *Atrien.* (Congruae), 27 iun. 1674, Dec. CCCLI—*Decisiones Recentiores,* Pars XVIII, tom. I, 654; S.R.R., *Vallisoletana* (Congruae), 11 ian. 1677, Dec. 1, n. 4—*Decisiones Recentiores,* Pars XIX, tom. I, 1; Reiffenstuel, *Ius Canonicum,* lib. III, tit. 25, n. 76; Barbosa, *Collectanea,* lib. III, tit. 5, c. 12, nn. 1-5; Leurenius, *Forum Ecclesiasticum,* lib. III, tit. 25, qu. 583, n. 3; De Luca, *Theatrum,* Tom. II, pars II, *De Pensionibus,* Disc. XVI, n. 4; Garcia, *De Beneficiis Ecclesiasticis,* Tom. I, pars I, c. 5, § 3, n. 373; Schmalzgrueber, *Ius Ecclesiasticum,* lib. III, tit. 25, n. 21.

"taxative."[61] This was evident also from the fact that the amount due to a cleric for his support, namely, his "salary," was fixed by diocesan statute or custom.[62]

In some regions an income of two thousand or three thousand *scudi* could be considered very modest for a bishop, whereas in some sections of the Kingdom of Naples, in Italy and in Dalmatia, an income of 500 *scudi* provided an ample and fitting allowance.[63] In the diocese of Atri, a bishop received 700 *scudi* for his support, and it was considered sufficient.[64] The Bishop of Policastro, the canonist Thomas De Rosa (+1695) considered 1,000 ducats or *scudi* scarcely sufficient.[65]

Naturally there was just as wide a diverenge of opinion on the amount required for the adequate support for pastors and vicars. In the seventeenth century the amount ranged from 36 *scudi* in one section of the Kingdom of Naples to over 400 in other sections of Italy.[66] In the eighteenth century, by diocesan statute, the sum of 36 *scudi* a year was considered a sufficient support for a cleric in one section of Italy,[67] while in other sections 60 and 70 *scudi* a year were demanded as the income for a priest who received his support from a pious foundation.[68] Even in the nineteenth

---

[61] S.C.C., *Cremonen.*, 23 iul. 1729, 13 aug. 1729—*Fontes*, n. 3351; S.C.C., *Brixinen.*, 22 aug. 1874—*Fontes*, n. 4229.

[62] Innocentius XIII, const. *Speculatores*, 4 nov. 1694, § 3—*Fontes*, n. 259; Benedictus XIII, const. *In supremo*, 23 sept. 1724, § 5—*Fontes*, n. 283.

[63] De Luca, *Theatrum*, Tom. II, *De Pensionibus*, Disc. XVI, n. 4.

[64] S.R.R., *Atrien.* (Congruae), 27 iun. 1674, Dec. CCCLI, n. 2—*Decisiones Recentiores*, Pars XVIII, tom. I, 654.

[65] De Rosa, *De Recta Distributione*, c. 1, n. 46.

[66] A decision of the Rota stated that the sum of 70 *scudi* was insufficient for a parish in the diocese of Valladolid, and that it should exceed 100 *scudi* in that locality.—S.R.R., *Vallisoletana* (Congruae), 11 ian. 1677, Dec. 1, nn. 4, 8—*Decisiones Recentiores*, Pars XIX, tom. I, 1. Garcia stated that in the Kingdom of Naples some pastors and vicars had an income of only 36 *scudi* a year.—*De Beneficiis*, pars II, c. 5, n. 117, u. 119; De Luca is the authority for the statement that some parishes had, and needed, an income of over 400 *scudi* a year.—*Theatrum*, Tom. I, *De Beneficio*, Disc. XC, n. 60.

[67] S.C.C., *Ariminen.*, 8 et 29 aug. 1722—*Fontes*, n. 3245.

[68] S.C.C., *Cremonen.*, 8 febr. 1738—*Fontes*, n. 3481 (60 ducats for support); S.C.C., *Burgi S. Domnini*, 24 maii 1727, 2 et 30 apr. 1729—*Fontes*, nn. 3327, 3346 (70 ducats for support).

century in a certain diocese in Italy, Sovana, the *congrua portio* of a priest was, by diocesan statute, only 30 *scudi* a year! This represented a minimum for support, and it is evident that it was so considered. The uncertain income from other sources augmented this slender allowance.[69]

Elsewhere there was a marked increase in the allowance for the support of a priest, in view of the general change in conditions consequent upon the Industrial Revolution. For instance, the sum of 180 Roman *scudi* was considered a just amount for the support of a cleric in northern Italy (then under Austria) in the latter part of the nineteenth century.[70]

Fortunately there is available an able summation of the legitimate expenditures made by a conscientious and conservative prelate, Bishop Thomas De Rosa, Ordinary of Policastro, who was also a canonist. The Bishop was demonstrating, by itemizing his expenditures, that the 1,000 *scudi* (or ducats) allowed for a bishop by the Council of Trent was scarcely sufficient, certainly not superabundant. The same expenses, *mutatis mutandis,* also applied to pastors and vicars.

> Indeed, not less than a thousand golden *scudi* are required for the decent support of a bishop. At least two hundred *scudi* a year are required for food and clothing, ten *scudi* a month being allowed for food, and eighty *scudi* a year for necessary personal clothing; for Benedictine abbots are allowed forty *scudi* for their wardrobe, and thus eighty for a bishop seems reasonable. Also, the bishop must have a master of his household who also serves as his chaplain. Likewise, he must have a personal servant who is also his barber and can, when the occasion arises, serve as a meat-carver and a secretary, to whom he must give at least eight *scudi* each month; also two servants, to whom he must give five *scudi* a month besides clothing, which is popularly called livery. Besides, he must have a cook to whom he cannot pay less than six *scudi* a month. All these expenses add up to five hundred and four *scudi.* If he should wish to provide board for them it will cost at least three ducats and a half

[69] S.C.C., *Soanen.,* 28 iul. 15 sept. 1838—*Fontes,* n. 4065.

[70] S.C.C., *Brixinen.,* 22 aug. 1874—*Fontes,* n. 4229.

a month, or, more liberally, four ducats and a half a month. . . .

The bishop must have a horse for riding through his diocese. The upkeep for the horse will cost 36 ducats, and if he has a team and a carriage it will cost 250 *scudi.* The linens and furnishings for the bishop and his household will cost 60 ducats a year. Something must be set aside for extending hospitality to his subjects when they come to see him, all the more so since by apostolic precept bishops are subject to the law of hospitality. Also, something must be devoted to the legitimate recreation of the bishop, which is permitted at least once a month. For a bishop is permitted decent recreation, as all the doctors hold, especially Laymann, Lugo, Sanchez, Molina, Reginald, Bardi and others; these recreations are taken by all religious, even those of the strict observance such as the Capuchins, the Cistercians, the Carthusians, the Camaldolese, the Jesuits, the Theatines, and others, not to mention other monks and congregations who are more lax and who live splendidly. All these (not including the expenses for the carriage, which must be omitted in some cities) constitute eight hundred and sixty ducats; consequently, only one hundred and sixty ducats out of a thousand are left.

But other things must be considered, such as trips which the bishop must make, maintenance of the episcopal residence, expenses for illness, expenses of the cathedral for candles, oil, and other supplies, since almost all bishops must defray these expenses. The bishop must also defend his rights in legal suits against the royal ministers and others, and this implies a considerable expense. I have omitted mentioning almsgiving, which cannot be neglected by a bishop without causing a great deal of scandal. . . .

Wherefore, from beginning to end, I conclude that the sum of a thousand ducats scarcely suffices for a bishop who wishes to live according to the regulations of the Fathers of the Church. I do not speak for worldly bishops, because for those who live luxuriously, *flens dico,* two thousand ducats do not suffice.[71]

The opinion of Bishop De Rosa was further evidence that the decision on the amount constituting the *portio congrua* depended,

[71] De Rosa, *De Recta Distributione,* c. 1, n. 40-47. The translation is furnished by the present writer.

if not determined by diocesan statute, on the opinion of clerics of sensitive (*timoratae*) conscience in that region, as reflected in the established customs.[72] In the event of a dispute the ordinary was the competent judge in causes concerning the amount due for a cleric's support, even if one of the litigants was the prelate of an exempt monastery and immediately subject to the Holy See.[73]

The cases or actions brought by clerics who demanded a more liberal income were handled by the bishop (or his delegate) in an informal "administrative" procedure; the action was brought under the right of sustenance (*ius alimentationis*). The cleric presented his petition (*libellus*), which contained a statement of his finances, and showed the alleged inadequacy of his income. A decision was made promptly, in accordance with the urgency of the complaint and in line with the legal maxim, *"Venter non patitur dilationem"* (literally, "The stomach can't wait"). Redress against the decision could be sought but the decision was effective immediately; the recourse could be invoked *in devolutivo* and not *in suspensivo,* that is to say, the interposed recourse lacked all effect of suspending the execution of the decision as rendered.[74]

In Belgium, the princes, in a declaration to a Synod of Malines, stated that if the pastors could not secure redress from their ordinary in the matter of decent support, they could appeal to the Royal Council, which would grant them financial help from the Royal Treasury.[75]

---

[72] Reiffenstuel, *Ius Canonicum,* lib. III, tit. 25, n. 76.

[73] Conc. Trident., sess. VII, *de ref.,* c. 7; Schmalzgrueber, *Ius Ecclesiasticum,* lib. III, tit. 39, n. 139. This was, actually, old legislation—c. 1, *de iure patronatus,* III, 12, in Clem.

[74] Schmalzgrueber, *Ius Ecclesiasticum,* lib. III, tit. 39, n. 140; Van Espen, *Ius Ecclesiasticum Universum* (5 vols., Lovanii, 1735), tom. II, par. II, sect. IV, tit. 3, c. 7, n. 9.

[75] Van Espen, *ibid.,* nn. 13, 14. "XIII. Edictum Principum Belgii directum ad Synodum Mechliniensem, art. 15, injungit Judicibus Regiis ut prompte et undilate exequi mandent per suos apparitores, quidquid in hac materia congruae portionis sive competentiae pastoralis fuerit vel provisionaliter vel definitive per Episcopos ordinatum.

XIV. Ulterius eodem Edicto, art. 16, declarant Principes esse suam mentem ut si contingat ipsos Ordinarios fore defectuosos in assignanda hac portione sive competentia ipsis Parochis, tunc licebit pastoribus recurrere ad Consilia Regia suarum respective Dioecesium, sed ad ipsorum querelas

Article 4. Obligation of Disposing of Superfluous Income

The determination of the amount constituting the sufficient support of the clergy involved, as a consequence, a discussion on the duty of giving all superfluous income from a benefice or a pension to some pious cause. The income from patrimony was not involved in this discussion. Superfluous income was that which was in excess of the amount necessary to maintain a cleric according to his legitimate needs.[76] Further, it was agreed that this obligation bound clerics *sub gravi.*[77]

The first question to settle was: how many sources of income were not included in the returns from the benefice or the pension? In some instances diocesan statutes helped in this determination. At any rate, it was patent that all earnings through the cleric's personal labor, if performed as a task extraneous to the discharge of the duties intimately connected with his office, was not a part of his returns from the benefice or the pension; such earnings were called *"bona ex industria," "bona quasi-patrimonialia," "bona industrialia,"* or by similar terms. This type of income included the payments received for teaching, for instructing in art, the stipends gained by preaching at other churches, and generally also the daily distributions which yielded to those who participated in the choral service, such as the chanting of the divine office.[78]

---

hac in parte provideatur; praesertim intervenientibus, si opus sit, Fiscalibus Regiis." Apparently the same system was observed in France.—Van Espen, *ibid.*, n. 12.

[76] ". . . episcopi et caeteri beneficiati totum id quod superest ultra propriam sustentationem tenentur erogare in pios usus, quod extra controversiam apud omnes est."—De Rosa, *De Recta Distributione,* cap. 2, n. 46; Conc. Trident., sess. XXV, *de ref.*, cc. 1. 9.

[77] Fagnanus, *Commentaria,* lib. III, tit. 25, c. 5, n. 5; Leurenius, *Forum Ecclesiasticum,* lib. III, tit. 25, qu. 585; Reiffenstuel, *Ius Canonicum,* lib. III, tit. 25, n. 22 sq., also n. 51; Schmalzgrueber, *Ius Ecclesiasticum,* lib. III, tit. 25, n. 22.

[78] Reiffenstuel, *Ius Canonicum,* lib. III, tit. 25, nn. 3, 14; Leurenius, *Forum Ecclesiasticum,* lib. III, tit. 25, qu. 582, n. 2. De Luca considered the choral distributions *"tamquam merx servitii et laboris personalis."—Theatrum,* Tom. I, *De Parochis,* Disc. XI, n. 8. Garcia, as an exception, thought that the daily distributions were a part of the returns of the benefice.—*De Beneficiis Ecclesiasticis,* pars II, c. 5, n. 321.

It was also agreed that the beneficiary acquired everything which through his frugal living he saved from his income for decent support; such savings were called "*bona parsimonialia.*" The *bona parsimonialia,* therefore, needed not to be given to pious causes. Whoever denied himself the elements of a decent living was considered to have saved from his expenses an amount which he could rightly reserve to himself.[79] Also, any beneficiary who at his own expense had improved the productivity of the lands which belonged to the benefice was permitted to keep the increased returns.[80]

It has been seen in the section which dealt with the composition of the *portio congrua* (Article 1) that it was controverted whether the offerings made at the time of funerals, weddings, etc., constituted a part of the *portio congrua.* Since no definite decision on this question was ever reached by the Roman Curia (circumstances of each particular case were always considered), no sharp line of distinction could be drawn about whether these *iura stolae* and "uncertain emoluments" belonged to the *congrua portio,* and thus there was not rendered any decision on whether the superfluous amount from such funds was to be devoted to pious causes.

The next question was the nature of the duty to devote the superfluous income to pious causes. Was it a duty of justice, with the consequent duty of restitution if one failed to perform the obligation, or was it a duty of charity, which when neglected did not entail a similar duty of restitution?

The older opinion, voiced by Fagnanus, was that the obligation was of a doubtful nature, and hence no restitution could be demanded.[81] In the later opinions, some doctors held that beneficiaries did not have ownership (*dominium*) of the excess income of the benefice, but were only the administrators of such excess funds; hence, if they did not properly dispose of the superfluous funds, they were to be held to restitution. It was contended that this was the probable opinion.[82] The opponents of this opinion contended

---

[79] Leurenius, *Forum Ecclesiasticum,* lib. III, tit. 25, qu. 583, n. 3; Reiffenstuel, *Ius Canonicum,* lib. III, tit. 25, n. 15; Schmalzgrueber, *Ius Ecclesiasticum,* lib. III, tit. 25, n. 21.

[80] Schmalzgrueber, *op. cit.,* lib. III, tit. 25, n. 20.

[81] Fagnanus, *Commentaria,* lib. III, tit. 25, c. 5, n. 5.

[82] Reiffenstuel (1642-1703) was the chief proponent of this opinion.—*Ius Canonicum,* lib. III, tit. 25, nn. 22-46.

that the beneficiary did acquire ownership (*dominium*) of all the income of the benefice or the pension, and hence could not be bound to make restitution of what was actually his.[83]

Leurenius, in following this opinion to its ultimate conclusion, stated that to incur a mortal sin a beneficiary had to spend wastefully on "parasites and games" four thousand gold ducats out of an excess of thirty thousand.[84] Schmalzgrueber, while illustrating the wide divergence of opinion on this subject, cited Hurtado as stating that a beneficiary fulfilled his obligation towards his duties of charity if he devoted from one-fourth to one-half of his superfluous income. De Lugo contended that a beneficiary committed a grave sin if he wrongly expended one-twentieth of his superfluous income, provided that such superfluous income represented a considerable sum. Schmalzgrueber thought that no definite rule about an amount could be given, but that more funds had to be squandered by a beneficiary to constitute a mortal sin than was required to constitute a mortal sin by theft, because the beneficiary had *dominium* of the income.[85]

Schmalzgrueber seemed to offer the best solution for the controversy regarding the duty of devoting one's superfluous income to pious causes. Passing over the controversy regarding the duty of justice versus the duty of charity, he argued that the obligation derived solely from the positive precept of the Church, since it could not be clearly established that any obligation arose from justice, or from charity, or from the virtue of religion (the obligation founded on the contention that the founders of benefices or the contributors to the Church intended their contributions not primarily for the support of clerics but for the cause of religion, and hence any surplus was to be devoted to pious causes).[86] The opinion

[83] Leurenius (1646-1723) was a proponent of this opinion, and cited St. Thomas (+1274), Covarrubias (+1577) and Gonzalez-Tellez (+ after 1673) as fellow proponents.—*Forum Ecclesiasticum,* lib. III, tit. 25, qu. 583, n. 4. Leurenius admitted that the interpretation of the pertinent passages in St. Thomas were also disputed, and thus reflected the intricacy of the controversy.

[84] ". . . qui ex superfluis 30,000 aureorum impenderet in parasitos et ludos 4,000"—*op. cit.,* lib. III, tit. 25, qu. 585.

[85] Schmalzgrueber, *Ius Ecclesiasticum,* lib. III, tit. 25, nn. 22, 23.

[86] Schmalzgrueber, *Ius Ecclesiasticum,* lib. III, tit. 25, n. 33; he cited the canonist Jacob Wiestner (1640-1709) as in agreement with this opinion.

of Schmalzgrueber became the common opinion in the Church in the years before the promulgation of the present Code.[87]

SECTION 2. SUPPORT BY TITULUS SERVITII DIOECESIS AND TITULUS MISSIONIS

The conversions of the newly colonized and developed lands of the world from the seventeenth to the nineteenth century brought an even greater demand for the recognition of new titles of ordination for the clergy. The salvation of souls was being handicapped by the lack of benefices, pensions and patrimonies to support the priests who were needed. Hence for ordination a greater use was made of service of the diocese as also of the title of service of the mission (*titulus servitii dioecesis, titulus missionis*).

The increased use of the *titulus servitii dioecesis* and the *titulus missionis* did not change in any way the concept of the amount due to the clergy for its support. These new titles merely meant new ways of achieving the end attained so well by the titles recognized at the Council of Trent. As will appear later, these new titles were accepted only after the Apostolic See was assured by the petitioning bishops that the clergy could be sufficiently supported through the returns from them.

Further consideration of the *titulus mensae* is here omitted, for it became designated as the title for the ordination of religious who did not take solemn vows and who did not therefore use the *titulus paupertatis,* the title in use for the ordination of religious who belonged to religious Orders.[88]

Article 1. Support by titulus servitii dioecesis

There was an increasing demand through the eighteenth and nineteenth centuries for the recognition by the Holy See of the title of service of the diocese (*titulus servitii dioecesis*) for ordination. The effects of the French Revolution and the growth of the

---

[87] Wernz, *Ius Decretalium,* III, n. 186, pp. 198-199.

[88] Leo XII (1823-1829) const. *Inter religiosas,* 11 mart. 1828—*Bull. Rom.* (*cont.*), XIII, 660; Leo XIII (1878-1903), const. *Conditae a Christo,* 8 dec. 1900, § II, n. VI—*Fontes,* n. 644; S.C. Ep et Reg., decr. *Quemadmodum,* 17 dec. 1890—*Fontes,* n. 2017.

Church in South and North America (especially in Mexico and the United States) made it necessary to recognize the support of priests under a title other than those which had been approved in the Council of Trent.

In France the hatred of the atheistic Republic of the Revolution gave way to the repressions of the Napoleonic government. According to Article 26 of the *Articles Organiques,* published on April 8, 1802, the French bishops were forbidden to ordain priests unless they enjoyed a patrimony with a revenue of three hundred gold francs a year. Compliance with this law would have prevented almost all ordinations. Consequently, despite the law, the bishops ordained priests according to the needs of the parishes, and these priests were assigned to parishes that could support them. The bishops were permitted to ordain these priests without any of the approved titles—the Holy See had not yet approved the title of service of the diocese—but the bishops were firmly enjoined to safeguard the decent support of the clergy.[89] Besides making a general statement of the principles concerning the decent support of the clergy, many of the French dioceses made specific provisions for a fund in support of the sick and indigent diocesan priests who had been ordained on the title of service to the diocese; these sick-funds were known as "*caisses de retraite,*" "*caisses de secours.*"[90]

---

[89] Many, *Praelectiones de Sacra Ordinatione* (Parisiis, 1905), nn. 146-147 (hereafter referred to as *De Sacra Ordinatione*). The Provincial Council of Auch (1851) declared (c. 96) that clerics in major Orders should have a title of benefice or patrimony, but provided that "pro temporis praesentis necessitate, super praefato titulo aut ipsius parte, annuente Apostolica Sede, cum clericis promovendis dispensant episcopi."—*Acta et Decreta Sacrorum Conciliorum Recentiorum, Collectio Lacensis* (7 vols. Friburgi Brisgoviae: Herder, 1870-1892), IV, col. 1189 (hereafter referred to as *Coll. Lac.*). Cf. the Provincial Council of Rheims (1849), c. 2—*Coll. Lac.,* IV, col. 124-125; the Provincial Council of Avignon (1849), c. 7, § 3—*Coll. Lac.,* IV, col. 34; the Provincial Council of Albi (1850), Decree II—*Coll. Lac.,* IV, col. 436-437; the Provincial Council of Bordeaux (1850), c. 7, § 1—*Coll. Lac.,* IV, col. 574; the Provincial Council of Sens (1850), c. 7—*Coll. Lac.,* IV, col. 893.

[90] The Provincial Council of Rheims (1859), c. 2—*Coll. Lac.,* IV, col. 124; the Provincial Council of Avignon (1849), c. 7—*Coll. Lac.,* IV, col. 34; the Provincial Council of Albi (1850), Decree 2—*Coll. Lac.,* IV, col. 436; the Provincial Council of Bordeaux (1850), c. 7—*Coll. Lac.,* IV, col. 574; Wernz, *Ius Decretalium,* II, n. 92.

The general use, therefore, by apostolic indult, of the *titulus servitii dioecesis* in France brought no change in the concept of the decent support of the clergy.

In Hungary, the same situation regarding the support of clerics prevailed, except that ordination on the title of service of the diocese was permitted by apostolic indult. The Provincial Council of Kalócsa (1863), defined the amount of support that should be accorded to clerics in major Orders, and in its next canon cited the apostolic indult which permitted bishops to ordain clerics for the service of the diocese; certainly, the same degree of support that was due to clerics from a benefice was thus implicitly accorded to clerics ordained under the title of service to the diocese.[91]

In Mexico the age-long custom of ordaining clerics to major Orders on the certain knowledge that the offerings of the faithful would provide a sufficient support was finally approved in 1879. The petition of the bishops in Mexico, as well as the wording of the rescript, made it abundantly clear that no ordinations were to be performed by bishops unless they were sure that the faithful could and would make sufficient offerings for the proper support of the clerics.[92] Later, by virtue of the Plenary Council of Latin America in 1899, permission to use this *titulus servitii dioecesis* was extended to all bishops of Latin America.[93]

The support of the clergy in the Thirteen Colonies of England was accomplished mostly by means of the returns from land estates. Two Jesuit priests acompanied the settlers of Lord Baltimore to Maryland, and in acordance with the stipulations made by Lord Baltimore with the Jesuit General and the general law governing the settlers, the Jesuit Fathers were allowed to claim and to cultivate land for their support.[94]

---

[91] Council of Kalócsa (1863), c. 15: "Qui ex indulto apostolico in servitium dioecesis absque titulo ordinantur presbyteri servire dioecesi obligantur."—*Coll. Lac.*, V, col. 686; cf. also c. 14—*loc. cit.*

[92] S.C.C., *ad Ecclesiam de Chiapas*, 21 iun. 1879—*Acta Sanctae Sedis* (*ASS*) (41 vols., Romae, 1865-1908), XII (1879), 569.

[93] Plenary Council of Latin America (1899), Tit. V. *De Ordine*, c. 7—*Acta et Decreta Concilii Plenarii Americae Latinae* (Romae, 1902), n. 582.

[94] John Gilmary Shea, *The Catholic Church in Colonial Days* (New York, 1886), pp. 47 ff. Cf. E. L. Heston, *The Alienation of Church Property in the United States*. The Catholic University of America Canon Law Studies, n.

The extent of the land belonging to the Jesuits was so considerable that it easily supported them and the needs of the Church in the colony. Despite the sad experience of the Catholics in Maryland at the hands of an armed invasion under the bitterly anti-Catholic Clayborne from Virginia, the Church in Maryland was able to support its clergy in general accordance with the manner prescribed by the Council of Trent—by means of the returns from a benefice. Bishop Carroll (1735-1815) later gave testimony of the independence of the priests in Maryland in virtue of their land holdings.[95] In the parishes where the pastor was supported, not from the proceeds of Church lands, but by free-will offerings of the parishioners, the ecclesiastical authorities reminded the faithful persistently that priests were to be given a decent support.[96]

Inasmuch as the first missionaries to the Colonies were Jesuits,

---

132 (Washington, D. C.: The Catholic University of America Press, 1941), p. 11.

[95] Shea, *The Catholic Church in Colonial Days,* p. 364. For a full treatment of the nature of the support of diocesan priests in the United States, cf. *The Nature of Support of Diocesan Priests in the United States,* by Kenneth R. O'Brien (Dissertation in Partial Fulfillment for the Degree of the Licentiate in Canon Law, Catholic University of America, 1948). It is difficult to classify the nature of the support for these early Jesuits. The priests, although they held the deed to various parcels of land, did not enjoy the income from that particular parcel; the income from all the land holdings constituted a common fund, which was apportioned to the various priests according to the decision of the Chapter meetings at Whitemarsh, Maryland. The system was unique, and probably could be better designated as support from the "common table" (*titulus mensae communis*) than from a benefice. The Jesuits themselves, and later the other clergy, did not consider this system a system of benefices.—T. Hughes, *History of the Society of Jesus in North America, Colonial and Federal* (2 vols., New York, 1908), Vol. II, *Documents,* Appendix I, p. 627.

[96] T. Hughes, *ibid.,* pp. 635-636; Peter Guilday, *A History of the Councils of Baltimore* (New York: Macmillan Co., 1932), pp. 62 ff.; Synod of the United States (1791), Statute 7—*Coll. Lac.,* III, col. 6. Later, after the suppression of the Society of Jesus in 1773, the secular priests and the former Jesuits (now secular priests) were supported from the income of the estates. This system of support could possibly be called a "community benefice" or a *titulus mensae communis,* but for lack of a more precise terminology and for convenience the writer will refer to this system as that of a benefice. It has been noted previously that this system of support was *sui generis.*

there was no problem concerning their *titulus ordinationis.* Even when the Society of Jesus was dissolved in 1773, the dissolution did not affect the well-established benefices of these priests.

Later, however, the acquisition of property for the support of the clergy did not keep pace with the increase of Catholics, both clergy and laity, in pioneer America, so that the clergy in many instances had to depend upon help from the foreign missionary societies, such as the Society for the Propagation of the Faith in France, the Leopoldinen-Stiftung in Austria, and the Ludwig-Missionsverein.[97] Although the priests were ordained under the *titulus missionis,* it is evident that the Church in America always insisted that a decent support was due to the clergy.[98] In fact, the early Jesuits were so conscious of the support that was due to clerics according to their dignity that it was one of the chief reasons for their decision to resist the appointment of a bishop to the newly founded United States. They insisted that there was no adequate means of support for a bishop.[99] The same Chapter that had adopted this resolution recognized also that all priests who had performed faithful service were not only to enjoy a decent support during the years of their active ministry, but also "in old age or infirmity."[100]

Finally, in 1908, when the Church in the United States passed under the jurisdiction of the Sacred Consistorial Congregation, the basis was laid for ordaining priests under the title of service of the diocese.[101] Early in January of 1909, Pope Pius X (1903-1914)

---

[97] The I Provincial Council of Baltimore (1829), Decretum 1—*Coll. Lac.,* III, col. 25; the III Provincial Council of Baltimore (1837), Decretum 2—*Coll. Lac.,* III, col. 56.

[98] The I Plenary Council of Baltimore (1852)—*Coll. Lac.,* III, col. 152.

[99] Guilday, *Life and Times of John Carroll* (2 vols., New York, 1922), II, 529 ff.

[100] Guilday, *op. cit.,* II, 529.

[101] Pius X (1903-1914) const. *Sapienti consilio,* 29 iun. 1908—*Acta Apostolicae Sedis, Commentarium Officiale* (Romae, 1909-), I (1909), 148 (hereafter referred to as *AAS*). A decree of the Sacred Congregation of the Consistory provided for the ordination of the students of the North American College in Rome under the title of service of the diocese.—S.C. Consist., 12 nov. 1908, ad XI, XII—*Fontes,* n. 2056.

ordered that clerics be ordained to major Orders under the title of service of the diocese.[102]

The evidence that the concept of support due to the clergy was not changed by the approval of the *titulus servitii dioecesis* is found in the statement by which it was introduced for consideration at the Vatican Council in 1870. Schema XIII proposed for consideration this new title of ordination, which left to the bishop the determination of the manner and the source of the support for the clergy thus ordained; the clergy could be supported from the offerings of the faithful, or by any other approved manner which guaranteed the proper support for them. The *Schema* specified that not only the current needs of the clergy were to be met, but that provision had to be made for support during illness or incapacity.[103]

Article 2. Support by titulus missionis

The *titulus missionis,* in regard to the support of clerics, differed little from the *titulus servitii dioecesis.* Both permitted the ordination of clerics to major Orders without the assured sufficient income of a benefice, pension or patrimony, and made the cleric rely on

[102] "In riposta alla sua lettera del 14 dicembre teste decorso, N. 420-d., mi reco a premura di significare alla S.V. Illma, che il Santo Padre ha stabilito, che d'ora innanzi, in tutti codesti Stati Uniti d'America Settentrionali, i chierici promovendi al Suddiaconato sieno ordinati 'titulo servitii ecclesiae' anziche 'titulo missionis' come il fu fatto finora."—*The Ecclesiastical Review* (from 1889-1905, and again from 1944 onward; *The American Ecclesiastical Review,* Philadelphia, 1889-1943; Washington, D. C., 1944-), XL (1909), 329. Although the title, *servitii dioecesis* or *ecclesiae* was not formally established as canonical until the promulgation of the present Code, it was accepted as legal.—Augustine, *A Commentary on the New Code of Canon Law* (8 vols., Vol. IV, 3. ed., St. Louis: Herder, 1925), IV, 472 (hereafter cited *Commentary*); McBride, *Incardination and Excardination of Seculars,* The Catholic University of America Canon Law Studies, n. 145 (Washington, D. C.: The Catholic University of America Press, 1941), pp. 151-152.

[103] "Curent autem episcopi sive per oblationes fidelium quorum erga Ecclesiam pietas eum in finem excitanda erit, sive per alia pro locorum opportunitate comparanda subsidia id efficere ut . . . eorum qui indigent inopia sublevari queat."—Vatican Council (1870), Schema XIII—*Coll. Lac.,* VIII, col. 667.

the free-will offerings of the faithful to whom he ministered. The great difference, canonically, lay in the oath of the cleric to remain in the service of the mission unless he received a proper dispensation from the oath he had taken. There was also, from the human viewpoint, the added sacrifice of laboring in a foreign land amid unpredictable and often hostile circumstances. Hence, clerics ordained under the *titulus missionis* were to be given a more thorough test of character than was exacted of those who received ordination under other titles.[104]

Although the difference in the wealth and the resources of the regions in which most missionaries labored demanded the acceptance by them of a lower standard of living than that to which they had been accustomed, no cleric could be ordained under this title unless there was a definite assurance of a sufficient sustenance for him.[105]

As was seen in the preceding article, the Church in the United States was under the jurisdiction of the Sacred Congregation for the Propagation of the Faith, and thus the clergy were ordained under the title of the mission. However, it cannot be asserted that the concept of the support due to the clergy was impaired or reduced in consequence of the clergy's ordination under this title.

The general increase in the prosperity of the Church in the United States was responsible for the improvement in the support of the clergy, and when the title of ordination was changed in 1908 from that of title of the mission to that of title of service of the diocese (or Church), the change brought no alteration of the concept of support due to the clergy. Although a cleric ordained under the title of the mission expected generally to be supported in a meager fashion, the support of such a cleric was sometimes as ample as that which was afforded the parish clergy in certain regions of impoverished Catholic countries.

---

[104] S.C. Prop. de Fide, instr. 27 apr. 1871, §§ 6, 7—*Fontes,* n. 4878.

[105] S.C. de Prop. de Fide, instr. 27 apr. 1871, § 1—*Fontes,* n. 4878; S.C. Prop. de Fide (C.P. pro Sin.), 7 aug. 1678, ad 9—*Fontes,* 4489; S.C. Prop. de Fide, decr. 18 aug. 1885—*Collectanea Sacrae Congregationis de Propaganda Fide,* n. 1641.

PART II

Canonical Commentary

CHAPTER VII

General Concept of Fitting Support of the Secular Clergy in the Present Code of Canon Law

In the present Code of Canon Law, the injunction to the ordinary to provide fitting support for the secular clergy is contained principally in canons 979 and 981:

> Canon 979, § 1.—Pro clericis saecularibus titulus canonicus est titulus beneficii, eoque deficiente, patrimonii aut pensionis.
>
> § 2. Hic titulus debet esse vere securus pro tota ordinati vita et vere sufficiens ad congruam eiusdem sustentationem, secundum normas ab Ordinariis pro diversis locorum et temporum necessitatibus et adiunctis dandas.
>
> Canon 981, § 1.—Si ne unus quidem ex titulis de quibus in can. 979, § 1, praeto sit, suppleri potest titulo servitii dioecesis, et, in locis Sacrae Congregationi de Prop. Fide subiectis, titulo missionis, ita tamen ut ordinatus, iureiurando interposito, se devoveat perpetuo dioecesis aut missionis servitio, sub Ordinarii loci pro tempore auctoritate.
>
> § 2. Ordinarius presbytero, quem promoverit titulo servitii ecclesiae vel missionis, debet beneficium vel officium vel subsidium, ad congruam eiusdem sustentationem sufficiens, conferre.

Prior to a consideration of the constitutent elements contained in the concept of fitting support due to the clergy, attention must be directed to a few pertinent facts.

First, it should be noted that this fitting support, *congrua sustentatio,* is due to every cleric in major Orders who is in good standing—subdeacons, deacons and priests.[1] A study of the amount

[1] Canon 980, § 2. Although the writer will occasionally use the popular term "salary" in referring to the allotment accorded to pastors and assistant pastors, the term is not to be interpreted in its civil law meaning; the difference between the canonical and civil law meaning of the word will be explained in Chapter VIII.

of support that is due specifically to each of the members of these different sacred orders will be made in a later part of the dissertation.

Also, it must be borne in mind that the term "fitting support" is defined, however roughly, in canon 979, which refers to ordination on the title of benefice, pension or patrimony; canon 981, which refers to ordination on the title of the service of the diocese or of the mission, offers no explanation at all of the term "fitting support." Canon 981 is a new law. It is obvious, therefore, that the concept of fitting support was interpreted primarily in terms of a benefice, pension or patrimony[2]—whatever constituted a suitable benefice, pension or patrimony constituted a *congrua sustentatio,* a fitting support. Later, because of the paucity of benefices, pensions and patrimonies, the Church permitted the ordination of clerics in major Orders on the title of service of the mission or service of the diocese, provided that the ordinary could guarantee them a fitting support;[3] this fitting support, however, remained the same as that secured from a sufficient benefice, pension or patrimony.[4] The elements of a fitting support as derived from a benefice, pension or patrimony remain the same when that support is derived from the title of service of the diocese or service of the mission.

In this country, where support of the clergy for the past century has been almost exclusively secured from the title of service of the mission or service of the diocese, there is a natural tendency to consider the support of the clergy without any reference to its original definition in relation to support from a benefice, pension of patrimony.[5] The inclination is to accept a *de facto* situation for a *de iure* concept.

The present Code, in its definition of fitting support, has not

[2] Cf. Chapter V, pp. 60 ff.

[3] Cf. Chapter VI, pp. 97 ff.

[4] Cf. Chapter VI, pp. 102, 103.

[5] At present, a parish in the United States is considered a benefice.—Augustine, *A Commentary on the New Code of Canon Law* (8 vols., Vol. VI, 3. ed., St. Louis: Herder, 1931), VI, 495; Vermeersch-Creusen, *Epitome Iuris Canonici* (3 vols., Vol. 2, 6. ed., Mechlinae, Romae: Dessain, 1940), II, 523; Beste, *Introductio in Codicem* (3. ed., Collegeville: St. John's Abbey Press, 1946), pp. 228, 229, 714.

changed the concept from that contained in the pre-Code law. This concept must therefore be interpreted according to the pre-Code law[6] in conformity with the decisions of the Holy See and the pre-Code commentators. Many of the modern commentators either refrain entirely from commenting on the concept of fitting support, or repeat the views of the pre-Code commentators.[7]

What, then, is meant today by the words of canon 979, § 1, that the support due to the clergy must be "sufficient for a fitting support in conformity with the rules of the Ordinary in accordance with the needs and circumstances of the respective localities and times?"

The most comprehensive and precise answer is given by a canonist of a country, Spain, that had many benefices:

> A fitting support must be understood in a generous way and without scrupulosity (*anxietate.*) It includes, according to the doctors, all that is necessary for food, clothing, housing, medical care and the preservation of health, the maintenance of servants according to the status of the beneficiary, decent relaxation, a moderate amount of liberality towards good causes, the demands of sociability, of hospitality that must be shown to friends and to the needy, of the payment of one's debts as well as those of

[6] Canon 6, 2°.

[7] The gradual seizure of church property throughout the world rendered nugatory much of the discussion of support of the clergy from benefices, patrimonies and pensions. Church property in England was completely confiscated in the sixteenth century; the property of the Church in France was confiscated in 1789; the confiscation of the church property constituting benefices was practically completed in Italy by 1890; the property of the Church in Germany suffered great depredations throughout the religious wars. In all these countries the clergy who were formerly supported by benefices or pensions were forced to secure support from a grant by the State or from the funds of the diocese. When the Church was confronted with such a situation the canonical commentators were discouraged from considering the support due to the clergy from benefices and funds that no longer existed.—A. Bonal, *Institutiones Canonicae* (2 vols., Parisiis, 1898), II, 106; G. Hergenröther, *Storia Universale della Chiesa* (Italian translation by Enrico Rosa, 6. ed., 6 vols., Firenze: Libreria Editrice Fiorentina, 1930), VI, 191-209, 345, 370-390; Charles Poulet, *A History of the Catholic Church* (translation by Sidney A. Raemers, 2 vols., St. Louis: Herder, 1945), II, 439-442.

> one's relatives, of prudent provision for the future, etc. All these must be supplied in accordance with the dignity of the person, the amount of the income (of the benefice, etc.), the merits and efforts for the Church of the person receiving the benefice. . . . The best norm is the prevailing usage among zealous holders of benefices.[8]

Of course, if a cleric is assured of receiving a sufficient pension when he retires he need not receive a salary sufficiently large to enable him to make provision for the future.

This opinion agrees with those of the prominent, older canonists, such as Schmalzgrueber,[9] Wernz,[10] Reiffenstuel,[11] Bouix (1808-1870),[12] and Grandclaude (1826-1900).[13] This opinion also agrees with and is an amplification of the opinion of the American pre-Code commentator, Doctor S. B. Smith (1845-1895):

> By *congrua sustentatio* is here meant not a scanty, but a comfortable and honorable support; that is, a living which supplies not merely the necessaries but also the comforts of life in keeping with the ecclesiastical state.[14]

The more noted modern commentators agree in general with the

---

[8] "*Honesta sustentatio* cum amplitudine et sine anxietate intelligenda est. Complectitur, iuxta doctores, omnia convenientia ad victum, vestitum, habitationem, morbos curandos et valetudinem conservandam, famulos sustentandos iuxta beneficiarii statum, honestam relaxationem, moderata munera facienda, respectus sociales, hospitalitatem amicis et egenis praebendam, debita sua suorum solvenda, prudentem futuri praevisionem, etc. Haec omnia iuxta personae dignitatem, redituum abundantiam, merita et labores beneficiati pro Ecclesia. . . . Optimam normam praebebit usus inter honestos beneficiatos vigens."—E. Regatillo, *Institutiones Iuris Canonici,* 2 vols., Vol. 1, 2. ed., Santander: Sal Terrae, 1946), I, 195.

[9] *Ius Ecclesiasticum,* lib. III, tit. 39, n. 137.

[10] *Ius Decretalium,* III, n. 186, pp. 198-199.

[11] *Ius Canonicum,* lib. III, tit. 5, n. 221.

[12] Bouix, *Tractatus de Parocho* (3. ed., Parisiis, 1880), p. 280.

[13] *Jus Canonicum* (3 vols., Parisiis, 1882-1883), I, 229.

[14] *Elements of Ecclesiastical Law* (3 vols., Vol. III, New York, 1888), III, 95, footnote.

opinion of Regatillo, but are very loath to enumerate all the elements that constitute a fitting support.[15]

In general, then, the determination of the fitting support of the clergy is governed by the following broad provisions:

1) it should include all that is necessary for a comfortable, secure living;
2) the degree of this comfortable, secure living is to be determined by
   a) the dignity and merits of the cleric, and
   b) the circumstances of place and time;
3) the amount of the income is to be determined by the ordinary.

SECTION 1. THINGS GENERALLY NECESSARY FOR A COMFORTABLE AND SECURE LIVING

Inasmuch as every cleric has a right to a comfortable secure living according to his status, it is necessary to determine first which things are necessary for the proper support of a cleric.

There is unanimity of opinion among the commentators on most of the elements deemed necessary for a comfortable and secure living—food, housing, clothing, medical care, almsgiving, recreation, the meeting of social responsibilities, the costs of hospitality, and provision for the future. There is dispute and even denial on the part of some authors regarding the cleric's duty to support his near-relatives,[16] and there is discussion about the amount to be

[15] Wernz-Vidal, *Ius Canonicum ad Codicis Normam Exactam* (7 tomes in 8, Vol. II, 3. ed., 1943; Vol. IV, pars 1, 1934; Vol. IV, pars 2, 1935; Vol. VII, 1937, Romae: Universitas Gregoriana), IV, pars 2, 249 (hereafter cited as *Ius Canonicum*); Cappello, *Tractatus Canonico-Moralis de Sacramentis* (3 vols. in 6, Vol. II, pars III, Romae: Marietti, 1935), Vol. II, pars III, 399 (hereafter cited *De Sacramentis*); Cappello, *Summa Iuris Canonici* (3 vols., Vol. II, 4. ed., Romae: Universitas Gregoriana, 1945), II, 535; Vermeersch-Creusen, *Epitome Iuris Canonici,* II, 169; Beste, *Introductio in Codicem,* p. 730; Augustine, *A Commentary on the Code of Canon Law,* VI, 537; Coronata, *Institutiones Iuris Canonici* (5 vols., Vol. II, 2. ed., Taurini: Marietti, 1939), II, 416; Coronata, *Tractatus Canonicus de Sacramentis* (5 vols., Vol. II, Taurini-Romae: Marietti, 1945), II, 105 (hereafter cited *De Sacramentis*).

[16] Regatillo, *Institutiones Iuris Canonici,* I, 195; Coronata, *Institutiones Iuris Canonici,* II, 416; Beste, *Introductio in Codicem,* p. 730; Augustine, *A Commentary on the Code of Canon Law,* VI, 537.

allotted for other elements of a cleric's living, such as housing and recreation, and provision for the future.

In regard to the duty of clerics to support near-relatives, there is a decision of the Sacred Congregation of Bishops and Regulars which illustrates the mind of the Church on this duty of nature incumbent on all persons, and therefore also on clerics.[17] An old and infirm retired pastor, who had received an annual pension of 900 marks from the government, was ordered by his Ordinary to live in a retreat for aged priests. Furthermore, his pension was cancelled because the Ordinary, by arrangement with the government, had utilized the funds allocated for the clerical pensions to build a retreat for aged and infirm priests. The aged and retired pastor refused to comply, and demanded that the Ordinary pay his pension. The Sacred Congregation upheld the plea of the aged pastor.[18]

The retired pastor submitted the following reasons for demanding the pension: he had expended a great deal of his private fortune on charity and therefore needed the pension to pay his expenses at the Jesuit College in which he resided; his health demanded occasional sojourns in the milder climate of Italy; his sick and dependent sister needed his continued financial assistance.

The Sacred Congregation replied strongly in the affirmative to the pastor's plea—"*Attentis omnibus, affirmative et amplius ad mentem.* . . ." The Sacred Congregation noted that the pension was due in justice to the retired pastor and that all his acts of charity (*pia opera*) were to be considered in reference to the payment of the pension. The Sacred Congregation thus certainly accepted the support of the pastor's infirm sister as one of his duties and works of charity.

Inasmuch as the duty of a son to support his parents is more grave than that which obliges him to support his brothers and

---

[17] H. Noldin-A. Schmitt, *Summa Theologiae Moralis* (24. ed., 3 vols., Oeniponte: Rauch, 1936), II, 266, 267.

[18] S.C. Ep. et Reg., *Posnanien. Pensio,* 18 maii 1906—*ASS,* XXXIX (1906), 485-461. The Sacred Congregation adverted to the fact that the retired pastor had long been pensioned before the retreat was built. It implied that the case would have been considered differently if the retreat had existed before the priest was pensioned.

sisters,[19] the decision of the Sacred Congregation certainly confirmed the right of the parents, to be supported, if they be in need, by their son, a priest. This duty establishes the correlative right of a priest to receive enough income to support at least dependent parents as well as sisters and brothers. The decision does not determine the extent of the obligation in the collateral line, but it would certainly extend to everyone in the direct line—to grandparents.[20]

One may also note here in passing that the decision of the Sacred Congregation is another evidence of the Church's position that the retired cleric is entitled to a suitable pension.[21] This question will be treated more fully later in Chapter X in regard to the support due to the aged and infirm clerics.

The Church also indicates its attitude towards the support of parents by clerics in its legislation on religious: a candidate is not to be permitted to enter the novitiate if his parents are dependent,[22] and if his parents become dependent after he has taken a vow of poverty, he may receive and send the money without violating the vow of poverty.[23]

The older canonists, notably Schmalzgrueber and Reiffenstuel, were specific about the amount of support a cleric should give his relatives. According to them, a cleric should afford the members of his family—parents, brothers and sisters—sufficient support to enable them to live according to their state in life, but not above it. The cleric should therefore be capable of enabling his brother to pursue his studies and of providing a sufficient dowry to his sister if the family cannot supply it. Also, if the cleric has any children, e.g., from a marriage before he received sacred Orders, he

---

[19] Noldin-Schmitt, *Summa Theologiae Moralis,* II, 266.

[20] In virtue of canon 542, 2°, a candidate for admission as a novice in a religious institute may not be admitted licitly to the novitiate if he has a dependent parent or grandparent.

[21] Canons 979, § 1; 1429; Wernz-Vidal, *Ius Canonicum,* IV, pars 1, 295, 298.

[22] Canon 542, 2°.

[23] Schaefer, *Compendium de Religiosis ad Normam Codicis Iuris Canonici* (3. ed., Romae: Herder, 1940), p. 700 (hereafter cited as *De Religiosis*).

is bound to support them and should therefore receive sufficient income for this support.[24]

Clerics should also be able, according to Schmalzgrueber, to assist, *mutatis mutandis,* their servants in the same way that they assist the members of their family.[25]

In regard to the living accommodations that should be accorded a cleric, it should be noted that the cleric is not expected to pay for these accommodations from the amount he receives as his fitting support. Suitable housing has always been afforded the clergy in addition to the amount of support received.[26] Hence, today no deduction should be made from a cleric's salary as payment for his room or house rent.

The amount and kinds of recreation permitted to clerics have never been defined. The Church has, however, frequently stated what clerics may not do for recreation. These regulations are contained principally in canons 138 and 140.[27]

The Church therefore contents itself with the general law that clerics should abstain from whatever dishonors the clerical state. The Church specifies some of these things in its universal law: practicing unbecoming arts, gambling, certain types of hunting, frequenting taverns, attending inappropriate theatrical shows, spectacles and presentations at which a cleric's presence would give cause for scandal.

By prohibiting certain types of unbecoming recreation, the Church insinuates that there are types of recreation becoming to the clerical state.[28] Certainly such elevating recreations as reading

[24] Schmalzgrueber, *Ius Ecclesiasticum Universum,* III, tit. 25, n. 25; tit. 39, n. 118; Reiffenstuel, *Ius Canonicum Universum,* lib. III, tit. 5, n. 222.

[25] Schmalzgrueber, *Ius Ecclesiasticum Universum,* lib. III, tit. 39, n. 118.

[26] G. Corazzini, *La Parrocchia* (Torino, 1900), p. 451; Wernz-Vidal, *Ius Canonicum,* IV, pars 2, 240.

[27] Canon 138.—Clerical ab iis omnibus quae statum suum dedecent, prorsus abstineant; indecoras artes ne exerceant; aleatoriis ludis, pecunia exposita, ne vacant; arma ne gestent, nisi quando iusta timendi causa subsit; venationi ne indulgeant, clamorosam autem nunquam exerceant; tabernas aliaque similia loca sine necessitate aut alia iusta causa ab Ordinario loci probata ne ingrediantur.

Canon 140.—Spectaculis, choreis, et pompis quae eos dedecent, vel quibus clericos interesse scandalo sit, praesertim in publicis theatris, ne intersint.

[28] Schmalzgrueber, *Ius Canonicum Universum,* lib. III, tit. 39, n. 121.

good literature, attending concerts, or studying art, are laudable and profitable. The playing of cards and attending respectable movies and plays are also permitted. Likewise, recreation by participating in or witnessing athletic games or sports, provided there is no unreasonable expenditure of money or time, is permitted; among such sports one may name golf, swimming, baseball, riding, football, tennis.

The amount of money and time permitted to clerics for indulging in permissible recreation is determined by the amount of their income and the demands of their duties.[29] It must be remembered, however, that such a time-consuming recreation as golf may through frequent indulgence contravene the regulations stating that pastors are not permitted to be absent from their parishes for over two months (continuously or interruptedly) in a year.[30]

The Church provides an opportunity for clerics to enjoy adequate recreation through its regulations on vacations. A pastor may be absent from his parish for two months during the year,[31] but he is required to provide a substitute to perform his duties during this absence.[32] The bishop is permitted to be absent from his diocese for three months during the year,[33] but he is required to be in his diocese during the more solemn parts of the ecclesiastical year, unless he is excused for some legitimate reason.[34] Although the Code does not provide specifically for a vacation for parish assistants, the pastor is empowered to allow them a vacation, the duration of which is generally decided by diocesan statute.[35]

---

[29] Schmalzgrueber, *loc. cit.*

[30] Canon 465, § 2.

[31] Canon 465, §§ 2, 3.

[32] Canon 465, § 4.

[33] Canon 338, § 2.

[34] Canon 338, § 3.

[35] The V Synod of the Archdiocese of Los Angeles decreed that assistants were to receive an annual vacation of three weeks.—V Synod of Los Angeles (1927), Statute 58—*Statuta Dioecesis Angelorum et S. Didaci* (St. Louis: Herder, 1927), p. 10. The Diocese of Toledo permits two weeks of vacation annually to assistants ordained for less than five years, and three weeks to those ordained more than five years.—I Synod of Toledo (1941), Decree 85—*Acta et Decreta Synodi Dioecesanae Toletanae Primae* (Toleti: Cancellaria Curiae Dioecesanae, 1941), p. 52.

To assist a cleric in using his opportunity for a vacation, many dioceses permit the pastor to pay for his own substitute as well as for the substitute of the assistant pastor from the parish funds.[36] The same dioceses also provide that the pastor and the assistant be paid a salary for a part or for all of the time spent in vacation.

It is obvious then that the Church favors the enjoyment of adequate recreation by clerics, and thus approves of such means as are needed for assuring enough income to enable them to secure that recreation.

The Church is, and always has been, very solicitous for an adequate care of the clergy in their old age or disability.[37] The income of the cleric, as was noted above, should be sufficient to enable the cleric to save enough for his support when he retires because of old age or disability, unless the cleric is assured of a sufficient pension upon retirement. The mind of the Church is obvious from the provisions in law for clerics who when resigning from benefices have not sufficient funds for their support. The ordinary is not allowed to permit a cleric who possesses a benefice

---

[36] The Diocese of Toledo permits the pastor to pay for his substitute from parish funds for two Sundays.—I Synod of Toledo (1941), Decree 61—*Acta et Decreta Synodi Dioecesanae Toletanae Primae,* p. 47; the Diocese of Seattle allows the pastor to pay from parish funds for a substitute for one month, and to pay for a substitute for the assistant for two weeks.—V Synod of Seattle (1938), Decree 79, §§ 1, 2—*Statuta Dioecesis Seattlensis* (Seattle: Metropolitan Press, 1938), p. 52; in Monterey-Fresno, the diocesan statute provides that the pastor may pay for his substitute from the parish funds.—I Synod of Monterey-Fresno (1929), Decree 74, § 3—*Statuta Dioecesis Montereyensis-Fresnensis* (Fresno: St. Columba Guild, 1929), p. 30; in Harrisburg the substitute for the pastor is also paid from the parish funds.—IX Synod of Harrisburg (1943), Decree 79—*Statutes of the Diocese of Harrisburg* (Harrisburg: Curiae Dioecesis, 1943), p. 62.

[37] Reiffenstuel, referring to the removal of clerics from a benefice because of an incurable disease and without provision for adequate support, wrote: ". . . si enim clerici aegrotantes tam inhumaniter tractarentur, caeteri deterrerentur a clericatu."—*Ius Canonicum Universum,* lib. III, tit. 6, n. 3. Even in China, where the Church is in straitened circumstances, provision is made for the support of retired priests,—"N. 92. Tempore infirmitatis, senectutis aut impotentiae cunctis ejus necessitatibus cum caritate providebitur."—*Praxis Missionalis in Vicariatu Apostolico de Ichang* (Wuchang: The Franciscan Press, 1935), p. 32.

to resign that benefice unless he has sufficient means of support,[38] and if the beneficiary is removed for a cause, he must be provided with sufficient means of income by being given another benefice or a pension.[39] If, because of some necessity, resignation of a benefice is permitted a cleric who has not sufficient funds for his support, the ordinary is empowered to confer the benefice on another cleric on the condition that the resigning beneficiary enjoy a pension from the benefice;[40] the pension thus levied can amount to one-third of the income of the benefice.[41]

In those parts of the world where the lack of benefices rendered the legislation of the Church inefficacious, the ordinaries provided for the support of the aged or disabled clergy by means of special arrangements which fulfilled the intention of the law. The ordinaries, in such sections, instituted insurance policies or pension plans for the clergy.[42] This system is still widely in use today.[43]

In those countries in which the State pays the salaries of the clergy, some provision is always made for the payment of pensions to the aged or disabled clergy.[44] Belgium, where the State pays the salaries of the clergy, has a singularly generous but involved system of pensions: the full pension—to which a priest is entitled if he has reached the age of 65 and has served in the ministry for 30 years—is the equivalent of the mean salary that the priest received during the last five years of his active ministry; partial pensions are paid to priests who because of infirmities have been

[38] Canon 1484.

[39] Canon 2154.

[40] Canon 1429, § 1.

[41] Canon 1429, § 2.

[42] Provincial Council of Rheims (1849), c. 2—*Coll. Lac.*, IV, col. 124; Provincial Council of Avignon (1849), c. 7—*Coll. Lac.*, IV, col. 34; Many, *Praelectiones de Sacra Ordinatione*, nn. 146-147; Wernz, *Ius Decretalium*, II, n. 92; I Plenary Council of Baltimore (1852)—*Coll. Lac.*, III, col. 152.

[43] In the Archdioceses of Baltimore and Washington, the premium is paid by the parish and the cleric, each paying half of the total cost. Similar systems are used elsewhere.

[44] *Sollemnis Conventio inter Sanctam Sedem et Rempublicam Poloniae*—*AAS*, XVII (1925), 385-386; *Concordat entre le Saint Siége et le Gouvernement de Lithuanie*, Article XXIV—*AAS*, XII (1920), 432. In Austria, a priest is retired at the age of 70 with a pension roughly equal to his salary.—*Besoldungsordnung*, Archdiocese of Vienna, September 1, 1947.

obliged to leave their duties and who have served at least ten years in the ministry. The lowest partial pension is one-half the amount of the full pension.[45]

It should be noted that the ordinary in such a country is still obliged to support members of the clergy who are not entitled to support from the State, e.g., priests who are obliged to retire or to leave their duties, but who have not yet served ten years in the ministry and are consequently not entitled to a pension from the State.[46] Also, if the pension or salary provided by the State is not sufficient for the just needs of the cleric, the ordinary is still obliged, if the means are available, to supply the support needed by the cleric. The assistance accorded by the State to the clergy does not abrogate the right and duty of the ordinary to provide support for the clergy.[47]

SECTION 2. THE INDIVIDUATING FACTORS DETERMINING THE DEGREE OF A COMFORTABLE AND SECURE LIVING

Article 1. Dignity and Merit of the Cleric

Regatillo states the traditional and commonly accepted opinion that the amount of income or living to which a cleric is entitled depends upon a number of factors, namely, the dignity and merit of the cleric as well as all those considerations which are understood as circumstances of place and time (including the amount of income of the parish or benefice).[48]

It is well established that a cleric is to receive recompense according to his ecclesiastical dignity. A bishop or a monsignor is

---

[45] The system of partial pensions in Belgium is the following: a priest who has served at least ten years receives half the full pension plus 1/60 of it for each year of service over ten years and less than 20 years; a priest who has served at least 20 years receives two-thirds of the full pension plus 1/30 of it for each year of service over twenty years and less than thirty.—Letter from the Embassy of Belgium, December 3, 1948, Washington, D. C.

It is interesting to note that this system of pensions was codified by a law of July 21, 1844.

[46] Canons 979; 980; 981.

[47] Canons 979; 980; 981.

[48] *Institutiones Iuris Canonici,* I, 195.

expected to have more obligations and to contribute more generously to deserving causes than a priest without any prelatial dignity.[49] For the same reason a pastor should receive a larger income than an assistant pastor.

It is also recognized that a cleric should be rewarded or recompensed according to his merit.[50] Merit includes the accomplishments of the cleric, such as sanctity, administrative ability, scholastic attainments, as well as labor and zeal in the ministry of the Church.[51]

---

[49] By the terms of the Concordat between the Holy See and the Government of Poland, signed in 1925, the salaries of the clergy were to be granted by a "point" system. A cardinal was to receive 2,500 points, plus 800 zlotys for expenses; archbishops were to receive 2,000 points, plus 600 zlotys for expenses; bishops were to receive 1,700 points, plus 600 zlotys for expenses; canons or members of chapters were to receive 600 points; pastors were to receive 270 points; professors in the seminary were to receive 600 points; assistant pastors were to receive 200 points (A zloty was then worth 25 cents).—*Sollemnis Conventio inter Sanctam Sedem et Poloniae Rempublicam* —*AAS,* XVII (1925), 282.

The following is the list of the salaries of the clergy in Belgium, paid by the Government:

Archbishop	373,500 francs
Bishop	298,800 francs
Vicar General of Archdiocese	85,590 francs
Vicar General of Diocese	76,680 francs
Canon of Archdiocese	61,230 francs
Canon of Diocese	56,640 francs
Pastor	40,710 francs
Assistant pastors and vicars	37,200 francs
Chaplain	37,200 francs

Letter from the Embassy of Belgium, December 3, 1948, Washington, D. C.

In France, a more complete and graduated system of salaries for the clergy is observed; in the Archdiocese of Paris, for instance, three different grades of assistant pastors are distinguished with a corresponding gradation in salary.—Letter of Emmanuel Cardinal Suhard, Archbishop of Paris, to his Clergy, January 20, 1948; *Instructions Pratiques,* Archdiocese of Paris, Oct. 24, 1947.

Austria has a similar system.—*Besoldungsordnung,* Archdiocese of Vienna, September 1, 1947.

[50] Regatillo, *Institutiones Iuris Canonici,* I, 195.

[51] In Europe, clerics who occupy highly responsible offices in the diocese, as the vicar general, canons and chancellor, receive increased remuneration in recognition of their increased responsibilities and labors.—*Besoldungs-*

The Church, conforming to its traditional policy of recognizing that learning renders a cleric more valuable for the work of the Church,[52] continues today to increase the remuneration for a cleric who has gained scholastic distinction.[53] Whatever increases the ability of the cleric for the work of the Church makes him eligible for more income. A cleric who by his learning is able to teach or to speak authoritatively renders a signal service to the Church.

Merit also includes the amount of labor or zeal expended in the care of souls. Thus a pastor who is entrusted with the care and administration of a large parish deserves more of an income than one who has the care of a small parish, *ceteris paribus.*[54] Also, the cleric who actually labors more in the care of souls—whether he be a pastor or an assistant pastor—deserves more than a cleric who does less labor. Of course it would be impossible for an ordinary to make adjustments in income according to merit for every cleric in his diocese, but he could apply the principle in a general way or in extraordinary cases. Justice demands that he who contributes more effort and better results in the work of the ministry be fittingly repaid.

It is interesting to note that even the States which confiscated the Church's property gradually came to develop a system of

---

ordnung, Archdiocese of Vienna, September 1, 1947; Letter from the Embassy of Belgium, Washington, D. C., December 3, 1948; Letter of Emmanuel Cardinal Suhard, Archdiocese of Paris, to his Clergy, January 20, 1948.

[52] Leurenius, *Forum Ecclesiasticum,* lib. III, tit. 25, qu. 583, n. 3; Schmalzgrueber, *Ius Ecclesiasticum Universum,* lib. III, tit. 39, n. 137; Reiffenstuel, *Ius Canonicum Universum,* lib. III, tit. 5, n. 221.

[53] Concordats generally recognize the merit of a seminary professor by according him a salary higher than that given to a pastor. In Poland, for example, a seminary professor was accorded 600 points in comparison with 250 accorded to a pastor. Even if the pastor received stole fee, which the professor did not, the difference was still notable.—*Sollemnis Conventio inter Sanctam Sedem et Poloniae Rempublicam—AAS,* XVII (1925), 282.

[54] In the Archdiocese of Paris, the pastors are divided into three different salary groups according to the number of assistant pastors they have (which is an index of the size of the parish). A pastor who has no assistants receives annually 86,300 francs; a pastor who has one, two or three assistants receives annually 87,550 francs; a pastor who has more than three assistants receives annually 88,800 francs.—Letter of Emmanuel Cardinal Suhard, Archbishop of Paris, to his Clergy, January 20, 1948.

recompense according to the merit of the cleric. France, which began in 1789 with granting only one type of salary to all clerics in accordance with its revolutionary aim of blind *egalité*, soon distinguished between "pastors of the first class" and "pastors of the second class" according to the importance of the parish. Later, a difference in allotment was made according to the age of the clergy, and a supplement was provided for the priests who had either to binate in their own parish or to provide Mass for a neighboring community.[55] A similar, equitable system was adopted by Belgium.[56]

The Church not only canonized this system of granting salaries

---

[55] In France, pastors of first class parishes who were under 70 years of age received 1,500 francs, and those who were 70 years of age or older received 1,600 francs. Pastors of second class parishes who were under 70 years of age received 1,200 francs, and those who were over 70 received 1,300 francs. Priests serving non-parochial churches (*succursales*) received 900 francs a year if under 60 years of age, if over 60 years they received 1,100 francs, and if over 70 years, 1,200 francs; those over 75 years of age received 1,300 francs. The pastor who binated was also given a supplement.—Bonal, *Institutiones Canonicae*, II, 106.

Assistant pastors in France, by a law of April 9, 1874, received a salary of 450 francs a year. This was augmented through a supplement granted by the municipality; the supplement could amount to 500 francs.—Bonal, *op. cit.*, II, 196.

In general, the same system is in force today in the Archdiocese of Paris.—Letter of Emmanuel Cardinal Suhard, Archbishop of Paris, to his Clergy, January 20, 1948.

[56] By a law of Belgium enacted on May 28, 1863, bishops were paid 16,000 francs a year, pastors of the first class were paid 2,047.5 francs (with no age differential), pastors of the second class were paid from 1,363 to 1,600 francs (according to age), priests attending non-parochial churches were paid from 950 to 1,200 francs (according to age), and assistant pastors were paid from 600 to 800 francs.—P. de Brabandére, *Compendium Juris Canonici* (2 vols., Brugis, 1866-1869), I, 452.

Today the following salaries are paid to the clergy in Belgium by the State:

Archbishop	373,500 francs
Bishop	298,800 francs
Pastor	40,710 francs
Assistant pastor	37,200 francs

The distinctions between pastors as well as those between assistant pastors have been discontinued.—Letter from the Embassy of Belgium, December 3, 1948, Washington, D. C.

to the clergy graded according to dignity and merit by approving Concordats and diocesan synods that embodied such a system, but on occasion directed that an increase in salary be directed to the cleric who had contributed the most labor. The Government of Italy granted an increase in the allotment to a parish whose pastor was a collegiate chapter that had named a vicar to perform all the parochial work. The chapter claimed that it should receive the increased allotment, but the Sacred Congregation of the Council upheld the plea of the vicar and awarded to him and his assistants the increase in the allotment, for they had performed the work of the ministry; it was also noted by the Sacred Congregation that the intention of the Government in granting the increase in the allotment was to recompense those priests who were engaged in the parochial work. The vicar was allotted an additional 300 lire, and a sum of 510 lire was to be divided among the assistants.[57]

In the United States there is not, and never has been, any consideration of the noble lineage of a cleric in determining his income. In other countries and in other centuries a cleric was supposed to receive more of an income if he was of the nobility, since such a status involved additional obligations.[58] Possibly such consideration is still given to priest-noblemen in other countries, but it has no application in our country.

In opposition to all the commentators who agree that the income of a cleric should be determined in accord with his dignity and merit, there is one dissenting commentator who denies that the qualifications of a cleric should be considered in the determining of his remuneration.[59] He does not explain fully, however, what he means by *"qualitates"* of clerics. If *"qualitates"* refers to the difference in ecclesiastical rank, his opinion is not admissible; if the term refers to the intellectual, administrative or moral excellence

---

[57] S.C.C., *Triventina,* 18 mart. 1905—*ASS,* XXXVIII (1905), 85.

[58] Schmalzgrueber, *Ius Ecclesiasticum Universum,* lib. III, tit. 39, n. 137; Reiffenstuel, *Ius Canonicum Universum,* lib. III, tit. 5, n. 221.

[59] Blat, *Commentarium Textus Codicis Iuris Canonici* (5 vols. in 6, Lib. III, pars I, 2. ed., Romae: Tipographia Pontificia, 1924), Lib. III, pars I, 405.

of the cleric, it is very difficult to see how this singular opinion could prevail over the opposing common opinion.

Article 2. Circumstances of Place and Time

There is no dissenting opinion on the meaning of the words of canon 979 that the fitting support of the different classes of clerics must be determined according to the circumstances or necessities of time and place—*pro diversis locorum et temporum necessitatibus.*[60] In a word, the income of the cleric must be determined in accord with his environment. Coronata is more emphatic than the others in averring that the difference in circumstances of time and place make impossible a general rule of the Church on this subject; he states that neither the Council of Trent nor the Code could establish a precise general rule.[61]

The clerics in a prosperous country are entitled to enjoy a better living in regard to housing, food, transportation and medical services than the clerics of a less fortunate country. A pastor in Italy or in England should not expect to have the same income as the pastor of a parish of equal size in New York or Chicago. Nor could a pastor moving from Brooklyn to South America expect to live, without causing scandal, in the manner to which he was accustomed. A priest can own a car in the United States without causing even comment (unless a diocesan statute forbids it), since it is quite usual for persons of moderate income to own a car; a priest owning a car in southern Italy or in Peru might cause grave scandal.

There is, of course, a considerable difference in economic conditions also within the confines of a country. Hence the income of clerics should differ according to the varied conditions of different sections of the country. In fact, there is a notable difference in the

---

[60] Blat, *Commentarium Textus Codicis Iuris Canonici,* lib. III, pars I, 405; Udalricus Beste, *Introductio in Codicem,* 534; Stephanus Sipos, *Enchiridion Iuris Canonici* (3. ed., Pécs; "Haladás, R. T.," 1936), p. 468, note; Wernz-Vidal, *Ius Canonicum,* IV, pars 2, 249; Cappello, *De Sacramentis,* II, pars III, 399; *Summa Iuris Canonici,* II, 535; Vermeersch-Creusen, *Epitome Iuris Canonici,* II, 169.

[61] Coronata, *De Sacramentis,* II, 105.

economic conditions of urban and rural parishes; different incomes may be accorded to priests in neighboring parishes.[62]

There is never, however, any justification for luxurious living on the part of the clergy, regardless of the wealth of the locality. Extravagance in living is completely foreign and abhorrent to the clerical life, no matter how opulent the economic condition of society may be.[63]

In brief, a cleric should receive an income sufficient to enable him to live with fitting dignity in conformity with the general economic conditions of his locality as well as the obligations to which he is subject.

SECTION 3. DETERMINATION OF THE AMOUNT OF THE INCOME BY THE ORDINARY

The Code provides that the determination of the income of the clergy is to be made by the Ordinary.[64] This is not only in conformity with his right of jurisdiction over his subjects, but is also necessitated by the diverse circumstances.

The Ordinary is to be guided in his determination of the income of the clergy by their difference in dignity and merit as well as by the difference in the circumstances of time and place.[65] In fact, one commentator thinks that the Ordinary should adjust the salary for each parish—an opinion which is hardly feasible, however much it would be recommended by equity.[66]

As expected, there is diversity of advice by the commentators on how the Ordinary should determine the income of clerics. One opinion prefers the Ordinary to ignore the prevailing customs and to lay down definite norms concerning the income of clerics; the opinion would advise him to be guided by the action of other

---

[62] M. Bargilliat, *Droits et Devoirs des Curés et des Vicaires Paroissiaux* (Paris, 1920), p. 409.

[63] Cappello, *Summa Iuris Canonici,* II, 535.

[64] Canon 979, § 2.

[65] Coronata, *De Sacramentis,* II, 105; Blat, *Commentarium Textus Codicis Juris Canonici,* lib. III, pars I, 405.

[66] ". . . qui tiendra compte des circonstances très variables dans les diverses paroisses."—Bargilliat, *Droits et Devoirs des Curés et des Vicaires Paroissiaux,* p. 409.

ordinaries.[67] Another opinion states categorically that the best norm is afforded through the usage that is current among respected beneficiaries.[68]

No one will deny the necessity of a definite law in a diocese on the income of the clergy, and it seems to be immaterial whether or not the ordinary follows the prevailing custom, provided that his decision is made in accordance with equity. Wherever underpayment of the clergy has prevailed as a current usage, the Ordinary is certainly not free to abide by that usage. If a cleric feels aggrieved by the decision of the ordinary concerning his income, the cleric can seek redress from the Sacred Congregation of the Council.[69]

The ordinary in his decision regarding the income of clerics is not of course to make the economic welfare of the clerics the highest norm. The principle, *"salus animarum suprema lex,"* obtains here, and if a region is capable of supporting a priest only in a meager fashion, the ordinary can assign someone to that parish. Of course the ordinary is bound in justice to furnish a priest in such circumstances with a decent support from diocesan funds if this be possible. But the penury of the diocese or the region should not prevent the appointment of a priest as pastor as long as the parish is capable of providing for the current living expenses of the priest.[70] A decision of the Pontifical Commission for the

---

[67] "*. . . et vere sufficiens,* ergo quoad redditus ex titulo de facto percipiendos *ad congruam eiusdem* 'ordinati' *sustentationem* in victu, vestitu, habitatione, aliisque, *secundum normas,* non iam consuetudine introductas, sed quae tamen prudenter condantur *ab Ordinariis* generaliter."—Blat, *Commentarium Textus Codicis Iuris Canonici,* lib. III, pars I, 405.

[68] "Optimam normam praebebit usus inter honestos beneficiatos vigens."—Regatillo, *Institutiones Iuris Canonici,* I, 195.

[69] This procedure is administrative, not judicial. It is fully described in the dissertation of the Rev. Kenneth A. O'Brien, *The Nature of Support of Diocesan Priests in the United States of America* (Washington, D. C.: The Catholic University of America Press, 1949).

[70] III Plenary Council of Baltimore (1884), Decree 273—*Acta et Decreta Concilii Plenarii Baltimorensis,* III, p. 157.

It is significant to note the provisions in law for the adequate support of the clergy in China. Although the dire poverty of the Church permits no conveniences to the clergy, there is recognition of and insistence on the observance of the principles of canon law concerning the support of the

Authentic Interpretation of the Code in 1945 makes it clear that a bishop may not leave a parish vacant because of the economic difficulties of the diocese.[71]

It should also be noted that if a cleric is able to support himself by his own labor—e.g., as a teacher, painter, singer, lecturer—such remuneration is not, canonically, a substitute for the fitting support due from the ordinary. The ordinary still owes the cleric a fitting support, and must supply it to him when it is possible. Of course in a mission territory the ordinary may find it impossible to supply such support for years, but whenever it becomes possible to supply such support the ordinary has the duty.[72]

---

clergy, not only during their active ministry, but also in the event of their retirement. The following excerpts are quoted from the *Praxis Missionalis* for the Apostolic Vicariate of Ichang, China:

"91. Cuilibet in nostro Vicariatu sub titulo Missionis ordinato, Vicarius Apostolicus secundum usum in hac Missione vigentem, sufficiens subsidium ad congruam ejusdem sustentationem conferet, pro quo scopo summa stipulatur annua major vel minor juxta circumstantias et necessitates, qua ipse sibi procurat necessaria ad vivendum. . . .

"92. Tempore infirmitatis, senectutis aut impotentiae cunctis ejus necessitatibus cum caritate providebitur.

"94. Omnes sacerdotes quotannis 300 Sacra secundum intentiones a Procuratore Missionis ipsis datas persolvunt. Reliquas Missas applicant sive (casu dato) juxta n. 50 et 93, sive ad intentionem liberam pro qua etiam stipendium accipere possunt de eoque libere disponere quin rationem reddant.

Aliae vero pecuniae omnesque praestationes fidelium occasione cujuscumque ministerii, sicut cuncta dona vel eleemosynae quae in pios usus (i.e., non mere intuitu personae) fuerint data, cedunt Missioni et de iis quotannis strictam rationem reddere tenetur Vicario Apostolico. Horum enim omnium plenum dominium non habent sed meram administrationem delegatam quippe quae, ex jure nostrae Missionis sunt bona ecclesiastica, vi contractus bilateralis in hunc sensum inter sacerdotem et Missionem libere initi.

"158, § 2. Cum dicente Christo, dignus sit operarius mercede sua, christianorum est, secundum antiquam consuetudinem, invitare missionarium et providere victui ejus durante missione; si forsan in aliquo loco pauci sint christiani et pauperes, missionarii ipsos adire ne recusent, sed obique faciles et paupertatis cultores se exhibeant."—*Praxis Missionalis in Vicariatu Apostolico de Ichang,* pp. 32, 57.

[71] Pontificia Commissio ad Codicis Canones Authentice Interpretandos, 3 maii 1945—*AAS,* XXXVII (1945), 149.

[72] Beste, *Introductio in Codicem,* p. 534; Sipos, *Enchiridion Iuris Canonici,* p. 468.

There is a general misconception that the fitting support of the clergy is to be interpreted as an irreducible minimum or bare subsistence level of living. Such is not the mind of the Church nor the law of the Church. The Church distinguishes between a fitting support and a minimum support in its legislation on the support that is to be accorded to the members of the clergy in various circumstances. The Church exhibits its concept of a comfortable but very moderate support of the clergy in the approved regulations and practices of religious congregations and orders whose members take the vow of poverty. The Church further illustrates its concept of a moderate but minimum fitting support of the secular clergy in its legislation on the support of priests burdened with insoluble debts.[73] The Church likewise expounds its concept of an absolute minimum or subsistence level of support in its legislation on the support to be accorded, in charity, to a deposed cleric.[74]

The regulations of religious orders and congregations offer an illustration of the Church's concept of a very moderately comfortable standard of living for the clergy. Although the solemn vow of poverty which forbids the owning and administering of private property does not involve any particular standard of living, the spirit of poverty commanded by the religious life enjoins a life of decent but very moderate human comfort. The object of the vow of poverty is the detachment from worldly goods and the using of material things only insofar as they are needed for maintaining a befitting life for the religious.[75]

The religious orders and congregations, except for those of very severe discipline, provide a standard of living which conforms to the moderation desired by the Church. The religious superior of a community is enjoined to provide everything that is needed for the support of the religious.[76] This provision for the living expenses of the religious is to be so comprehensive that it will take care of

---

[73] Canon 122.

[74] Canon 2303, § 2.

[75] Pierre Bastien, *Directoire Canonique* (Abbaye de Maredsous, 1904), p. 141; Albert Battandier, *Guide Canonique pour les Constitutions des Instituts à Voeux Simples* (6. ed., Paris: Gabalda, 1923), p. 180; Schaefer, *De Religiosis*, p. 682.

[76] Schaefer, *De Religiosis*, p. 701.

even miscellaneous items such as carfare, stationery, etc. Hence, there will be no need for the religious to keep a small sum of money, *peculium dependens,* for such needs.

Although a candidate should not be allowed to take religious vows if near-relatives are dependent upon him,[77] if his parents become dependent upon his support after he has taken the vow of poverty he still is bound to support them—presupposed that he is the only possible source of income for them. To receive money for the support of one's dependent parents is not contrary to the vow of poverty.[78] In practice the religious congregation or order will send the needed money to the dependent parents or permit the cleric to engage in such work—e.g., by being a chaplain in the armed forces—as will secure to him enough for the support of his dependent parents.

Since therefore, by rule and practice, congregations and orders permit religious to support their dependent parents, the secular clergy should also be guaranteed enough income to support dependent near-relatives.

The Church in its legislation exemplifies the minimum fitting support that is due to a cleric who is in good standing. Canon 122 guarantees to a cleric in good standing, but burdened with insoluble debts, whatever he needs for his just living expenses while also recognizing the obligation of the cleric to pay his debts when possible. Canon 122 states:

> Clericis qui creditoribus satisfacere coguntur salva sint quae ad honestam sui sustentationem, prudenti ecclesiastici iudicis arbitrio, sunt necessaria, firma tamen eorumdem obligatione creditoribus quamprimum satisfaciendi.

This provision of law is called the *beneficium competentiae.*

Although the amount of the support provided for in canon 122 is to be determined by the ecclesiastical judge, it is agreed by many canonists that in practice the amount granted should correspond to that which is determined by civil law in such cases.[79] The civil

---

[77] Canon 542, 2°.

[78] Schaefer, *De Religiosis,* p. 700.

[79] Regatillo, *Institutiones Iuris Canonici,* I, 150; Ioannes Chelodi, *Ius Canonicum de Personis* (3. ed., Vicenza: Società Anonima Typografica, 1942), p. 184.

law provides generally that an insolvent debtor be protected against the seizure of those things that will be necessary for his sustenance.[80]

The Concordats of the Holy See with the Governments of Italy, Belgium and Lithuania state specifically that by the *beneficium competentiae* clerics are to be accorded the same treatment as State employes who are insolvent.[81] In some countries this allowance for the sustenance of the insolvent debtor is a fraction of his income; for instance, in Austria the civil law protects one-third of a debtor's income from any exaction for the payment of a debt.[82]

---

[80] J. Brys, *Juris Canonici Compendium* (Bruges: Desclée, 1947), p. 221; Beste, *Introductio in Codicem,* 181. The following excerpts from the law of the District of Columbia illustrate the attitude of the civil law towards providing *a beneficium competentiae* for a debtor who is insolvent:

15-493 (24:313) Earnings—Exemptions.

"The earnings, not to exceed $100.00 each month of all actual residents of the district of Columbia who provide for the support of a family in said District, for two months next preceding the issuing of any writ or process from any court or officer of and in said District against them, shall be exempt from attachment, levy, seizure. . . ." Mar. 3, 1901, 31 Stat. 1363, ch. 854, § 1107—*Code of Laws for the District of Columbia,* Title 15, Sec. 403.

401 (24:311) Exempt property of householder—Property in Transitu—Exception—Debt for wages.

"The following property, being the property of the head of a family or householder residing in the District of Columbia, shall be exempt from distraint, attachment, levy, and sale on execution or decree of any court in the District.

First: All wearing apparel belonging to all persons and to all heads of families being householders.

Second: All beds, bedding, household furniture, stoves, cooking utensils, and so forth, not exceeding $300 in value.

Third: Provisions for three months' support, whether provided or growing.

Fourth: Fuel for three weeks.

Fifth: Mechanics' tools and implements of the debtor's trade or business amounting to $200.00 in value. . . .—Mar. 3, 1901, 31 Stat. 1362, ch. 854, § 1105—*Code of Laws for the District of Columbia,* Title 15, Sec. 401.

[81] ". . . que les honoraires et autres appointements que les ecclésiastiques touchent à raison de leur office sont exempts de toute saisie dans la même mesure ou le sont les honoraires et les appointements des employés de l'Etat." —A. Van Hove, "Le Concordat entre le Saint-Siège et le Gouvernement Italien," *Nouvelle Revue Théologique* (Paris, 1869), LVI (1929), 522.

[82] Vermeersch-Creusen, *Epitome Iuris Canonici,* I, 214.

In the United States the clergy are in this matter plainly subject to the civil law.

If the ecclesiastical judge determines, without any relation to the civil law, the amount to be allowed to the insolvent cleric for his support, it seems certain that the amount should correspond to the cleric's income from his benefice or pension: for a pastor in the United States, such an income would correspond to his salary —which is supposed to be sufficient for his support. Hence an insolvent cleric would be liable to the exaction of only such offerings which are not connected with the income from his benefice or his "salary" as pastor, such as the offerings for sermons not delivered in his parish, stole fees, donations, Mass stipends, etc.[83] In those cases in which the stole fees or stipends constitute a part of the benefice (very rare or non-existent in the United States), all the constituent parts of the benefice would be exempt from seizure for debts.[84]

It is clear then from the consensus of opinion on the interpretation of canon 122 that the Church considers the cleric's income through his benefice, pension or "salary" to be his minimum fitting support, exclusive of any other emoluments given on the occasion of acts of the sacred ministry. As indicated above, this concept of the Church is not operative in those countries in which a Concordat specifically provides for the amount of the *beneficium competentiae* or in which the clergy are *de facto* subject to the civil law.

Lest there be any misunderstanding, the provisions of the *beneficium competentiae* do not apply to a priest who has contracted an insoluble debt in bad faith, by fraud, or through culpable negligence.[85] It should also be remembered that the *beneficium competentiae* is not a cancellation of a debt, but the deferment of payment of a just debt.

---

[83] Vermeersch-Creusen, *Epitome Iuris Canonici,* II, 554; Wernz-Vidal, *Ius Canonicum,* IV, pars 2, 241.

[84] Vermeersch-Creusen, *Epitome Iuris Canonici,* II, 554. This question will be treated more fully in the section which deals with the superfluous goods of a cleric that must be given to the poor or to pious causes. Cf. pp. 196 ff.

[85] Coronata, *Institutiones Iuris Canonici,* I, 215; Septimius Vecchiotti, *Institutiones Canonicae* (19. ed., 3 vols., Augustae Taurinorum, 1886), I, 408; Chelodi, *Ius Canonicum de Personis,* p. 184.

The Church also makes provision in its legislation for the minimum support to be accorded to a cleric in bad standing. This standard of living is the most basic in the legislation of the Church. If, unhappily, a priest has been deposed and is really in need, the ordinary is bound in charity to provide at least a minimum support for the unfortunate cleric. This duty of the ordinary is enunciated in canon 2303, § 2.

> Sed hoc ultimo in casu [depositionis], si clericus vere indigeat, Ordinarius pro sua caritate, quo meliore modo fieri potest, ei providere curet, ne cum dedecore status clericalis mendicare cogatur.

Obviously, this minimum support is not supposed to furnish the deposed cleric with the comforts accorded to the cleric in good standing, but burdened with insoluble debts, who is being protected by the *beneficium competentiae.* Nor is this minimum support to be as large as that which is to be afforded to the cleric who, although not deposed, has been deprived of his benefice but still has a claim upon a respectable support.[86]

It is clear, then that when the Church states that a cleric in good standing is to be accorded a fitting support, it does not mean that this is to be accepted in a minimum sense, but rather in a moderate and liberal sense. Had the Church intended that a cleric in good standing should receive only the necessities of life or a parsimonious living, it would not have ruled separately regarding the mere provision for the living expenses of the deposed cleric (canon 2303, § 2) the *congrua sustentatio* due to a cleric in good standing (canon 979, § 2), the *honesta sustentatio* to be accorded to a cleric in good standing but burdened with insoluble debts (canon 122), and the *honesta sustentatio* to be provided for the cleric who has been deprived of his benefice (canon 2299, § 3).

In summary, it is warranted to conclude that the following elements constitute the fitting support due to the clergy:

1) a moderately comfortable and secure living, which comprises besides suitable food, clothing and housing, adequate medical

[86] Canon 2299, § 3. The amount of the support to be given to a cleric who, though not deposed, is deprived of his benefice or pension will be treated more fully in Chapter XII, "The Support of Delinquent Clerics."

care, decent recreation, provision for the future, support of one's near-relatives if they are in want;

2) the amount of this support is to be determined in accord with
   a) the ecclesiastical dignity and merit of the cleric,
   b) the circumstances which reflect the economic condition of the locality in which and the community among which the cleric is ministering;
3) the ordinary is to be the judge of the amount accorded to clerics for their support.

It is obvious from a glance at the above elements constituting a fitting support that no definite amount can be indicated as the measure of support that is due to the clergy of a whole nation. It is instructive, however, to note the opinion of Augustine (1872-1943), one of the first commentators on the Code in the United States. Writing in the early 1920's, he thought that about $1,000 per year was the minimum income for a priest living on a patrimony; he considered that this amount "would just about afford a decent living."[87] Because of the rise in the cost of living, the estimate of Augustine would amount to about $2,400 a year, which is the total income a year for many pastors in the United States.

It is interesting to note that at the time of the French Revolution the General Assembly in Paris voted to allow each cleric, regardless of ecclesiastical rank, a home, a garden of half an acre, and a yearly allowance of 1,200 francs;[88] the clergy of course also received stole fees and Mass stipends in addition to this allowance. This allotment was considered a very harsh treatment of the clergy, befitting the anti-religious character of the Revolution. Today, allowing for the devaluation of the franc, the provision of the Revolutionary Assembly seems generous in comparison with the income accorded to the clergy by some Governments.

SECTION 4. OBLIGATION OF GIVING SUPERFLUOUS INCOME TO THE POOR OR TO PIOUS CAUSES

The income of a cleric from his benefice or pension is intended for his legitimate support, not for his personal enrichment. Hence

---

[87] *A Commentary on the New Code of Canon Law,* IV, 467.

[88] Bonal, *Institutiones Canonicae,* II, 106.

the Church rules that the superfluous income of a cleric from this benefice or pension—that is, whatever is more than is needed for his fitting support—must be given to the poor or to pious causes.[89] Only Cardinals enjoy the privilege of disposing freely of their income from a benefice.[90]

This law of the Church concerning superfluous income applies to that part of the income which is received from a benefice or a pension, not to the income from any other sources. This law concerning superfluous income from a benefice applies to the "salary" received by pastors in this country who were ordained on the title of service of the diocese. As stated before, it is incontestably established that parishes in this country constitute a benefice, and that the "salary" of the pastor is a beneficial income.[91]

Canonists divide the income of the clergy into the following categories:[92]

1. beneficial income—that which comes directly from the benefice, such as salaries paid by the governments to the clergy in consideration of the church property confiscated by these governments, "salaries" of pastors as

---

[89] Canon 1473.

[90] Canon 239, § 1, n. 19.

[91] S.C. Consist., 1 aug. 1919—*AAS,* XI (1919), 346-347; Letter (Private) of Apostolic Delegate, U. S., 10 nov. 1922—T. L. Bouscaren, *The Canon Law Digest* (2 vols., Milwaukee: Bruce, 1934-1944), I, 149; Jerome D. Hannan, "The Cleric's Last Will," *The Jurist* (Washington, D. C.: The Catholic University of America School of Canon Law, 1941-), VIII (1948), 57-58; Jerome D. Hannan, *The Canon Law of Wills* (Philadelphia: The Dolphin Press, 1935), nn. 306-313; Vermeersch-Creusen, *Epitome Iuris Canonici,* II, 522-523.

Coronata, agreeing with Vermeersch-Creusen, points out that the present canonical concept of the dowry of a parish, which permits the offertory collections in our parish churches to be considered the dowry ("certae et voluntariae fidelium oblationes"—canon 1410), is more wide and comprehensive than the former concept.—*Institutiones Iuris Canonici,* II, 361; Beste, *Introductio in Codicem,* p. 730; Augustine, *Commentary on the Code of Canon Law,* VI, 537; Woywod, *A practical Commentary on the Code of Canon Law* (revised by Callistus Smith, 10. ed., 2 vols., New York: Joseph F. Wagner, 1946), I, 136.

[92] Cappello, *Summa Iuris Canonici,* II, 535; Wernz-Vidal, *Ius Canonicum,* IV, pars 2, 239; Vermeersch-Creusen, *Epitome Iuris Canonici,* II, 554.

paid in this country by diocesan statute, contributions or taxes according to a fixed rate paid by the faithful, the income from founded Masses accruing to the holder of a benefice;
2. patrimonial income—that which comes from testaments, gifts, donations;
3. quasi-patrimonial—that which comes from acts of the ministry which are not an integral part of the office held by the beneficiary, though they are performed in virtue of the office, such as stole fees; also the voluntary offerings of the faithful, the daily allowance or distributions permitted to canons, the stipends for founded Masses when the endowment fund is not attached to the office held by the beneficiary;[93]
4. parsimonial income—that which through frugal living is saved from the amount allotted for the fitting support of the clergy.

There is considerable discussion whether stole fees are to be included in the beneficial income, or whether they are to be considered part of the quasi-patrimonial income. Although this question has not been definitely settled, it is generally accepted that stole fees are quasi-patrimonial income, unless it has been specifically determined that they belong to the beneficial income.[94] It is not questioned that stole fees (within the amount determined by the ordinary or by custom), the income from founded Masses, and also the offerings of the faithful can be made a part of the beneficial income.[95] So far, the ordinaries in the United States have not

[93] A warmly proposed recent opinion holds that everything which accrues to a cleric from his office, except stole fees, is a part of the beneficial income.—W. F. Allen, "Parish-Benefice Revenue," *The Jurist,* VIII (1948), 331.

[94] Vermeersch-Creusen, *Epitome Iuris Canonici,* II, 554; Wernz-Vidal, *Ius Canonicum,* VI, pars 2, 241.

[95] Canons 1410; 826, § 3, Vermeersch (1858-1936) thought that, even if the stole fees are made part of the beneficial income, the income which is derived through stole fees is not subject to the law concerning the disposition of superfluous income from a benefice.—*Epitome Iuris Canonici,* II, 554. De Meester agrees with this opinion.—*Juris Canonici et Juris Canonico-Civilis Compendium* (nova editio, 3 vols. in 4, Vol. III, pars I, Brugis, 1926), III, pars I, n. 1424, p. 348. The opposite opinion seems to

stated that stole fees form part of the income which derives from the parochial benefice.

Therefore, in the United States, the beneficial income which is subject to the law governing the disposal of superfluous goods is the salary of the pastor; the salary of the assistant is not an income from a benefice, but an emolument paid for his services.[96] Of course, if an ordinary were to decree, when establishing a parish, that the stole fees from part of the beneficial income, the income accruing from the stole fees would be subject to the provisions of canon 1473.

Hence, according to the present status, a pastor who receives a "salary" just sufficient for supplying his needs for a fiitting support is free to dispose of or to save all the income he may have from stole fees, donations, Mass stipends which are not part of the beneficial income, etc., likewise, he may dispose freely of all the income he enjoys from his own labor, such as lecturing, writing, music, etc. Also, if a pastor enjoys a benefice that is just capable of supporting him in a fitting manner and he lives very frugally—economizing on food, electricity, fuel—that portion which he thus saves becomes his own property and can be disposed of in any way; he has earned it by his own privation, and is not obliged to give it to the poor or to pious causes. In a word, a pastor can freely dispose of all his quasi-patrimonial and parsimonial income as well as his patrimonial income (which is really his private income, established in a manner that will guarantee its perpetuity and security).

---

be more acceptable and commonly held.—Coronata, *Institutiones Iuris Canonici,* II, 416; Wernz-Vidal, *Ius Canonicum,* II, 382.

Special arrangements are made in some mission countries whereby each priest is obliged to celebrate 300 Masses annually according to the intentions submitted by the Procurator of the Missions (who retains the stipends for the expenses of the vicariate or prefecture), and all stole fees and offerings of the faithful on the occasion of a spiritual ministration, unless made *intuitu personae,* must be used for the expenses of the mission.—*Praxis Missionalis in Vicariatu Apostolico de Ichang,* n. 94, p. 32. Such stole fees and offerings can hardly be said to constitute a part of the income of the benefice, for the priest must give an account of their administration each year; a beneficiary has no obligation to furnish a report on how he disposed of his beneficial income.

[96] Canon 476, § 1; Hannan, "The Cleric's Last Will," *The Jurist,* VIII (1948), 60.

However, if a pastor does not need for his fitting support all that is allotted to him as his salary, he is obliged to devote this superfluous amount to the poor or to pious causes. In view of the many demands made upon a pastor, especially those of charity, this possibility seems rare. If a pastor's salary thus exceeds his expenses for a fitting support, he is not obliged to devote any of his quasi-patrimonial or parsimonial income to the poor or to pious causes.[97]

The obligation of devoting the superfluous income from one's benefice to the poor or to pious causes is a grave duty of religion, but is most probably not a duty of justice. Hence, if one contravenes this obligation he is not bound to restitution.[98]

A cleric can fulfill the obligation of devoting his superfluous goods to the poor by giving to his own indigent relatives.[99] If there are no poor in the parish, the money can be given to a religious organization in the parish or to any good cause.

---

[97] It must be remembered that there is discussed here simply the obligation which derives from the law of the Code; a priest who possesses wealth, regardless of its source, is certainly subject to the law of charity.

[98] Vermeersch-Creusen, *Epitome Iuris Canonici,* II, 554; Beste, *Introductio in Codicem,* p. 371; Cappello, *Summa Iuris Canonici,* II, 535; Coronata, *Institutiones Iuris Canonici,* II, 415. Augustine on the contrary held that this is an obligation of strict justice.—*A Commentary on the New Code of Canon Law,* VI, 537.

[99] Cappello, *Summa Iuris Canonici,* II, 536.

CHAPTER VIII

Fitting Support of Pastors

The ordinary, whose office it is to decide the amount that constitutes the fitting support of a pastor, must consider the following factors:[1]

1) the things necessary for the pastor's secure and comfortable living in the light of his existing needs;
2) adjustment of the allotment according to the
   a) dignity of the pastor,
   b) merits of the pastor,
   c) circumstances of the whole environment.

Section 1. Things Necessary for a Secure and Comfortable Living for a Pastor

First, a pastor is to be afforded a comfortable and secure living according to his needs. A pastor does not receive wages or remuneration as a wage earner, i.e., in exact proportion to and payment for his hours of work. A pastor, in that he enjoys a benefice, is to be supported as an individual in consideration of the sacred office and clerical status with which he is vested.[2] He is paid for what he is, as well as for what he does. Obviously, consideration must be given to him not only as a member of the clerical state with certain obligations flowing from his office, but also as an individual with possibly singular needs.

Naturally, a pastor has a right, together with all clerics enjoying benefices, to the elementary needs of suitable housing, food and clothes, decent relaxation, prudent provision for the future, support

---

[1] Canon 979, § 1; Regatillo, *Institutiones Iuris Canonici,* I, 195; Cappello, *Summa Iuris Canonici,* II, 535; Vermeersch-Creusen, *Epitome Iuris Canonici,* II, 169; Beste, *Introductio in Codicem,* p. 730; Coronata, *Institutiones Iuris Canonici,* II, 416.

[2] Canons 1409, 1410; Vermeersch-Creusen, *Epitome Iuris Canonici,* II, 523.

for dependent relatives, a sufficient allowance for moderate demands of charity and hospitality, and proper medical care. Normally these basic requirements are generally the same for all clerics. But if a cleric has need of a special type of food or medical care, or a particular type of housing, he should receive it.[3] These demands must be kept within reasonable bounds, for no cleric is entitled to luxury or ostentatious living.[4] It is not unreasonable, however, to go occasionally to a location where the climate is favorable for a physical ailment, or to request food that is necessary for a prescribed diet. A pastor could reasonably request to be assigned in a location that favored his health.

Although it is always agreed that a pastor has a right to the necessities of daily life for himself, it is not so universally recognized that he also should receive enough to enable him to support his dependent near-relatives.[5] Scandal and disedification could certainly be occasioned if the needy parents, brothers or sisters of a pastor were not assisted by him. Enough assistance should be available to enable them to live in decent comfort, but not in any ostentatious, or extravagant manner. The older canonists held that a cleric could support his near-relatives in the manner befitting their station in life.[6] Today society is not so distinctly stratified that one could readily determine to what station in society the family of the pastor pertains, but the members of his family should certainly be accorded a respectable living. The cleric's duty to support his parents is not exclusively his; he shares that responsibility according to the measure in which his brothers and sisters lack an income along with the ability to provide one in the needed proportionate amount.

The Code also provides that the pastor enjoy a certain amount of proper and needed relaxation.[7] The pastor is permitted to be

[3] S.C. Ep. et Reg., *Posnanien.*, 18 maii 1906—ASS, XXXIX (1906), 461.

[4] Cappello, *Summa Iuris Canonici*, II, 535.

[5] Regatillo, *Institutiones Iuris Canonici*, I, 195; S.C. Ep. et Reg., *Posnanien.*, 18 maii 1906—*ASS*, XXXIX (1906), 458-461; Beste, *Introductio in Codicem*, p. 730; Coronata, *Institutiones Iuris Canonici*, II, 416.

[6] Schmalzgrueber, *Ius Ecclesiasticum Universum*, lib. III, tit. 25, n. 25; *ibid.*, tit. 39, n. 118; Reiffenstuel, *Ius Canonicum Universum*, lib. III, tit. 5, n. 222; Fagnanus, *Commentaria*, lib. III, tit. 25, c. 5, n. 19.

[7] Regatillo, *Institutiones Iuris Canonici*, I, 195.

absent from his parish a maximum of two months during the year—which time of absence may be intermittent or continuous.[8] This time of permitted absence may be used for vacation. Hence, if a pastor takes an occasional trip or is absent for a few days, this time is to be computed as part of the permitted two months' absence from the parish. An occasioned absence of just a few hours is not to be computed.[9]

The ordinary is permitted to regulate the length of the vacation allowable for pastors, and he may protract or shorten the maximum period of absence as established in the law of the Code.[10] Generally the maximum of a two months' vacation for pastors is not allowed in the United States; a few dioceses permit it.[11] Of course, if the physical or mental condition of a priest so demands, the ordinary could permit him to be absent long enough to enable him to recuperate completely.

Since a pastor is permitted to be absent for the purpose of a vacation, he should likewise receive enough income to enable him to plan his absence as a vacation. Also, since on such a vacation he is legitimately absent from his benefice, he is permitted to receive his salary as well as the stole fees for that time. However, the Ordinary may decree that a pastor receive his salary for the extent of the vacation that is permitted by the diocesan statute, and then further provide that if the pastor so wishes he may fill out the full two months of vacation which is permitted by the Code, but that he do so without further compensation from the parish. This arrangement is observed in the dioceses of Seattle and Monterey-Fresno.[12]

---

[8] Canon 465, § 2; Vermeersch-Creusen, *Epitome Iuris Canonici,* I, 401.

[9] Vermeersch-Creusen, *loc. cit.*

[10] Canon 465, § 2.

[11] The Dioceses of Toledo and Seattle permit a two months' vacation for pastors.—I Synod of Toledo (1941), Decree 93—*Acta et Decreta Synodi Dioecesanae Toletanae Primae,* p. 52; V Synod of Seattle (1938), Decree 79, § 1—*Statuta Dioecesis Seattlensis,* p. 52.

[12] The Diocese of Seattle allows a pastor to receive his salary for one month of vacation, but further permits him another month of vacation without pay.—V Synod of Seattle (1938), Decree 79, §§ 1, 2—*Statuta Dioecesis Seattlensis,* p. 52. The Diocese of Monterey-Fresno allows a pastor a vaca-

It is especially important that a pastor receive—and use for that purpose—enough to enable him to further his academic interests. Learning, especially in the sacred sciences, is absolutely essential for a successful ministry,[13] and no priest is to be allowed to become a pastor unless he shows sufficient knowledge of these sciences.[14] Ordinarily a priest is required to undergo an examination before the synodal examiners to prove his fitness for appointment as an irremovable pastor,[15] and preference for appointment should be shown, *ceteris paribus,* to the priest who excelled in the clerical examinations.[16] Conferences of the clergy should be held several times a year with a view to stimulating the study of the sacred sciences.[17]

Obviously, then, the pastor has a right and duty to allocate a portion of his income for the increase of his knowledge in those branches of learning that will be of advantage to him in the work of the ministry. Learning which is advantageous to the work of the ministry is not limited to the theological sciences. The Church has taught that all knowledge ennobles man,[18] and that erudition is particularly desirable for clerics entrusted with the direction of souls.

A pastor also has a right to suitable means of transportation for performing the duties of his office. This fact is recognized by the statutes of many dioceses.[19] The ordinary means of transportation

---

tion of 62 days a year, but he can receive a salary for only 31 days of this time.—I Synod of Monterey-Fresno (1929), Decree 74—*Statuta Dioecesis Montereyensis-Fresnensis,* p. 30.

[13] Canons 129, 130.

[14] Canon 459, § 2.

[15] Canon 459, § 3, 3°.

[16] Canon 130, § 2.

[17] Canon 131.

[18] Barbosa, *Iuris Ecclesiastici Universi Libri III* (Lugduni, 1660), n. 21, c. 28, X, *de praebendis et dignitatibus,* III, 5. Wernz-Vidal, *Ius Canonicum,* II, 182-189.

[19] Some dioceses permit the pastor to pay for the upkeep of a car, used for parish duty, from the parish funds, e.g., the Diocese of Harrisburg—IX Synod of the Diocese of Harrisburg (1943), Decree 89, § 1—*Statutes of the Diocese of Harrisburg,* p. 66. The Diocese of Toledo allows each priest an allotment of one hundred dollars per year for automobile expenses—I Synod of Toledo (1941), Statute 396—*Acta et Decreta Synodi Dioecesanae*

in the United States for people of moderate income is the automobile, and it would be very unreasonable to deny to a pastor that which is commonly considered necessary for the fulfillment of the duties of his office.

There are very few sections of the United States in which because of the extent of his parish a pastor does not need an automobile to enable him to respond promptly to sick calls and Communion calls, or to make the normal parish visits, social calls and business errands. Of course, a pastor does not have a right, except in extraordinary circumstances, to a very expensive car, but he does have a right to one which is suited to the demands of his advancing years and appropriately corresponds to the distinction which his parish enjoys. Prudence and the proper disinterestedness in material comfort will determine which type of car the pastor should secure.

The ordinary has the right to make regulations concerning the possession and use of automobiles by the clergy.[20] The public order and the spiritual welfare of souls may make it necessary for him to forbid his priests to have cars unless specific permission has been obtained. Such regulations could be necessary when an ostentatious display of expensive cars threatens to result in the disedification of the faithful.

Toletanae Primae, p. 120. The Diocese of Fargo allows the Board of Directors to grant an allotment of two hundred dollars a year to a pastor for transportation expenses if the parish has no mission, and three hundred dollars a year if the parish has one or more missions.—Synod of the Diocese of Fargo (1941), Decree 681—*Liber Synodalis Fargensis* I (Milwaukee: Bruce, 1941), p. 134.

[20] In the Diocese of Harrisburg, the pastor alone is permitted to own a car in his name or in that of the parish. Two assistants may use the car for parish business with the approval of the pastor.—IX Synod of Harrisburg (1943), Decree 15—*Statutes of the Diocese of Harrisburg,* p. 6.

The Diocese of Monterey-Fresno permits the pastor to buy a car for the use of the priests while performing parish duties—I Synod of Monterey-Fresno (1929), Decree 136, § 1—*Statuta Dioecesis Montereyensis-Fresnensis,* p. 44.

The Archdiocese of Los Angeles forbids priests to buy expensive cars.—V Synod of Los Angeles (1927), Statute 38—*Statuta Dioecesis Angelorum et Sancti Didaci,* p. 7.

Together with other clerics, a pastor has a right to security against penury in old age or disability.[21] This security can ensue when a pastor is given an income which will enable him to save enough to take care of eventual retirement because of old age or disability. The modern, world-wide threat of disastrous inflation almost makes it impractical to expect a pastor to save enough to provide security for himself; the value of money can depreciate so quickly that a moderately large fund of money no longer is a guarantee of security.[22] It would certainly be better for a pastor to invest his saving in something of real value that will continue to produce an income suitable for his support. This simply substitutes one problem for another—who will advise the cleric which investment is absolutely guaranteed?

A very equitable system, and practicable in some sections of the United States, for the providing of support for a disabled or retired pastor is the continuance of his salary by the parish he has left.[23] This allotment would constitute a pension, for the ordinary can require that the newly appointed pastor assume the obligation of paying a pension to his predecessor.[24] This system seems particularly suitable for the United States, where generally the pastor's salary represents only a small fraction of the total income of the parish.[25] The payment of the pension to the retired pastor would

---

[21] ". . . securus pro tota ordinati vita."—Canon 979, § 2. Cf. also canon 980, § 1.

[22] If the period from 1550-1560 was considered a time of great economic upheaval and merited the appellation, "Revolution of Prices," because prices increased threefold, what is to be said of our times when within fifty years wags and prices have increased fivefold!—Ferguson, *Landmarks of Economic Thought*, p. 28.

[23] Canon 1429, §§ 1, 2. This system has been found practicable in many sections of our country as well as in other countries. In the Diocese of Limerick, Eire, retired pastors are given an allowance of 208 pounds a year. Part of this comes from an allotment made by the parish they have left, and the rest is contributed by the diocesan Sick Clergy Fund.—Letter from the Archbishop's Palace, Limerick, October 20, 1948.

[24] Canon 1429, § 1.

[25] In many parishes in the dioceses of the eastern part of the United States the total of the salaries paid to the clergy represents only five to ten per cent of the income of the parish.

constitute a negligible expense for many parishes in the eastern part of the United States.

Some dioceses arrange a "beneficial fund" that furnishes payments to pastors (as to other clerics) who are retired because of old age or sickness. Payments are made by the clergy to this fund and this renders them eligible for the benefits when they become old or sick. This system may be equitable and would fulfill the requirements of law for the support of the clergy if the payments are sufficient. If the payments are insufficient for the proper support of sick or old pastors, such pastors have a right to demand more support from the ordinary; the institution of a beneficial fund that does not grant sufficient support to needy members of the clergy does not absolve the Ordinary from his obligation of providing sufficient support for the clergy.[26]

Although the Church has great solicitude for the welfare of the pastors, its primary concern is the welfare of the souls of the faithful, and hence the ordinary can establish a parish if there be need for it even if the parish income is very meager.[27] In fact, canon 1415, § 3, provides for such an emergency and allows the

[26] A more complete discussion of the method of arranging a pension or support of the aged and disabled clergy is found in Chapter X, pp. 259-269.

The Archdiocese of Paris has a commendable system of supporting old and disabled clerics. The clergy who enjoy an income above a certain figure contribute a certain proportion of their income to the Aid Fund of the Clergy (Entr' Aide du Clergé) of the Archdiocese; the Archdiocese completes the funds from its own resources (largely consisting of proceeds from the contribution known as the "Denier du Culte"). Those who receive as their allotment less than 55,000 francs a year make no payment to the Aid Fund, and this sum is tax-exempt in all clerical allotments. Those who receive from 55,000 to 60,000 francs a year pay 10% on their taxable income; those receiving from 60,000 to 80,000 francs pay 15% of their taxable income; those receiving from 80,000 to 100,000 francs pay 20% of their taxable income; and those receiving 100,000 francs a year pay 25% of their taxable income.—*Instructions Pratiques,* October 24, 1947, Archdiocese of Paris.

In the Archdiocese of Dublin, Eire, each pastor contributes two pounds a year, and assistants one pound a year, to the Diocesan Clerical Fund which supports disabled and aged priests; the major part of this fund is supplied from bequests.—Letter from the Chancellery of the Archdiocese of Dublin, October 21, 1948.

[27] Canon 1415, § 3; Pontificia Commissio ad Codicis Canones Authentice Interpretandos, 3 maii 1945—*AAS,* XXXVII (1945), 149.

ordinary to erect parishes on quasi-parishes when needed, even if a fitting support for the pastor is not available, but on condition that at least a bare support (necessities of life) is available from the current income of the parish.[28]

The III Plenary Council of Baltimore (1884), in dealing with this difficulty of fitting support for pastors, urged priests in charge of missions (these missions corresponded to parishes, for priests were then ordained *"ad titulum missionis"*) to be content with their income, if they did not receive the amount of salary allowed them by diocesan statute, as long as they received enough for food, clothing and shelter.[29] The same statute strongly urged priests not to take their salary from the capital funds of the parish. The statute did not, however, thus forbid priests to reimburse themselves from the capital funds for their current expenses if the income of the mission or parish was insufficient for such expenses. The provision of this statute seems still to be in effect; the conciliar enactment stands, *non contra sed praeter Codicem.*[30]

This statute of the III Plenary Council intended to provide for a particular situation; it did not intend to supplant the general law

[28] Canon 1415, §§ 1, 3. "Notabilis exceptio hoc canone statuitur qua beneficium erigi posse dicitur etsi congrua dos non habeatur. Notandum tamen est Codicem non absolute a tota dote dispensare, quod naturae beneficiorum repugnare videtur, sed solum a dote congrua."—Coronata, *Institutiones Iuris Canonici,* II, 366.

It is certainly the mind of the Church that parishes, benefices, or chaplaincies are to be discontinued if they are not able to provide even the necessities of life. Innocent XIII in his apostolic constitution of May 23, 1723, *Apostolici ministerii,* wrote: ". . . statuimus et mandamus quod Episcopi ad beneficiorum et capellaniarum, quae nullum certum redditum habent, suppressionem statim deveniant. De aliis vero beneficiis, et capellaniis, quarum certus annuus fructus ad memoratam saltem tertiam congruae partem non ascendit, decernimus nulli in posterum conferendam esse primam tonsuram ratione iuris assequendi aliquod ex dictis beneficiis, et capellaniis."—*Fontes,* n. 280, § 10, Benedict XIII, in his apostolic constitution *In supremo,* September 23, 1724, § 8, repeated the same words.—*Fontes,* n. 283.

[29] III Plenary Council of Baltimore (1884), Decree 273—*Statuta et Decreta Concilii Plenarii Baltimorensis III,* pp. 156-157.

[30] John D. M. Barrett, *A Comparative Study of the Councils of Baltimore and the Code of Canon Law,* The Catholic University of America Canon Law Studies, 83 (Washington, D. C.: The Catholic University of America, 1932), p. 101.

on the support of the clergy. The rapid growth of the nation presaged relief for the pastors of poor missions. Moreover, inasmuch as the statute admitted that pastors who did not receive their full salaries likewise did not receive the full remuneration which was their due,[31] it is obvious that the III Plenary Council did not wish to derogate from the general law which insisted on provision for the fitting support of pastors. The statute merely wished to insure adequate care of souls at a time when economic conditions were poor; it asserted the sovereignty of the basic principle, "*salus animarum suprema lex.*"

In connection with the consideration of the ordinary's right to assign a pastor to a parish that is not able to afford his fitting support or full salary, there arises the question whether the pastor can later recover from the parish or the ordinary the arrears in salary due to him. The III Plenary Council stated categorically that such arrears need not be paid as long as the pastor received enough for his shelter and sustenance.—". . . et Episcopus vel dioecesis nulla lege tenetur salarii defectum supplere, si qua de causa sacerdotes missionarii illud vel nullum vel justo minus acceperint, dummodo tamen juxta monitum Apostoli (I Tim. VI, 8) necessaria ad alimenta et tegumenta non desint."[32]

The statute of the III Plenary Council therefore did not definitely settle all questions concerning the payment of salaries in arrears. The Council insisted that the pastor cannot collect salaries in arrears if he enjoys enough income for his current basic support; but what is to be done if the pastor has been forced to supply, from his own saving, some of these basic necessities? Does the pastor then have a right to arrears in salary and, if so, to what extent? Further, it seems that the ordinary could pay the arrears in salary to a pastor, since the statute of the III Plenary Council simply states that neither he nor the diocese is held to make the payments; it does not forbid the ordinary to make the payments or to allow the pastor to re-imburse himself from the later returns of the parish. The statute of the III Plenary Council thus afforded

[31] III Plenary Council of Baltimore (1884), Decree 273: ". . . si qua de causa sacerdotes missionarii illud vel nullum vel justo minus acceperint."—*Acta et Decreta Plenarii Concilii Baltimorensis III*, p. 157.

[32] Decree 273—*Acta et Decreta Plenarii Concilii Baltimorensis III*, p. 157.

only a directive and a general protection to the ordinary and to the diocese from the claims of priests for arrears in salary.

Since the advent of the Code some dioceses in the United States have promulgated statutes that enlarge on the provisions of Statute 273 of the III Plenary Council by making specific provision for situations not covered by the Statute. The Synod of the Diocese of Toledo (1941) enacted a statute which declares that salaries in arrears are not to be paid. This provision is contained in Statute 398: ". . . salaries are not cumulative over the years; neither can they be paid out of borrowed funds. . . . If economic conditions have reduced the parish income to the point where adjustment of obligations is necessary, the pastor will adjust all salaries pro rata."[83]

Other dioceses have made specific regulations on the time within which salaries in arrears can be collected. The Archdiocese of Los Angeles decreed, in 1927, that salaries must be paid within the year in which they are due, and that they cannot be collected after that year.[84] The Diocese of Monterey-Fresno decreed in 1929 that salaries owing for more than a year can not be collected.[85] The statutes of the Diocese of Fargo grant discretionary power to the Board of Governors, entrusted with the adjudication of problems of salary, to grant payment to the pastor of arrears in salary during the course of the following year.[86]

Such diocesan statutes are properly warranted. They are not contrary to the Code; rather they follow in general the tenor of Canon 1415, § 3. They are intended for emergencies and unusual circumstances, and do not supplant the general law that guarantees a fitting support to pastors. They admit that the pastor has a right to more than his bare subsistence if the parish income can afford to pay more; they further admit that his right to a bare subsistence must be respected at all times.

---

[83] *Acta et Decreta Synodi Dioecesanae Toletanae Primae,* p. 121.

[84] Synod of Los Angeles (1927), Decree 207, § 4—*Statuta Dioecesis Angelorum et S. Didaci,* p. 35.

[85] I Synod of Monterey-Fresno (1929), Decree 139, § 2—*Statuta Dioecesis Montereyensis-Fresnensis,* p. 45.

[86] I Synod of Fargo (1941), Decree 689—*Liber Synodalis Fargensis I,* p. 135.

SECTION 2. ADJUSTMENT OF THE PASTOR'S ALLOTMENT ACCORDING TO DETERMINING FACTORS

Article 1. Dignity of the Pastor

The dignity of the pastor means in this country his ecclesiastical rank. In Europe, besides the ecclesiastical rank of the pastor, the nobility of the cleric was accounted as a mark of dignity and was to be considered in the assignment of a suitable income to the pastor.[37] In the United States no titles of nobility are recognized and hence, among secular priests, dignity is determined solely through their ecclesiastical rank.

The income of a pastor is conditioned by his ecclesiastical dignity.[38] The increase in income is not only consonant with the honor of the dignity conferred but is also necessitated by the increased demands made upon the dignitary.

The conferral of an ecclesiastical dignity—promotion to the position of a papal chamberlain or a domestic prelate and elevation to the episcopacy—always brings added expenses. These expenses come not only from the purchase of the required official vestments and the maintenance of a fitting standard of living, but also from the great increase in demands to promote charitable and civil causes. Certainly those pastors who are auxiliary bishops, domestic

[37] Barbosa, *Repertorium Iuris Civilis et Canonici* (Lugduni, 1675), lib. III, tit. 5, c. 28, n. 21; Schmalzgrueber, *Ius Ecclesiasticum Universum,* III, tit. 25, n. 21; *ibid.,* tit. 39, n. 137; Reiffenstuel, *Ius Canonicum Universum,* lib. III, tit. 25, n. 78. These authors also considered excellence in learning as a reason equal to nobility for an increased allotment for support. Special consideration for the learning of a priest, in allotting his support, has become obsolete in this country.

[38] By the terms of the Concordat between the Holy See and the Government of Poland, bishops and canons were to receive considerably more than pastors with no added ecclesiastical rank.—*Sollemnis Conventio inter Sanctam Sedem et Poloniae Rempublicam*—*AAS,* XVII (1925), 282. In many countries of Europe, e.g., Austria, France, Belgium, an increase in remuneration is allotted to the vicar general, the canons and the chancellor because of their dignity and responsibility. In many of our dioceses these offices are filled by pastors who thereby merit additional remuneration.—*Besoldungsordnung,* Archdiocese of Vienna, Sept. 7, 1947; Letter from the Embassy of Belgium, Washington, D. C., December 3, 1948; Letter of Emmanuel Cardinal Suhard, Archbishop of Paris, to his Clergy, January 20, 1948.

prelates or papal chamberlains have more expenses than pastors who do not have such rank and honors. These added demands cannot be ignored. An ecclesiastical dignitary must have sufficient income to permit him to fulfill honorably the duties of his position.

The Church has always recognized that an ecclesiastical dignitary is expected to be liberal in encouraging pious and good causes.[39] The ecclesiastic must show himself the leader in causes that aid religion and the general welfare. But such duties always bespeak the need of an increase in income for meeting these demands.

Thus, in the United States where an auxiliary bishop is frequently the pastor of a large parish, the bishop could be allowed by the ordinary to take a salary larger than that allowed to other pastors. His increased obligations make such an arrangement necessary. If the ordinary assigns the auxiliary bishop to a large parish with the intention of allowing the stole fees to recompense him for his increased needs, these stole fees would not thereby necessarily be considered a part of the income from his benefice, and subject therefore to the provision of canon 1473 (with the consequent duty of devoting his superfluous income from them to the poor or to pious causes). The stole fees are not a part of the beneficial income unless the Ordinary so ordains.[40]

Article 2. Merit of the Pastor

Although a pastor is supported in consideration of his sacred office and status as a cleric, the Church honors the law of equity that recompense should also be made according to merit. A cleric is supported by a benefice primarily because of his office—not because of the demands of commutative justice; but the benefice to which a cleric is assigned should be commensurate with his merits. Merit should be a determining factor in the size or kind of benefice assigned to a cleric.[41]

---

[39] De Rosa, *De Recta Distributione*, p. 8; Reiffenstuel, *Ius Canonicum Universum*, lib. III, tit. 25, nn. 78, 82; Leurenius, *Forum Ecclesiasticum*, lib. III, tit. 25, q. 83, n. 2.

[40] Vermeersch-Creusen, *Epitome Iuris Canonici*, II, 554; Wernz-Vidal, *Ius Canonicum*, VI, pars 2, 241.

[41] Regatillo, *Institutiones Iuris Canonici*, I, 195; Cappello, *De Sacramentis*, II, pars III, 399. This view is in accord with the teaching of the older

Merit relates not only to special accomplishments, such as scholastic excellence[42] or special talent,[43] but also to the amount of labor expended in the work of the ministry.

Thus, a priest who is a professor in the seminary (assuming that such a position is a benefice) is entitled to remuneration according to his eminence in learning.[44] If a pastor has mastered a subject that is of special value in the care of souls or in the work of the diocese, he should be rewarded accordingly. Such rewards not only conform to the law of justice but encourage scholarship and learning, which honor and enhance the clerical state.[45]

---

canonists: Rebuffus, *Tractatus,* n. 63; De Luca, *Theatrum,* tom. II, pars II, *De Pensionibus,* Disc. XVI, n. 4; Leurenius, *Forum Ecclesiasticum,* lib. III, tit. 25, qu. 583, n. 3; Schmalzgrueber, *Ius Ecclesiasticum Universum,* lib. III, tit. 39, n. 137.

It is obvious also from the law of the Church on the transferral of pastors that the merit of the pastor cannot be ignored—he who merits a good or large benefice cannot arbitrarily be assigned a lesser benefice.—Canons 2147; 2157; 2163, § 2.

[42] Canons 139, § 2; 459, § 3, 2°, 3°.

[43] Canon 459, § 2.

[44] In accordance with the terms of the Concordat between the Holy See and the Government of Poland, seminary professors are paid more than twice as much as pastors.—*Sollemnis Conventio inter Sanctam Sedem et Rempublicam Poloniae*—*AAS,* XVII (1927), 282. Inasmuch as these payments as made by the Governments are to be considered as beneficial income (Vermeersch-Creusen, *Epitome Iuris Canonici,* II, 525), the amount of the payments made to seminary professors shows the mind of the Holy See.

It must be remembered, however, that a priest can be a teacher without drawing his support from a benefice; for example, a priest could be engaged as a teacher by means of a contractual agreement. His remuneration, then, is not income derived from a benefice, but a definite salary or wage received on the terms of the contract.

[45] The necessity of adequately rewarding clerics according to their learning in order to insure the good of the Church is trenchantly expressed by Fagnanus, when writing in the seventeenth century concerning the status of canons. "Una [ratio] est propter evidentem necessitatem, id est, cum ob tenuitatem praebendarum non reperiuntur qui velint acceptare canonicatus, et ita ecclesia debito servitio destituitur. Altera est propter utilitatem, quia licet reperiantur non tamen sunt idonei et convenientes dignitati ecclesiae cathedralis, puto quia sunt simplices et idiotae, et meliores non inveniuntur.—*Commentaria,* lib. III, tit. 5, c. 33, n. 5.—The force of this passage is better understood when one recalls that Fagnanus won the reputation of being "magnus rigoristarum princeps."

A pastor should also be rewarded according to the amount of work he performs in the ministry. The term "work" here comprehends not only the duties of administering the sacraments, of preaching, instructing and visiting the parishioners, but also the duties of administering and supervising the activities of a parish.[46]

It is the custom in some countries, and such a custom is entirely in accord with the provisions of canon law, to graduate the salaries of pastors according to the size or importance of the parish. In the Archdiocese of Paris, for instance, the salaries of pastors are increased with the number of assistants assigned to the parish, which number is an indication of the number of souls in the parish.[47]

Even when the salary of the pastor is not graduated according to the number of assistants, the income of the pastor is conditioned by the size of the parish because of the increase in the stole fees. Whether or not the stole fees constitute officially a part of the beneficial income, they contribute, in this country, a considerable and steady augmentation to the income of the pastor. Thus, although the salaries of all pastors may be identical, the pastor with the larger or more opulent parish receives a larger income. Hence the ordinary rewards the more zealous and competent pastors by appointing them to the larger and more important parishes.

Article 3. The Circumstances of Place and Time

Since the fitting support of the clergy is gauged by the obligations and necessities of the clergy in their particular community, the fitting support of the clergy must be judged according to the conditions of the place and the times. The Code, recognizing this fact, states that the support is to be determined *"pro diversis locorum et temporum necessitatibus."*[48] The present legislation is but a repetition of the teaching of the older canonists.[49]

---

[46] S.C.C., *Triventina,* 18 mart. 1905—*ASS,* XXXVIII (1905), 85.

[47] As of the end of January, 1948, a pastor with no assistants received 76,400 francs a year, a pastor with from one to three assistants received 77,650 francs a year, and the pastor with more than three assistants received 78,900 francs a year.—Letter of Emmanuel Cardinal Suhard, Archbishop of Paris, to his Clergy, January 20, 1948.

[48] Canon 979, § 2.

[49] De Luca, *Theatrum,* tom. II, pars II, *De Pensionibus,* Disc. XVI, n. 4; Rebuffus, *Tractatus,* n. 76; Gonzalez-Tellez, *Commentaria,* s.v. *competens,*

It is obvious therefore that the amount in the support of the clergy will depend on the general standard of living in the community and the region. This does not mean that in an abjectly poor region the pastor has a right only to a bare subsistence, and that on the contrary in a very wealthy region the pastor can live luxuriously.[50] It means that he is to be afforded a support that is in keeping with his clerical needs, and that these needs naturally will increase in a more opulent parish; but in any circumstances a priest must eschew whatever is alien to the priestly dignity.

The ordinary could, therefore, determine that the remuneration due to pastors be conditioned by the circumstances in their parish. This need not mean that a pastor in a rural parish would receive less than a pastor in a city parish; frequently the rural pastor has much greater transportation expenses than the pastor in the urban parish. Generally the increase in stole fees in the larger parishes is sufficient to supply the pastor with the needed funds for the increased obligations, but the ordinary could justly decree that pastors who are burdened with unusually large obligations should receive an increase in their allotment.

The question that naturally arises in the United States is whether the present system of assigning an identical allotment to every pastor in the diocese, regardless of the difference in obligations and needs, is in accord with the prescriptions of Canon Law.

The answer seems to be that if this general salary is sufficient for guaranteeing a fitting support for every pastor in the diocese it is certainly just. Uniformity in this matter does not necessarily constitute an injustice. Furthermore, the difference in stole fees according to the size of the parish serves to reward adequately those pastors who have large and important parishes. Although the stole fees, as stated earlier, do not constitute a part of the beneficial return unless the ordinary so decrees, nevertheless they form a steady and considerable part of the income of a pastor in this country, and hence can be reckoned as a reliable source of income.

---

lib. III, tit. 5, c. 16; Reiffenstuel, *Ius Canonicum,* lib. III, tit. 25, n. 76; Schmalzgrueber, *Ius Ecclesiasticum,* lib. III, tit. 25, n. 20.

[50] Cappello, *Summa Iuris Canonici,* II, 535.

However, if a pastor, because of the dependence of his parents or other members of the family, or in consequence of some physical ailment, cannot meet his obligations from the salary accorded him or from the stole fees he receives, he certainly has a right to petition the ordinary for a larger salary. He has a right to more than the standard salary if that salary is not sufficient. A law or a custom in a diocese stipulating a certain amount as the salary of a pastor does not abolish the right of a pastor to a greater amount if he needs that amount for his fitting support.

There seems to be no reason why the just claims of a pastor cannot be secured according to the present system in the United States. The vast majority of the pastors are certainly accorded a fitting support through the salary which, as augmented by the stole fees and Mass stipends, gives them a comfortable margin of security; the exceptional cases—those whose obligations cannot be met with their income—could be accorded a suitable increase by the ordinary. These exceptional cases would not be so numerous (on the assumption that the salary accorded to pastors is generally sufficient) as to constitute an unmanageable problem for the ordinary.[51] If the ordinary receives a disturbingly large number of requests for increases in allowance, he may well consider making an adjustment in the general allowance for all pastors.

To discard or to change abruptly the system of identical salaries for all pastors as prevailing in most of the dioceses in the United States might seriously disturb the public order by affecting the morale of the clergy. A certain uniform dignity is by means of the present system accorded to all pastors alike, even though it is realized that pastors of the more important parishes receive a considerably larger income. But if a priest were assigned as pastor in a distant and small parish with a much smaller salary than that which is accorded to other pastors, he might feel aggrieved. The general tradition in this country, namely of according like salaries to all pastors, has naturally created a habit of thought and ex-

---

[51] The procedure for petitioning an increase in salary is of a summary character; a *libellus* is submitted by the petitioning priest, and the Ordinary will render a prompt hearing and decision. The ordinary may, of course, delegate a judge for this.—Rebuffus, *Tractatus,* n. 55; Schmalzgrueber, *Ius Ecclesiasticum,* lib. III, tit. 39, nn. 138-139.

pectancy in the minds of priests. This temper of mind has been of great value in a country where marked divergencies occur in the economic conditions of neighboring parishes; pastors who by law are entitled to a like salary—even if not all of them can collect that salary—enjoy a like prestige and dignity, which tends to make the pastor of the small and poor parish accept his sacrifice more willingly. This temper of mind is therefore very advantageous in securing the final purpose of the priesthood—the salvation of souls.[52]

Since the fitting support of a pastor depends upon many variable circumstances, it is impossible to determine a just or equitable sum for the support of pastors over the entire United States. However, it seems that the estimate made by Augustine[53] in the late twenties, namely that $1,000 was needed for the support of a priest by a pension, was reasonable. If $1,000 was necessary for affording a decently comfortable pension at that time, then at least $2,400 (the aggregate from all sources of income) would be necessary now for supporting a pastor in the active ministry in the eastern part of the United States, and for enabling him to make some provision for retirement in old age or illness, but he would hardly require that same amount if he were assured of receiving a sufficient pension upon retirement. This amount would not include any expenses for board and lodging, but it would meet all expenses for transportation.

This amount may seem like an exorbitant minimum, but an itemization of the expenses of a pastor engaged in the active min-

---

[52] It is not the purpose of this dissertation to discuss the feasibility or advisability of changing the present system of support for the clergy. Some priests are of the opinion that the present system should be so revised that all priests in the diocese receive a definite allowance, sufficient for all their needs, and that all income from stole fees, Mass stipends, etc., be remitted to the Chancery, so that they may be divided and shared by all. This system would, it is urged, equalize the burden of the ministry and benefit the impoverished clergy in the poor parishes. In fact, some efforts at establishing a general sharing by the priests of the diocese in the stole fees accruing throughout the diocese have been made in at least one diocese. These changes would require, of course, a considerable alteration of the present system as outlined by the Code.

[53] *A Commentary on the Code of Canon Law,* IV, 467.

istry—allowance being made for insurance or savings in case of disability, as well as for contributions to charity besides the normal expenses—will prove that it is a conservative estimate. It is granted that a pastor could (as many do) live on less than that amount, but consideration is here given to what the pastor should receive to enable him to discharge all his obligations. Naturally, some of the obligations of a pastor—such as charitable donations and hospitality—may be ignored if he does not enjoy a sufficient income, but persistent omission of all donations to charitable causes would redound to the discredit of the clergy.

Lest there be any misunderstanding about the right of a pastor to a fitting support and regarding the nature of that support, it must be recalled that this support is not due to the pastor or to any cleric unless he performs his duties. A pastor is supported in consideration of his sacred office. If he does not perform the duties of that office he is not entitled to the accruing support. Consideration is not given here to pastors who by misconduct have been suspended or deposed (these cases will be treated in Chapter XII), but only to pastors who are negligent in the discharge of their parochial duties. A pastor who is obliged by the law of residence to be present for duty in his parish is bound to restitution, *pro rata,* for any illegitimate absence from his parish.[54] A pastor can, of course, be removed from office for protracted and persistent absence from his parish.[55] It is assumed that the pastor performs his duties while present in the parish; if he is guilty of negligence even while present in the parish, he may also be removed from office.[56]

Thus a pastor who receives a salary of $125 per month and is illegitimately absent from his parish (having taken the maximum vacation allowed by the ordinary or by the Code)[57] for a week within a period of a month is bound to restitution for seven-thirtieths of his salary. The money is to be given to the ordinary,

---

[54] Canons 465, § 1; 2381, § 1. Vermeersch-Creusen, *Epitome Iuris Canonici,* I, 402; III, 370.

[55] The process for removal is described in canons 2168-2175.

[56] Canons 2182-2185.

[57] Canon 465, §§ 1, 2; Vermeersch-Creusen, *Epitome Iuris Canonici,* I, 401.

if this can be done without incriminating the pastor, or, if restitution to the ordinary is impossible, to the poor or to pious causes.[58] Furthermore, the restitution is to be made even if no charge or sentence is made against the pastor.[59] The ordinary can also, in the case of persistent and flagrant negligence of duty, deprive a pastor of part or of all of his beneficial income.[60]

SECTION 3. OBLIGATION OF GIVING SUPERFLUOUS INCOME TO THE POOR OR TO PIOUS CAUSES

As stated previously, the income of the pastor from his benefice or pension is intended for his legitimate support according to his clerical status and office, not for his personal enrichment, and consequently any superfluous income from his benefice or pension must be devoted to the poor or to pious causes.[61] The definition of the phrase "income from benefice and pension" has already been discussed.[62]

---

[58] Canon 2281, § 1; Beste, *Introductio in Codicem,* p. 991; Vermeersch-Creusen, *Epitome Iuris Canonici,* III, 370.

[59] Beste, *Introductio in Codicem,* p. 991; Vermeersch-Creusen, *Epitome Iuris Canonici,* III, 370.

[60] Canons 2183, 2184; Cappello, *Summa Iuris Canonici,* III, 390; Vermeersch-Creusen, *Epitome Iuris Canonici,* III, 208-209.

[61] Canon 1473; cf. Chapter VII, pp. 132 ff.

[62] Cf. Chapter VI, pp. 73-80.

CHAPTER IX

Fitting Support of Assistant Pastors

To understand the principles determining the income of an assistant pastor, one must understand his canonical position. An assistant pastor is a priest assigned by the ordinary to a parish to assist the pastor in his duties.[1] Generally the assistant pastor is deputed to help in the pastoral work of the whole parish, but he can be deputed to assist in only a section of the parish,[2] and the delineation of his obligations and rights is made by the ordinary, by the pastor, or by the diocesan statutes.[3] He is therefore directly under the guidance and supervision of the pastor,[4] and may be removed from his position for insubordination to the pastor.[5] An assistant pastor is removable at the will of the Ordinary, unless he enjoys a benefice;[6] if he enjoys a benefice, he must be removed according to the procedure by which pastors are removed and for the same reasons, with the additional reason of insubordination.[7]

Although an assistant pastor may enjoy a benefice (erected

---

[1] "Si parochus propter populi multitudinem aliasve causas nequeat, iudicio Ordinarii, solus convenientem curam gerere paroeciae, eidem detur unus vel plures vicarii cooperatores, quibus congrua remuneratio assignetur."—Canon 476, § 1.

[2] "Vicarii cooperatores constitui possunt sive pro universa paroecia sive pro determinata paroeciae parte."—Canon 476, § 2.

[3] "Eius iura et obligationes ex statutis dioecesanis, ex litteris Ordinarii et ex ipsius parochi commissione desumantur; sed, nisi aliud expresse caveatur, ipse debet ratione officii parochi vicem supplere eumque adiuvare in universo paroeciali ministerio, excepta applicatione Missae pro populo."—Canon 476, § 6.

[4] "Subest parocho, qui eum paterne instruat ac dirigat in cura animarum, ei invigilet et saltem quotannis ad Ordinarium de eodem referat."—Canon 476, § 7.

[5] Canon 477, § 2.

[6] Canon 477, § 1.

[7] Canon 477, § 2.

specifically for the support of an assistant pastor)[8] such benefices are practically non-existent in this country.[9] Normally an ordinary in this country assigns an assistant to a parish with the understanding that he will remain there only so long as the work of the parish necessitates an assistant for the pastor; this lack of perpetuity of assignment prevents an assistant's position from being a benefice.[10]

Furthermore, an assistant pastor, unlike a pastor, does not occupy an ecclesiastical office in the strict sense of the term.[11] Although canon 476 refers to the "office of the assistant pastor," the term "office" in this canon is used only in a broad and indefinite sense.[12]

It follows therefore that the basis on which an assistant pastor is remunerated is different from that of pastors. Whereas a pastor, who occupies an office in the strict sense of the term, receives an income from a benefice attached to an office, an assistant pastor does not occupy an office nor does he enjoy a benefice. Therefore canon 476, § 1, refers to the "fitting compensation" (*"congrua remuneratio"*) due to the assistant pastor, while the income of a pastor who enjoys a benefice is called, in canon 979, § 2, a "fitting support" (*"congrua sustentatio"*). The remuneration due an assistant pastor is a salary, in a qualified sense of the term, paid to him in view of his labors.[13] The compensation of an assistant pastor

[8] Canons 476 and 477, § 2.

[9] Beste, *Introductio in Codicem,* p. 715.

[10] Canon 1412; Cappello, *Summa Iuris Canonici,* II, 514; Beste, *Introductio in Codicem,* p. 715; Coronata, *Institutiones Iuris Canonici,* II, 358; Wernz-Vidal, *Ius Canonicum,* II, 202.

[11] Canon 145; Beste, *Introductio in Codicem,* p. 199; Vermeersch-Creusen, *Epitome Iuris Canonici,* I, 233.

[12] Stanislaus Woywod, *A Practical Commentary on the Code of Canon Law,* I, 175.

[13] S.R. Rota, *Salisburgen.* (Diminutionis beneficii parochialis), 1 aug. 1911, coram R. P. D. Francisco Heiner—*AAS,* III (1911), 575; Innocentius XIII, const. *Apostolic ministerii,* 23 maii 1723, § 13—*Fontes,* n. 280; Benedictus XIII, const. *In supremo,* 23 sept. 1724, § 10—*Fontes,* n. 283.

The canonical meaning of the term "salary" or remuneration of an assistant pastor is not the same as the term "salary" in its civil sense, in which it signifies a payment on a contractual agreement. According to the United States Internal Revenue Code, the term "salary" always implies a contract

follows the laws of commutative justice more closely than the beneficial income of a pastor or of any cleric enjoying a beneficial income; likewise, any priest who holds a position which is not a benefice should be paid a just salary for his labors in conformity with the laws of commutative and social justice.[14]

The ordinary determines the amount of compensation, or salary, due to an assistant pastor.[15] The ordinary in making his decision on the amount of salary to be paid an assistant pastor is to use, in general, the same considerations he employs in determining the income of the pastor. The assistant pastor has a right to the necessities of life, to provision for the future, to support for dependent near-relatives, and to the effective discharge of those obligations which derive from his clerical status, such as the purchase of books for continuing his studies, the making of donations to charity, and the enjoyment of suitable recreation.[16] The measure by which the assistant is to be compensated (thus determining the manner in which he will be able to meet his obligations) is determined by the quality of his labor as well as the

---

of employment.—*Davis* v. *Fall River,* 155 Mass., 96, 29 N.E. 202. The term "salary" involves a specific contract for a certain sum for a definite period of time.—54 *Corpus Juris,* 1124-1125. Patently, these elements of a salary are not found in the remuneration given to an assistant pastor.

Also, according to the Social Security Act, the United States Government considers the remuneration of Protestant ministers as not involving any contractual relationship.—*"Hearings Relative to the Social Security Act Amendments of 1939 before the Committee on Ways and Means," House of Representatives, Seventy Sixth Congress, First Session* (revised printing, Washington, D. C.: U. S. Government Printing Office, 1939).

For an exhaustive treatment of the nature of the income of the clergy according to the cviil law, confer the dissertation of Kenneth R. O'Brien, *The Nature of Support of Diocesan Priests in the United States of America.*

[14] Those priests who are permitted by their bishops to engage in work which is not connected with a benefice and the remuneration for which provides support for them—such as teaching at a university or occupying a position at the National Catholic Welfare Conference in Washington—are entitled to a salary in the strict sense of the term, and should be paid in proportion to their professional competence.

[15] Canon 476, § 1.

[16] Regatillo. *Institutiones Iuris Canonici,* I, 195; canons 476; 129; 130; confer Chapter VII, pp. 111 ff.

amount of his labor;[17] the amount of the compensation will depend also upon the income of the parish and the circumstances of the region.

In brief, although an assistant pastor, in common with all who have received major Orders, must be supported fittingly in view of his clerical status, he is chiefly remunerated for what he does—for the quality of his labor and the amount of that labor.[18]

The quality of the work of the assistant—a factor which in this country is not operative generally for conditioning an assistant's salary—depends upon the ability, merit and experience of the priest in the work of the ministry. The same qualifications that increase a pastor's efficiency, such as learning and zeal, also increase the assistant's efficiency and are deserving of reward.[19] An assistant who has labored in the ministry for a number of years is considered to be more experienced than a recently ordained assistant, and therefore has a right to more than one who has just been ordained. Thus, in some sections of France there are various grades of assistants, as there are various grades of pastors, with a corresponding gradation of salary.[20] In the same Archdiocese, if an

---

[17] ". . . determinare in ea quantitate quae pro suo prudenti arbitrio et conscientia conveniens videbitur, ratione videlicet habita redditüum et emolumentorum ecclesiae parochialis in qua deputati fuerint, necnon inspectis conditionibus loci, numero animarum, qualitate laboris, et quantitate impensarum, quas commissi officii necessitas postulaverit."—Innocentius XIII, const. *Apostolici ministerii,* 23 maii 1723, § 13—*Fontes,* n. 280. Benedict XIII, in his constitution *In supremo,* September 23, 1724, repeated the same words.—*Fontes,* n. 283.

[18] ". . . vicarii cooperatores quibus congrua remuneratio assignetur."—Canon 476, § 1.

[19] Canons 130, § 2; 459, § 3, 2°, 3°; Rebuffus, *Tractatus,* n. 63; Leurenius, *Forum Ecclesiasticum,* lib. III, tit. 25, qu. 583, n. 3; Schmalzgrueber, *Ius Ecclesiasticum,* lib. III, tit. 39, n. 137.

[20] The following is a list of the salaries of assistant pastors in the Archdiocese of Paris as of January 20, 1948:

Assistants (lowest grade)	60,900 francs
Second assistants	62,150 francs
First assistants	63,400 francs

Letter of Emmanuel Cardinal Suhard of Paris, to the Pastors, January 20, 1948.

assistant is named an administrator of a parish, his salary is increased to compensate for the new duties inherent in the position.[21]

Besides the consideration he receives for the quality of his work, an assistant pastor is to be recompensed according to the amount of his work in the sacred ministry.[22] The Church has recognized this elementary principle of justice both in its legal decisions and through its approbation of arrangements whereby priests receive a supplement to their salary for extraordinary services.[23] In some cases the supplement actually exceeded the amount of the salary accorded to an assistant pastor.[24] Of course, this principle of recompense for performance must not be reduced to the point of assigning a price for each rendering of spiritual ministry and thus immeasurably harming, rather than assisting, the sacred cause to which the priest has dedicated his life. Any semblance of venality must be avoided.

The amount of recompense to be accorded an assistant pastor—as in the case of a pastor—is also conditioned by the economic circumstances of the region and the income of the parish. Obviously, an assistant pastor in a section where the standard of living is high has more expenses and can expect to receive more than assistant pastors in a poor parish.[25]

The appointment, however, of an assistant pastor does not depend exclusively upon the affluence of the parish to which he is appointed.

---

[21] An administrator who was formerly an assistant of the lowest grade receives 62,900 francs, and an administrator who was formerly a second assistant receives 64,150 francs a year.—Letter of Emmanuel Cardinal Suhard of Paris, to the Pastors, January 20, 1948.

[22] Canon 476, § 1; Innocentius XIII, const. *Apostolici ministerii,* 23 maii 1723, § 13—*Fontes,* n. 280; Benedictus XIII, const. *In supremo,* 23 sept. 1724, § 10—*Fontes,* n. 283; S.R. Rota, *Salisburgen.* (Diminutionis beneficii parochialis), 1 aug. 1911, coram R. P. D. Francisco Heiner—*AAS,* III (1911), 575; S.C.C., *Triventina,* 18 mart. 1905—*ASS,* XXXVIII (1905), 85.

[23] Pastors and assistant pastors were given supplements for binating or for other works of the ministry that were unusual.—Bonal, *Institutiones Canonicae,* II, 196.

[24] Assistant pastors in France, by a law passed in 1874, who received only 450 francs a year could be accorded a supplement of 500 francs for extra services—Bonal, *loc. cit.*

[25] Cf. Chapter VIII, pp. 150, 151.

There is no reason why an ordinary cannot assign an assistant pastor, as he can a pastor, to a parish which needs the help of an assistant but is not financially capable of according him a just remuneration.[26] The cause which justifies the appointment of a pastor in such circumstances—the good of souls—justifies also the appointment of an assistant pastor, for that consideration is the final reason for the ordination of both the pastor and the assistant pastor. The minimum support owed to an assistant pastor is that with which he can meet his current living expenses; an ordinary could not expect a priest to serve at his own expense.[27] If the reduced income of the parish forces a reduction in the allotment to the pastor and his assistants, the allotments should be reduced proportionately.[28]

In the United States, the regulations on the collecting of arrears in salary are identical for pastors and assistant pastors.[29]

In determining the amount of the salary of the assistant, there should be a close relation with the amount allotted to the support of the pastor. An assistant pastor who discharges the same duties as the pastor, and who in the minds of the parishioners occupies a position in the parish very similar to that of the pastor, is also generally burdened with the same expenses as those of the pastor. Naturally because of the dignity of his position, his duties of administration, and his seniority in the priesthood is certainly entitled to more than the assistant pastor, even if their expenses are equal. But since the income of the assistant pastor should be sufficient to cover his expenses,[30] his income should not be greatly inferior to that of the pastor, on the assumption of course that the pastor does not receive an excessively high income.

Generally most of the ordinary expenses in a large parish in

---

[26] Canon 1415, §§ 1, 3; Coronata, *Institutiones Iuris Canonici,* II, 366; III Plenary Council of Baltimore (1884), Statute 273—*Statuta et Decreta Concilii Plenarii Baltimorensis III,* pp. 156-157.

[27] Innocentius XIII, const. *Apostolici ministerii,* 23 maii 1723, § 10—*Fontes,* n. 280.

[28] I Synod of Toledo (1941), Statute 398—*Acta et Decreta Synodi Dioecesanae Toletanae Primae,* p. 121.

[29] Cf. Chapter VIII, pp. 145, 146.

[30] Canon 476, § 1; Innocentius XIII, const. *Apostolici ministerii,* 23 maii 1723, § 13—*Fontes,* n. 280; Bouix, *Tractatus de Parocho,* p. 635.

the United States are the same for both pastor and assistant pastor. The cost of maintaining a car, of supporting dependent relatives, and of purchasing clothing and books is always equal. Possibly the greatest difference in expense arises from the demands of charity; the pastor is certainly expected to contribute to more causes and to contribute more generously than the assistant pastor. The pastor certainly also is likely to have more medical expenses and greater insurance or savings charges in making provision for the old age which impends more proximately for him than for the assistant.

It is informative to note the proportion between the pastor's and the assistant pastor's salaries as determined in Concordats approved by the Holy See. The Government of Poland in its Concordat agreed to pay vicars, including assistant pastors, about three-fourths of the amount allotted to pastors,[31] an assistant pastor being accorded two hundred "points," and a pastor two hundred and seventy "points." The same proportion is observed in other places in Europe where the faith has been long established and an equitable system could be developed without excessive interference from penal laws and persecutions.[32]

---

[31] *Sollemnis Conventio inter Sanctam Sedem et Rempublicam Poloniae—AAS,* XVII (1925), 285.

[32] In the Archdiocese of Paris, where there are many gradations in salaries of both pastors and assistant pastors, the lowest-salaried assistant receives 60,900 francs, and the highest-salaried pastor (those with more than three assistants) receives 78,900 francs a year.—Letter of Emmanuel Cardinal Suhard, of Paris, January 20, 1948.

In both England and Ireland the income of the clergy is derived mostly from stole fees and from the collection on Easter and Christmas which is devoted to the support of the parish clergy. In the Archdiocese of Westminster, pastors are allowed, where it is possible to do so, to take a salary of 100 pounds a year, and to give assistant pastors a salary of 40 pounds a year.—Letter from the Archbishop's House, Westminster, November 8, 1948. In the Diocese of Limerick, in the few parishes where the assistant lives with the pastor, the assistant pastor receives a nominal salary of 22 pounds a year!—Letter from the Diocesan Palace, October 20, 1948. It is evident therefore that the salary or the remuneration which assistant pastors receive in England and Ireland is greatly akin to the nature of the income from a benefice; certainly their salary is far inferior to the income they receive from Mass stipends, donations, stole fees, etc.

In Belgium, where the Government pays the salaries of the ministers of

Although the basic source of income for an assistant pastor is the salary, the amount of which is determined by diocesan statute or by decree of the ordinary, the assistant pastor has other sources of income. He has a right to those offerings which are grouped under the term *iura casualia*—Mass stipends, offerings or donations made on the occasion of a ministration which is not a right or duty of the pastor, e.g., for preaching or for attendance at a funeral or nuptial Mass, offerings made to the assistant by way of customary usage, statutory reputation, or will of the donor.[33] The income derived through the custom or practice (sometimes recognized by statute) of giving the Easter and Christmas collection to the pastor and the assistants is possibly the most remunerative of the incidental fees (*iura casualia*).[34]

The income from the incidental fees (*iura casualia*) is supposed to be only supplementary to the salary or the *portio congrua* of the assistant pastor.[35] However, in many places, including certain sections of the United States, the incidental fees frequently equal the salary; the relative stability and sizable amount of the incidental fees possibly constitute the chief factors in keeping unchanged the low salaries of assistant pastors.

An assistant pastor does not have a right to the stole fees;[36] stole fees are offerings made on the occasion of the administration of the sacraments or of parish functions such as funerals, marriages, baptisms, etc.[37] These stole fees belong to the pastor, even if the

---

religion, a pastor receives 40,710 francs a year, and an assistant pastor receives 37,200 francs a year (one dollar is equal to 43.87 Belgian francs).—Letter from the Embassy of Belgium, December 3, 1948, Washington, D. C.

In Austria, the basic salary of an assistant pastor is four-fifths the amount of the salary of a pastor.—*Besoldungsordnung*, Archdiocese of Vienna, September 1, 1947.

[33] Brys, *Juris Canonici Compendium*, I, 481.

[34] This custom is observed and approved in at least some sections of Ireland, England and the United States.—Letter from the Archbishop's House, Westminster, November 8, 1948; Letter from the Archbishop's Palace, Limerick, October 20, 1948.

[35] Brys, *Juris Canonici Compendium*, I, 481.

[36] Canons 463, §§ 1, 3; 1507, § 1; Vermeersch-Creusen, *Epitome Iuris Canonici*, I, 399; Coronata, *Institutiones Iuris Canonici*, I, 582; Cappello, *Summa Iuris Canonici*, I (4. ed., 1945), 477.

[37] Canon 462.

assistant pastor performs all the duties for the performance of which they are given. The assistant is entitled only to that portion of the offering which exceeds the amount of the regular fee and which he knows was intended as a donation made to him.[38] The assistant pastor who performs the functions for which the stole fees are offered is compensated by the salary he receives.

Contrary to the general law of the Code, one opinion contends, and is supported by practice in some places, that custom or diocesan statute can establish a division of the stole fees between the pastor and his assistants; the share of the assistant constitutes a part of the income of the assistant.[39] This opinion (and the practices which conform to it) runs counter to the general law of the Code, which provides not only that the *iura stolae* belong to the pastor, but further states that the only stole fee which the bishop is empowered to regulate is that for funerals.[40] The other stole fees must be established by a decree of a provincial council, and these decrees are ineffective unless they have been approved by the Holy See.[41] In the absence of the establishment of stole fees by a provincial council, it seems that custom could supply the defect of a provincial decree.[42]

However, it is undeniably true that in many places, both in this and in other countries, the pastor is obliged by statute to share his stole fees with his assistants according to a certain *ratio*. The Diocese of Harrisburg has a statute decreeing that in parishes where there are two or more priests, the stole fees shall be divided into as many parts as there are priests, plus one, of which the pastor shall receive two parts and each assistant one part.[43] Thus a pastor with one assistant receives two-thirds of the stole fees, a pastor with two assistants receives one half of the stole fees (each assistant receives a fourth) and a pastor with three

---

[38] Canon 463, § 3.

[39] Bargilliat, *Droits et Devoirs des Curés et des Vicaires Paroissiaux*, p. 410.

[40] Canon 1234, § 1. This canon provides that the ordinary must solicit the advice of his consultors in determining the fee for funerals.

[41] Canon 1507, § 1.

[42] Canons 1410 and 463, § 1.

[43] IX Synod of Harrisburg (1943), Decree 33, § 4—*Statutes of the Diocese of Harrisburg*, p. 48.

assistants receives two-fifths of the stole fees (each assistant receives one-fifth). The same system is observed at least in many part of Ireland and England.[44] In France also, the pastors must share their stole fees with their assistants.[45]

This system of decreeing the sharing of stole fees could be established legally in two ways: by apostolic privilege[46] or by custom.[47] The approbation of these statutes and customs by the Holy See constitutes a privilege.[48] The system could also have legal sanction without the granting of an apostolic privilege—as the result of an immemorial custom. Such an immemorial custom is not specifically reprobated by the present Code, and therefore could have legal force. Such a system of sharing stole fees could also arise simply through the agreement of the pastors who consented to share their stole fees while still maintaining their right to the stole fees; in such an event each pastor would individually have the right to discontinue at will sharing the stole fees. Of course, this voluntary sharing would have no value in stabilizing the system legally; hence it has no application in considering the legal validity of the system established through apostolic privilege or custom. (If the ordinary, in erecting a parish, were to decree that the stole fees constitute part of the income of the benefice, the pastor would then pay the assistant pastor by sharing with him the stole fees; this arrangement, however, rarely if ever occurs in the United States.)

There is another great difference between the income of an assistant pastor and that of a pastor—the income of the assistant pastor is not subject to the law which calls for an expending of the excess income in favor of the poor or of other pious causes. The income of the assistant pastor is remuneration for services, and the law concerning excess income applies only to income

[44] Letter from the Archbishop's Palace, Limerick, October 20, 1948; Letter from the Chancellery of the Archdiocese of Dublin, October 21, 1948. Letter from the Archbishop's House, Westminster, Nov. 8, 1948.

[45] Bargilliat, *Droits et Devoirs des Curés et des Vicaires Paroissiaux*, p. 410.

[46] Canon 63.

[47] Canons 27, § 1, 28.

[48] Beste defines a privilege as "lex privata aliquod speciale et permanens beneficium aut favorem contra vel praeter ius concedens."—*Introductio in Codicem*, p. 119.

from benefices.[49] However, if the assistant pastor enjoys the income of a benefice—as occurs frequently in Europe[50]—his excess income is subject to the prescriptions of canon 1473. Of course, benefices could be erected for the support of the assistant pastors in this country, and in consequence thereof such income would be subject to the prescriptions of canon 1473, but hitherto no such erection of benefices has occurred.

Upon this consideration of the provisions of the Code concerning the remuneration of assistant pastors, there naturally arises the question whether the prevailing system of remunerating assistant pastors in the United States conforms to the provisions of the Code. Two salient points must be considered: is it comformable to the law to pay all assistants in the diocese the same salary? and, is the amount which is paid sufficient?

In regard to the first point, whether it is conformable to the law to pay all assistants in the diocese the same salary, it must be stated that such an arrangement is proper if all the assistants have the same obligations, perform them in approximately the same manner, and receive a sufficient remuneration which enables them to live in a fitting manner. Actually, almost all assistants in the United States have the same obligations and duties; the differences in their duties arise from the peculiar circumstances in the parish or from the condition of the pastor. If in addition to the normal duties of an assistant pastor the priest must perform other duties —such as being practically the administrator of the parish because of the illness or disability of the pastor, or serving as a member of the diocesan tribunal or as a director of charities—he should receive extra remuneration,[51] that is, whenever the diocese is able to afford it. Of course, if the assistant priest is situated in a parish that has very few duties and then is assigned to some extra-

---

[49] Coronata, *Institutiones Iuris Canonici*, II, 416; Beste, *Introductio in Codicem*, p. 730; Vermeersch-Creusen, *Epitome Iuris Canonici*, II, 526.

[50] Woywod, *A Practical Commentary on the Code of Canon Law*, I, 174; Coronata, *Institutiones Iuris Canonici*, II, 361.

[51] In the Archdioceses of Paris and Vienna, extra remuneration is paid to priests who perform tasks in addition to the normal duties of their position.—*Besoldungsordnung*, Archdiocese of Vienna, September 1, 1947; Letter of Emmanuel Cardinal Suhard, Archbishop of Paris, to his Clergy, January 20, 1948.

parochial duty such as those described above, the salary he receives as an assistant pastor is mostly a remuneration for the performance of the extra-parochial duties.

It is assumed that the assistant pastors generally perform their duties in the same manner. If an assistant pastor is notably negligent, the ordinary could remove him and apply other punitive measures. Usually those assistant pastors who are outstanding in the performance of their parochial duties receive an equitable reward in the form of donations and larger incidental fees than less zealous assistant pastors. Certainly the ordinary is empowered to increase the salary of assistants according to their experience and ability in discharging their duties, as is done in France.

In the interest of the public order, the ordinary should be prudent and circumspect in arranging such a system of graded salaries for assistant pastors lest it arouse contention. Possibly the most prudent way to arrange such a system would consist in instituting a gradation in salary according to seniority of service, with an augmentation of the salaries of those who are assigned to special extra-parochial duties.

The salary of the assistant pastor should also be sufficiently large to enable him to pay all his legitimate expenses and to live conformably to his clerical status. If because of unusual expenses —such as the support of dependent near-relatives, or the cost of protracted illness—his salary is not sufficient, he should be accorded an increase commensurate with his needs. The sacerdotal dignity of the assistant pastor is never separable from his remuneration. The assistant pastor is paid not only for what he does, but also for what he is; he is paid not only for the services he renders, but also a means to support him according to his needs in a manner befitting the clerical state.

The final consideration concerns the approximate amount an assistant pastor should be paid in the United States. Naturally, no rule can be made for the entire United States with its great divergence of conditions. An assistant pastor in the eastern part of the United States—situated in a section that enjoys a high standard of living and in a parish that requires the use of an automobile—needs an income of about $1,800 a year; this amount would be the aggregate of his income from his salary, Mass stipends and share in the stole fees. This amount seems needed if he is to pay all his obligations and expenses, exclusive of the contributions to be given if he needs to support his parents, and exclusive also of the expenses for board and room. It will be noted that this approximation comprises about three-fourths of the amount estimated as a minimum for the needs of a pastor in the eastern part of the United States.[52]

If this amount seems excessive it must be recalled that it is intended to cover all the legitimate obligations of an assistant pastor. The demands of charity—including contributions for the erection of seminaries, hospitals, schools, etc.—form a considerable part of the needs of an assistant pastor. In this respect the clergy in this country are subject to more demands than the clergy in Europe. Many of the expenses of the Church in Europe have been met during the course of the centuries by the munificent donations of charitable persons who endowed institutions, dioceses and parishes; in the United States the expenses for constructing and maintaining our educational and charitable institutions come from the contributions of the faithful, and the clergy are rightly expected to furnish an example of generosity to the laity. An assistant pastor is not an isolated individual free of obligations to the community and the parish. As a spiritual leader he has, and must recognize, the obligations which are imposed on him by his position.

In summary, an assistant pastor is entitled to that support which he earns by his labor and which is due him as a priest. He is entitled to a living which should be characterized by the restraint imposed by his sacred profession, but which should also be sufficient for all the demands—personal, charitable, social—imposed by that sacred calling.

---

[52] Cf. Chapter VIII, p. 153.

CHAPTER X

Fitting Support of Priests in Special Circumstances

SECTION 1. SUPPORT FOR PRIESTS ENGAGED IN STUDY

"Ignorance is the mother of all errors and greatly to be avoided by all priests of God," declared the IV Council of Toledo in Spain, when it summed up very succinctly, in a negative way, the attitude of the Church towards learning.[1] Pope Honorius III (1216-1227) stated, in a positive manner, the regard of the Church for learning when in the following words he referred to clerics who qualified as teachers of theology: ". . . qui, cum docti fuerint, in Dei ecclesia velut splendor fulgeant firmamenti, ex quibus postmodum copia possit haberi doctorum, qui, velut stellae, in perpetuas aeternitates mansuri ad justitiam valeant plurimas erudire. . . ."[2]

Inasmuch as each truth proceeds from Him who is the Truth, the pursuit of truth finally and inevitably leads to the knowledge of God, the Supreme Wisdom. Consequently priests, who are God's ministers to men, cannot disregard the cultivation of those studies which are as it were a participation in the knowledge of God, and a path to the acknowledgment of His dominion over us. Pope Pius XI (1922-1938) called attention to this fact again in our generation, and reiterated the need of learning as an instrumental agency in the work of the priesthood.[3]

Naturally the Church provides in the Code for the proper inculcation of knowledge necessary for the work of the ministry, as well as for the encouragement of learning that will be helpful and conducive to that work. The Church defines in the Code those studies—principally the sacred sciences of theology and philosophy

[1] IV Council of Toledo (633), c. 25—Bruns, I, 231.

[2] C. 5, X, *de magistris, et ne aliquid exigatur pro licentia docendi,* V, 5.

[3] Pius XI, litt. apost. *Officiorum omnium,* 1 aug. 1922—*AAS,* XIV (1922), 449; litt. encycl. *Ad catholici sacerdotii,* 20 dec. 1935—*AAS,* XXVIII (1936), 5; cf. also the Encyclical Letter of Pius X (1903-1914), *Pascendi,* 8 sept. 1907—*ASS,* XL (1907), 640; *Fontes,* n. 680.

—which are necessary for one ordained as God's priest.[4] The Code further establishes the method by which the priest is to retain and refresh his knowledge of these essential studies—by an examination each year during at least his first triennium in the priesthood,[5] and by attendance at conferences on theological and liturgical questions several times a year.[6] A further encouragement and stimulus to the study of the sacred sciences is furnished by the rule that those who have excelled in the triennial examinations or have secured graduate degrees in the theological sciences should, *ceteris paribus,* be given prior consideration in the conferring of benefices and offices.[7] Moreover, before a priest may be appointed as an irremovable pastor, he shall successfully undergo an examination in theology.[8]

The Church is also rightly interested in encouraging the study of the secular sciences that aid the work of the priestly ministry.[9] The II Plenary Council of Baltimore (1866) urged priests in our country to abet their work for souls by cultivating the knowledge of the sciences suitable for this purpose.[10] Pius XI urged priests

---

[4] The seminary course should include a two-year course in philosophy and a four-year course in theology together with the study of Scripture, Church history, canon law, sacred oratory and ecclesiastical music. There should also be lectures in pastoral theology, and instructions in the methods of catechizing, in the hearing of confessions, visiting the sick and consoling the dying.—Canon 1365.

Before a candidate may receive Orders he must successfully pass an examination concerning the Order he is to receive, and candidates for sacred Orders must also undergo an examination in theology.—Canons 996, §§ 1, 2; 1380.

[5] Canon 130, § 1.

[6] Canon 131.

[7] Canons 130, § 2; 1380.

[8] Canon 459, § 3, 3°.

[9] Provincial Council of Cologne (1850), c. 36—*Coll. Lac.,* V, col. 379; Provincial Council of Prague (1860), c. 3—*Coll. Lac.,* V, col. 418; Provincial Council of Utrecht (1865), c. 2—*Coll. Lac.,* V, col. 911. Pius XI, litt. encycl., *Ad catholici sacerdotii,* 20 dec. 1935—*AAS,* XXVIII (1936), 33-34.

[10] II Plenary Council of Baltimore (1866), Decrees 170, 177—*Acta et Decreta Concilii Plenarii Baltimorensis II,* pp. 105, 107.

to cultivate those sciences which are the patrimony of all cultivated men, in order to forward the work of the sacred ministry.[11]

Although the Church encourages the pursuit of those studies which are helpful to the vocation of the priest, the Church rightly prescribes that special permission be obtained for a cleric to practice professions which are alien to the dignity of the priesthood, or which tend to embroil the priest in secular affairs.[12]

It is obvious, then, that an ordinary can and should appoint priests to pursue those branches of knowledge that are necessary and helpful to the work of the diocesan curia as well as the direction of souls.[13] Within the past few decades there has been such a broadening of knowledge and systematization of certain activities, as in the field of education and in the works of charity, that priests must enter many new fields of study. Thus in addition to the need for priests properly trained in the theological sciences and in canon law, many dioceses now need priests trained in the modern methods of charitable and sociological work, education, labor organization and youth work. The general welfare of the Church permits, if it

---

[11] Pius XI, litt. encycl. *Ad catholici sacerdotii*, 20 dec. 1935—*AAS*, XXVIII (1936), 34.

[12] Thus it is forbidden, without an apostolic indult, to practice the profession of medicine or surgery, or to act as a notary public except in the ecclesiastical curia, or to accept public offices that entail secular jurisdiction or administrative duties.—Canon 139, § 2.

Further, a cleric may not, without permission of his ordinary, act as agent for the goods and property of lay people, or assume secular offices which impose the obligation of rendering an account, or act as an attorney in secular courts except for the good of the Church or for a charitable cause.—Canon 139, § 3.

[13] "Quoties et quandiu id, iudicio proprii Ordinarii, exigat Ecclesiae necessitas, ac nisi legitimum impedimentum excuset, sucipiendum est clericis ac fideliter implendum munus quod ipsis fuerit ab Episcopo commissum."—Canon 128.

Commenting on the meaning of the word *"munus"* in this canon, Beste states: "Munus latissime sumitur pro quocumque officio in dioecesi, quod ad salutem animarum vel bonum religionis confert, etsi non curatum, e.g., parochi vicarii, cappellani, moderatoris scholarum paroecialium, rectoris orphanotrophii aliusve pii instituti. Quod praesertim apud nos valet, ubi clerici generatim titulo servitii dioecesis ad subdiaconatum promoventur."—*Introductio in Codicem*, p. 183. Cf. also Coronata, *Institutiones Iuris Canonici*. I, 219.

does not demand, that the ordinary should direct priests to secure scholastic degrees in these studies, even when it entails attending appropriate schools after ordination.

Priests who have been directed by the ordinary to pursue studies after their ordination are entitled to a fitting support.[14] They are entitled to this support not only in view of their title under which they were ordained to sacred Orders,[15] but also as a fitting recompense for their labor in behalf of the diocese. Certainly if to an assistant pastor there is due a fitting compensation (*remuneratio congrua*) for his efforts in a parish,[16] the priest who is preparing himself, at the command of his ordinary, for special work in the diocese is entitled to a just recompense for his labors. Pope Honorius III referred to clerics pursuing higher studies as "laboring in the vineyard of the Lord."[17]

It is helpful for the present purpose to note the system employed by the Church in former centuries in order to secure for dioceses a sufficient number of priests trained as teachers in the theological sciences. It was decreed at the III Latern Council (1179), in canon 18, and again at the IV Lateran Council (1215), in canon 11, that each cathedral was to support a *magister,* and each metropolitan cathedral was to support a theologian, who would instruct priests and laymen in the sacred sciences; the *magister* and the theologian were to receive a canon's prebend without becoming a canon.[18]

Further, the theologian and the *magister* were solemnly forbidden to accept any gratuities for their services, so that all who desired instruction would have equal and easy access to their services. Pope Honorius further provided, besides reiterating the commands of the previous legislation, that if those clerics who had been sent to continue their studies at a university or similar place of learning did not receive from other sources an income sufficient to enable them to continue their studies, the diocese was to contribute to their support; he further decreed that both teachers and students should receive by permission of the Holy See the income from their

[14] Cf. Chapter IX, pp. 151 ff.

[15] Canon 980, § 1.

[16] Canon 476.

[17] C. 5, X, *de magistris,* et ne aliquid exigatur pro licentia docendi, V. 5.

[18] *Histoires des Conciles de l'Eglise,* V, seconde partie, pp. 1101, 1341.

benefices and prebends while absent from their benefices or chapters, even though the absence for study might last for five years.[19] A severe penalty was meted out to those canons who received the income from their prebends while they were supposedly pursuing studies but were actually enjoying vacations.[20]

The Council of Trent renewed the legislation which permitted beneficed clerics (who were consequently obliged to observe the law of residence) to receive the income from their benefices or prebends while absent for the purpose of study.[21] The same practice could be permitted today.[22]

Since the earlier law of the Church, which has not been even partially abrogated by the legislation of the present Code of Canon Law, remains in effect,[23] it is evident that an ordinary who directs a priest[24] to leave his work in the diocese and to undertake advanced studies must provide that he be fittingly supported. This fitting support must be interpreted according to the principles described in Chapters VII and VIII, namely, as sufficient for a cleric's lodging, food, clothing, proper recreation, support of dependents, adequate medical care, some donations to charity, expenses of transportation (an item of considerable moment if the school is very distant), books and other supplies necessary for the prosecution of the studies. Likewise, the reasons which excuse an ordinary from

---

[19] ". . . quibus, si proprii proventus ecclesiastici non sufficiunt, praedicti necessaria subministrent. Docentes vero in theologica facultate, dum in scholis docuerint, et studentes in ipsa integre per annos quinque, percipiant de licentia Sedis Apostolicae proventus praebendarum et beneficiorum suorum, non obstante aliqua alia consuetudine vel statuto, cum denario fraudari non debeant in vinea Domini operantes."—c. 5, X, *de magistris, et ne aliquid exigatur pro licentia docendi,* V, 5.

[20] C. 12, X, *de magistris, et ne aliquid exigatur pro licentia docendi,* V, 5.

[21] Conc. Trident, sess. V, *de ref.,* c. 1.

[22] D'Angelo (1885-1930) suggested that a cleric in leaving a benefice for the purpose of study could be accorded a pension from that benefice.—*Tasse e Pensioni nel Codice di Diritio Canonico* (2. ed., cor. et ampl., Torino: L.I.C.E., 1927), p. 122, nota 2.

[23] Canon 6.

[24] The same rule of fitting support would apply to a subdeacon or deacon who instead of being ordained to the priesthood would be commanded to engage in special studies. The support that should be accorded to subdeacons and deacons is treated in Chapter XI, *infra,* pp. 183-185.

the payment of a fitting support or of a just remuneration to his clerics would also be applicable in the case of support due to clerics engaged in graduate studies.[25]

The amount of salary paid to a priest engaged in study should, in conformity with the legislation of the Church, have some relation to the status of the priest before he began his studies. The legislation of the Church on the support of clerics engaged in graduate studies, the demands of equity, and the canons which protect a cleric against being transferred without a cause to a lesser benefice support this contention.[26] Thus, if a pastor or a cleric who possesses a benefice is directed to undertake graduate studies, he should be paid the income he enjoyed from his benefice (minus the daily allowances which yield to those canons who participate in the choral duties).[27] A priest who has been an assistant pastor, or would have been an assistant pastor if he had not been directed to continue his studies, should receive the salary of an assistant pastor if he is sent to undertake graduate studies. In general, the priest who is studying should receive the same salary he would have received had he remained on duty in the diocese.

The salary due to a priest who is engaged in graduate study for the benefit of the diocese should not be interpreted to mean only a supply of Mass stipends or occasional donations that prove insufficient for the payment of the priest's expenses. The priest should at regular intervals be paid a sufficient amount to cover all necessary expenditures and to enable him to live in a manner befitting his clerical dignity.

If an ordinary, because of the penury of the diocese, cannot afford to pay a just remuneration or a fitting support to priests engaged in study for the diocese, he could command priests to undertake these studies if there is a necessity commensurate with the amount of hardship or inconvenience caused.[28] The minimum

---

[25] III Plenary Council of Baltimore (1886), Statute 273—*Acta et Decreta Concilii Plenarii Baltimorensis III,* pp. 156-157; canon 1415, § 3.

[26] Canons 2163; 2147.

[27] Canon 395, § 3.

[28] Coronata, *Institutiones Iuris Canonici,* I, 219; III Plenary Council of Baltimore (1884), Statute 273—*Acta et Decreta Plenarii Concilii Baltimorensis III,* pp. 156-157.

support that must be afforded a priest in such a case is the payment of all his current expenses.[29] These current expenses would include expenses for transportation and all expenses incidental to his studies besides the amount needed for his lodging, food, clothing, medical expenses and support of dependent relatives. There should be few dioceses within the United States in such straitened financial circumstances that they can afford to pay only the current expenses of priests assigned to advanced study.

In summary, the priest engaged in study at the command of or with the permission of his ordinary is performing a duty that is as commendable and as worthy of remuneration as the work of the pastoral or curial ministry in the diocese, and should be recompensed accordingly.

SECTION 2. SUPPORT FOR DISABLED AND AGED PRIESTS

Although the question of adequate provision for the support of aged and disabled clerics has been treated in discussing the support due to disabled or aged pastors and assistant pastors,[30] no specific consideration was given to the applicability of the provisions of the Code to the conditions in the United States. A problem arises from the fact that the provisions of the Code for granting pensions to the retired clergy[31] postulate the ordination of the clergy principally on the title of benefice and the consequent support from the benefice for whose tenure the cleric was ordained, whereas in the United States most of the secular clergy are ordained on the title of service of the diocese and are supported, if pastors, successively by several benefices, while assistant pastors are never accorded a benefice.

There are two methods of arranging a system of pensions according to the Code:

1. by using his power to impose a moderate exaction on all beneficiaries for any special cause, the Ordinary can impose an occasional exaction and thus establish a common fund for the support

---

[29] III Plenary Council of Baltimore (1884), Statute 273—*Acta et Decreta Concilii Plenarii Baltimorensis III*, pp. 156-157.

[30] Cf. Chapters VII, pp. 116-117; VIII, pp. 142 ff.; IX, p. 158.

[31] Canon 1429, § 2.

of disabled or aged priests;[32] this would be an extraordinary method of establishing a pension fund;

2. the ordinary can impose a pension that will endure for the lifetime of the beneficiary on any benefice at the time of the conferral of the benefice on the new incumbent. The pension will be to the benefit of a retiring pastor or vicar (therefore including an assistant pastor) who served that parish.[33]

An investigation of the application of each method will show their advantages and disadvantages for providing pensions to retired priests in this country.

1. The ordinary, by using his power to impose a moderate, occasional exaction on all beneficiaries, would be able to levy a tax only on the pastors (who comprise almost the sole beneficiaries in the dioceses in the United States). The pastors would be obliged to bear the burden of the fund that would be used in aid not only of retired or disabled pastors, but of all disabled or retired priests of the diocese. This system would seem to impose an unfair burden on the pastors' incomes. Actually, a system similar to this is used in the Archdiocese of Paris, but in Europe there are more beneficiaries in a diocese than in a diocese in the United States. In European dioceses the beneficed clergy include not only the pastors but almost all the priests of the diocese, including the canons, seminary professors, and in many cases the assistant pastors. It must also be remembered that the exaction permitted to the ordinary by canon 1505 applies only to extraordinary cases, and could not without an indult be made a regular, annual tax on the beneficed clergy; it could be applied only occasionally,[34] and would scarcely be suitable for establishing a fund for pensions.

2. A retiring beneficiary can be granted a pension from the benefice he is vacating, and an assistant pastor can be granted a pension, in case of retirement or disability, from the parish he served.[35] Certain problems arise from the application of this provision of law in our country.

---

[32] Canon 1505.

[33] Canon 1429, §§ 1, 2.

[34] Beste, *Introductio in Codicem*, pp. 745-746.

[35] Canon 1429, § 2. For information on the manner of computing and arranging a pension, cf. Appendix I.

Unfortunately, the system of providing pensions for retired clerics as contained in canon 1429, § 2, is not applicable to many of the secular clergy in the United States.[36] Canon 1429, § 2, envisages a situation wherein most of the priests will be ordained on the title of a benefice or will, before their retirement, come to enjoy the income of a benefice, which income will be large enough to afford them a suitable pension when they retire, besides adequately supporting the new incumbent in the benefice. Besides, canon 1429, § 2, envisages a rather permanent assignment of priests to parishes, so that even if an assistant pastor retires while assigned to that parish he will have the right to draw a suitable and sufficient pension from the parish-benefice.

This system for providing pensions, as outlined in canon 1429, § 2, does not apply to the condition of the majority of priests in the United States. First, a cleric in the United States is not ordained to major Orders on the title of a benefice by which he will be supported during his active ministry, and from which he will draw a pension when he retires. A cleric in the United States is ordained on the title of service of the diocese. He knows not which or how many parishes he will serve as pastor or as assistant pastor during his active ministry. In fact, the title of service of the diocese was approved because there were not sufficient benefices for the support of the priests needed for the care of souls in a diocese.

Further, a cleric ordained on the title of service of the diocese is seldom assigned for the rest of his active ministry to a certain parish. A secular priest, generally, serves in the course of his ministry several parishes successively. Parishes which are heavily burdened with debt would be loath to welcome the appointment

---

[36] The provisions of canon 1429, § 2, in restricting the granting of pensions on parochial benefices to priests who served that parish as pastors or vicars seem to work hardships also in countries other than the United States. Coronata comments strongly on canon 1429, § 2: "De iure ferendo, si semel nostrum votum exprimere liceat, optandum est ut Ordinariis maior circa hoc libertas relinquatur. Sunt etiam apud nos paroeciae pinguissimae quarum reditibus subveniri posset facile vicariis cooperatoribus, qui saepe saepius in magna versantur paupertate, cum non spernenda populi christiani admiratione. Utinam concedatur Ordinariis locorum modus his incommodis subveniendi, concedendo ipsis ius pensiones imponendi etiam beneficiis paroecialibus."—*Institutiones Iuris Canonici,* II, 381.

of an assistant pastor, however much his services were needed, if his possible retirement would prove another burden to the parish. The same is true of parishes with low incomes, even if there is no outstanding debt. Under a system of pensions the ordinary could feel induced to assign assistant pastors to parishes on the basis of their ability to supply them with a pension in the event of retirement, rather than on the basis of need for their services in the parish. The prevalent attitude in this country, arising from the whole complexus of existing conditions, is that a cleric ordained on the title of service of the diocese as the title implies, looks to the diocese for provision for his support in case of retirement;[37] a secular priest, in the event that he retires, does not expect to secure support from the parish from which he retires (especially if he is an assistant pastor) unless that parish is wealthy.

Unfortunately, while it seems that the Code has not provided a practicable system of securing support for retired priests ordained on the title of service of the diocese, the conciliar legislation in the United States devised a system which in part has proved contrary to the provisions of the Code, and thus has been in part abrogated.[38]

The III Plenary Council of Baltimore (1884), after due consideration of the existing conditions in the United States, decreed as a preferable method of supplying support for priests in need a general tax on the parishes to establish a fund for the support of such priests—a tax which is contrary to the provisions of canon

[37] There is evidence, in the conciliar legislation, of the prevalence of this attitude in the United States also in the last century. Statute 90 of the II Plenary Council provided that if a retired pastor could not be supported from the income of the parish from which he retired, his support was to come from the donations of the clergy and laity of the diocese.—II Plenary Council of Baltimore (1886), Statute 90—*Concilii Plenarii Baltimorensiis II Acta et Decreta,* p. 66. The III Plenary Council, profiting from the experience of dioceses in the intervening years, decreed that the ordinaries should establish a fund for the support of retired or indigent priests by imposing a tax on all the parishes. This diocesan fund was to be administered under the direction of the ordinary.—III Plenary Council of Baltimore (1884), Statute 71—*Acta et Decreta Concilii Plenarii Baltimorensis III,* p. 36. This provision of the III Plenary Council has become abrogated through the law contained in canon 1505 of the Code.

[38] Canon 6, 1°.

1505 of the present Code.[39] The Statute also provided alternative methods of providing support for priests if this method of taxation proved too vexatious for parishes already burdened with too many appeals. The ordinary could impose an exaction on the salary of each priest in the diocese; or in lieu of the impracticability of the

---

[39] Although the decree of the III Plenary Council was designed to secure sufficient support for all priests, it naturally had particular relevance to the needs of indigent or retired priests, as is evident from the context of the decree.

"Statuimus igitur ac decernimus, ut in singulis nostris dioecesibus Episcopi, inito prius cum clero suo consilio, quamprimum constituant modos mediaque opportuna, quibus subsidia ad decentem illorum sacerdotum sustentationem elargienda praesto habeantur. Quem in finem ab Episcopo aerarium vel gaza instituatur, imposita taxa singulis paroeciis, quae opportuna videbitur. Huic pecuniae juxta normas clare definitas administrandae commissio presbyterorum, ipso Episcopo praeside, praeponantur.

"Si quis vero Episcopus, ob frequentes ad populum de pecunia appellationes, hanc novam taxam imponendam non esse judicaverit, ab aequitatis ac justitiae tramite alienum non erit, taxam annuam ipsismet dioecesis sacerdotibus imponere, quae singuli pro rata salarii pecuniam contribuant.

"Modus alius praedictae necessitati prospiciendi in eo est, ut societas mutui subsidii inter presbyteros constituatur, quae societas aerarii seu pecuniae congestae administrationem, item Episcopo praeside, curabit. Huic societati unusquisque sacerdos dioecesi adscriptus nomen dare urgeatur."—III Plenary Council of Baltimore (1884), Statute 71—*Acta et Decreta Concilii Plenarii Baltimorensis III,* p. 36.

The first two paragraphs of this statute seem clearly contrary to the provisions of canon 1505, which permits the ordinary to levy only a moderate exaction on the beneficiaries in the diocese for meeting some special need of the diocese. This permissible moderate taxation is not to be imposed annually or regularly, and is contemplated only for an unusual and exceptional, not constant, necessity.—Beste, *Introductio in Codicem,* p. 756; Vermeersch-Creusen, *Epitome Iuris Canonici,* II, 575.

Hence the opinion of Barrett, namely, that the provisions of Statute 71 of the III Plenary Council of Baltimore are "*praeter Codicem* and still binding," is patently inadmissible.—Barrett, *A Comparative Study of the Councils of Baltimore and the Code of Canon Law,* p. 39. Although the first two paragraphs of Statute 71 are *contra Codicem,* the third paragraph seems to be, as Barrett states, *praeter Codicem* and still binding (unless abrogated through a contrary general custom).

It seems from the commentary of Barrett that he considered the provisions of Statute 71 of the III Plenary Council only in relation with the provisions

other two methods, the ordinary could form a mutual assistance society among the clergy, which society was to be directed by the ordinary. The second method proposed is also abrogated in consequence of the provisions of canon 1505, for the reasons already submitted.

At present, therefore, when it is impossible to supply from the income of the parish a suitable pension to a priest retiring from the parish (canon 1429, § 2), the support for a retired priest should be provided according to the last paragraph of Statute 71 of the III Plenary Council of Baltimore, that is, by establishing a clerical mutual assistance society.

What is to be done if the ordinary cannot secure a fitting support for retired priests either by arranging a pension according to the provisions of canon 1429, § 2, or by establishing a clerical mutual assistance society? The easiest solution may consist in the Ordinary's request that a collection for the support of retired priests be taken up in all the parishes. The Code does not forbid that an annual collection of voluntary offerings be solicited for the support of the clergy; it only forbids that a constantly recurring tax be imposed.[40]

---

of canons 981, § 2, 1484 and 2154, and not in relation with canon 1505, which is the canon through which the first two paragraphs of Statute 71 have become abrogated.

Statute 71 of the III Plenary Council was the result of the experience of the bishops in the United States who had tried other means of providing support for priests in need. The II Plenary Council of Baltimore had decreed in 1866 that the support of the retired pastor or disabled priest was to come primarily from the parish he had served, and, if this parish proved too poor to render such support, the clergy and the faithful of the diocese were to supply the needed support.—II Plenary Council of Baltimore (1866), Statute 90—*Acta et Decreta Concilii Plenarii Baltimorensis II*, p. 66.

The II Plenary Council had thus decreed a system which closely resembled that for which permission is now made in canon 1429, § 2, but the system had proved impracticable, and the III Plenary Council (1884) devised a system which discarded that portion of Statute 90 of the II Plenary Council with which canon 1429, § 2, has practically become identified. It favored the last part of Statute 90, which provided support for priests in need by means of a tax levied on all parishes (which part of the Statute has now been abrogated through canon 1505).

[40] Canon 1505.

Certainly, the generosity of the faithful, spurred by their appreciation of the services rendered by their clergy, should guarantee the success of a collection solicited for the support of the retired clergy. In fact, it is a common experience to hear comments by the devout laity on the lack of a suitable retreat for aged or retired priests as well as concern for their welfare, generally expressed by the question, "What do they do for priests who retire?" The fund established by the receipts from an annual collection in behalf of the retired clergy has been found by some dioceses to be ample for the fitting support of the retired clergy. Such a fund would also be the recipient of many bequests, so that eventually, sufficient capital would be amassed to enable the ordinary to dispense with the annual collection.

If an ordinary feels that the proper support of the retired clergy cannot be left to the uncertain results of a collection, he could very properly apply to the Holy See for an indult which would permit him to levy a tax on the parishes in the diocese in order to insure enough funds for the proper support of the retired clergy. There is no doubt about the solicitude of the Holy See for the proper support of the indigent and retired clergy, and this solicitude would guarantee a sympathetic hearing for the plea seeking the indult, especially if the ordinary could show that the canonically prescribed methods of supporting the retired clergy were unavailing or not feasible in his diocese.

In conclusion, the following summary of the methods to be employed in providing a sufficient support for the retired clergy is submitted:

1. The Code prescribes that the ordinary may establish suitable pensions for retiring pastors or assistant pastors from the income of the benefice from which they retire (canon 1429, § 2);
2. If the method of securing pensions for the retired clergy as outlined in canon 1429, § 2, cannot be adopted, the ordinary should establish, if possible, an effective clerical mutual assistance society, as was decreed in Statute 71 of the III Plenary Council of Baltimore;

3. If the foregoing methods cannot be applied or if they prove ineffective, the ordinary may institute a collection in the parishes of the diocese for the support of the retired clergy.
4. If the foregoing methods prove impracticable in his diocese, the ordinary may also apply to the Holy See for an indult to allow him to levy a moderate tax on the parishes to establish a fund for the support of the retired clergy.

CHAPTER XI

Fitting Support of Subdeacons and Deacons

The Code states that no one can be ordained to sacred Orders without a canonical title of ordination, in virtue of which title the ordained cleric is to be supported in a manner befitting his clerical state; whoever permits a cleric to be ordained to sacred Orders without a canonical title of ordination, unless authorized by an apostolic indult, must furnish such a cleric with the necessities of life.[1] If a bishop ordains a cleric to sacred Orders with the understanding or pact that the cleric will not demand support from him, such an agreement or pact is null and unenforceable.[2]

Inasmuch as the concept of the fitting support of priests—as pastors and assistant pastors—has been treated in previous chapters, this chapter will consider exclusively the support which is due to other clerics in sacred Orders, that is, to subdeacons and deacons.

Subdeacons and deacons are entitled to those things which in Chapter VII, pages 111 ff., were enumerated as necessary for the fitting support of clerics, with the exception that subdeacons and deacons can hardly expect an allowance from the ordinary for donations to charitable causes or for social obligations. Except possibly for extraordinary cases, subdeacons and deacons are not expected to contribute substantially to charitable causes or to have social obligations involving notable financial expenses. They have, therefore, a right to all personal living expenses and to other sums necessary for the maintenance of their status as seminarians, as well as for the support of dependent members of their families, if

[1] Canon 980, § 1.—Ordinatus in sacris, si titulum amittat, alium sibi provideat, nisi, iudicio Episcopi, eius congruae sustentationi aliter cautum sit.

§ 2. Qui citra apostolicum indultum, suum subditum in sacris sine titulo canonico scienter ordinaverint aut ordinari permiserint, debent ipsi eorumque successores eidem egenti alimenta necessaria praebere, donec congruae eiusdem sustentationi aliter provisum fuerit.

[2] Canon 980, § 3.—Si episcopus aliquem ordinaverit sine titulo canonico cum pacto ut ordinatus non petat ab ipso alimenta, hoc pactum omni vi caret.

such relatives cannot be supported by other members of the family.[8] Of course, an ordinary can refuse ordination to sacred Orders to a cleric in minor orders if he has dependent relatives whose support would be a too great burden upon the finances of the diocese.

Since support is due to a cleric in major Orders in virtue of his title of ordination, it seems certain that he should not be obliged to pay for his expenses in the semiary from the time of his reception of subdiaconate. If he volunteers, however, to pay his expenses and thus to assist the diocese, he is rendering a great service. In those dioceses, therefore, in which the seminarians are asked to agree to repay to the ordinary, in whole or in part, the expenses of their course in the seminary, specific exception should be made for the expenses incurred during the time in which they were in major Orders.

It also follows that the ordinary has a right to assign to a cleric in major Orders any reasonable duties. Generally, of course, subdeacons and deacons are engaged in studies preparatory to the reception of ordination to the priesthood. During the summer months, however, the ordinary has the right to request a subdeacon or deacon to assist a pastor in a parish, or to do catechetical work; such clerics, of course, have a right to support while performing such duties.

Although all clerics in major Orders have a right to a fitting support, there is more elasticity in the concept of what constitutes a fitting support for deacons and subdeacons than in that affecting the support of priests and clerics of higher rank; obviously these lower major Orders do not connate a dignity equal to that which attaches to the higher major Orders. Consequently a greater latitude is permissible in determining the extent of the fitting support owed to such clerics and in employing the means for guaranteeing or securing that support.

---

[8] The provisions of the Code of Canon Law concerning the support of deacons and subdeacons are fulfilled by means of the support that is accorded in the major seminary, especially as accorded by the major seminaries in most parts of Europe, in which everything is supplied to the seminarians, even all items of clothing.

It is a practice in many dioceses for the ordinary to permit even subdeacons during the vacation months to perform work such as typing or clerking, which is not incongruous with the status of such a cleric, in order to assist his family.

CHAPTER XII

The Support of Delinquent Clerics

The diverse penalties imposed on delinquent clerics imply, on the part of their ordinaries, certain duties in regard to the support of such clerics. The Code provides that every secular cleric who has received major Orders is entitled to support unless he has been guilty of such a crime that he suffers deposition, perpetual deprivation of the clerical habit, or degradation.[1] Even if he is deposed but repentant, the ordinary is obliged in charity to afford him at least a minimum of support; the cleric, however, has no claim in justice to this support.[2]

The duty of an ordinary in regard to the support of delinquent clerics can be conveniently studied according to the main division of penalties into censures and vindicative penalties.

Section 1. Support for a Cleric Under Censure

Since a censure is a penalty which is inflicted only on a person who is both delinquent and contumacious, and from which the person must be absolved when he proves himself penitent, the Ordinary has no duty to provide support for a cleric who has incurred a censure which, either after sentence has been pronounced or by the commission of the crime, involves the loss of income. Obviously, a cleric cannot expect support from the Church while contumaciously persevering in a sin to which is attached a censure, since he can free himself of the censure and sin by amending his bahavior.

---

[1] Canons 980, § 1; 2298, 6°; 2299, § 3; 2303; 2304; 2305; Smith, *Elements of Ecclesiastical Law,* III, 95; Sipos, *Enchiridion Iuris Canonici,* p. 947; Stephen A. Findlay, *Canonical Norms Governing the Deposition and Degradation of Clerics,* The Catholic University of America Canon Law Studies, n. 130 (Washington, D. C.: The Catholic University of America Press, 1941), pp. 167 ff. (hereafter referred to as *Deposition and Degradation of Clerics*).

[2] Canon 2303, § 2.

[3] Canons 2241; 2255, § 1; 2266; 2280.

There are three kinds of censures which may be imposed on delinquent clerics: excommunication, interdict, and suspension.[4] These censures have different effects upon the income of the cleric upon whom they are imposed. The censures of excommunication and personal interdict, after the declaration or imposition of such censures, deprive a cleric of the income from all ecclesiastical dignities, offices, benefices and pensions[5] which amounts to deprivation of practically all the income received from the Church.[6] The effects of suspension on the income of a cleric are separable.[7] In addition to the general suspension which involves the exclusion of a cleric from the exercise of his office and from the enjoyment of income from his benefice, there is also suspension *a beneficio* (from the benefice), suspension *ab officio* (from the office), suspension *a divinis* (from sacred functions), and suspension *ab ordinibus* (from orders), which involve deprivation of some or all of the income of a cleric who has incurred such a penalty.[8]

The censure of suspension from the benefice deprives a cleric of his income from that benefice, but permits him to live in the parish house and to administer the goods of the benefice; if he takes any of the income of the benefice, he is obliged to restitution.[9] Hence, if the pastor of a parish in the United States incurs the censure of suspension from the benefice, he would be deprived of his salary.

The censure of suspension from the office does not take away from a cleric the income from his benefice, his pension, or, if he has been ordained on the title of the service of the diocese or of the mission, his salary, or the enjoyment of the living quarters

[4] Canon 2255.

[5] Canon 2266; Coronata, *Institutiones Iuris Canonici,* IV, 213.

[6] An excommunicated cleric may receive a stole fee or an offering for administering the sacraments on those unusual occasions when he is so permitted to exercise his sacred ministry.—Canon 2261. These occasions are so few and the income from them so irregular and small that it would be almost negligible.

[7] Canon 2278, § 2; Wernz-Vidal, *Ius Canonicum,* VII, 335; Vermeersch-Creusen, *Epitome Iuris Canonici,* III, 289.

[8] Canons 2278 § 2; 2279; Vermeersch-Creusen, *Epitome Iuris Canonici,* III, 290.

[9] Canon 2280; Wernz-Vidal, *Ius Canonicum,* VII, 334.

which have been assigned to him.[10] Of course, such a cleric is deprived of certain other income, such as stole fees and similar emoluments which would have accrued to him from the performance of those acts of the sacred ministry which under the suspension he is forbidden to exercise.

Likewise, the censures of suspension *a divinis* and *ab ordinibus* (as well as suspension from any or all of the sacred Orders) deprive a cleric upon whom they are imposed of the income which he would have received had he not been barred from the exercise of those sacred Orders.[11] As in the case of clerics who have been excommunicated, but upon whom a declaratory or condemnatory sentence has not been pronounced, the faithful may for any just reason petition a suspended priest to administer to them the sacraments or sacramentals, especially if no other minister is available; however, the faithful may petition the sacraments of penance and extreme unction from a priest suspended by a declaratory or condemnatory sentence only in danger of death.[12]

It seems that in none of these cases of censure is the bishop obliged to extend support to the cleric thus affected because the cleric, by his penitence, can secure absolution from his sin and the censure attached to it. It must be remembered, however, that even after a cleric has been absolved from a censure and is therefore free of its effects in regard to his income, the ordinary can inflict, as a punishment for his misdeed, a vindicative penalty that will deprive him of part or all of his income.[13] The duty of the bishop to support a cleric in such an eventuality will receive consideration in the next section.

SECTION 2. SUPPORT FOR CLERICS SUFFERING VINDICATIVE PENALTIES

Vindicative penalties are those which are intended directly for the expiation of a delict and for restoring the disturbed public order; therefore their duration does not depend upon the penitence of the

---

[10] Canons 2279, § 1; 2280, § 1; Coronata, *Institutiones Iuris Canonici,* IV, 253.

[11] Canon 2279, § 2, 2°, 3°; Coronata, *Institutiones Iuris Canonici,* IV, 253.

[12] Canons 2284; 2261.

[13] Canons 2286; 2291, 12°; Vermeersch-Creusen, *Epitome Iuris Canonici,* III, 294; Wernz-Vidal, *Ius Canonicum,* VII, 343.

cleric.[14] Vindicative penalties are remitted by dispensation, not by absolution; their remission is *in forma gratiae*, not *in forma iustitiae*. An appeal may be made to the Ordinary or to the competent authority for granting the dispensation,[15] but the appeal is not made in the name of justice, and therefore may be refused. In this respect the remission of vindicative penalties differs widely from that of censures. However, in more urgent cases, if the cleric cannot observe the penalty for a secret sin without betraying publicly his guilt, he may appeal to his confessor for a dispensation; the confessor must have recourse, if possible, to the ordinary or to the Sacred Penitentiary within a month.[16]

Vindicative penalties may be imposed for a temporary or a perpetual duration, or for an unspecified duration of time—*ad nutum superioris*.[17]

Although there are many different kinds of vindicative penalties, consideration is here given only to those which affect the income of clerics. The principal vindicative penalties affecting the income of clerics upon whom they are imposed are: temporary of perpetual suspension either *ab officio* or *a divinis*,[18] deprivation of one's benefice or office,[19] deprivation of some right connected with an office or benefice,[20] deposition,[21] perpetual privation of the clerical habit[22] and degradation.[23]

---

[14] Canons 2286; 2291; 2298. The great majority of the delinquent clerics with whom the ordinary must deal are those upon whom vindicative penalties have been imposed or will be imposed, since the unfortunate cleric usually does not approach the ordinary until he is penitent and has secured absolution from any censure he may have incurred.

[15] Canon 2289; Beste, *Introductio in Codicem*, p. 948; Vermeersch-Creusen, *Epitome Iuris Canonici*, III, 295.

[16] Canon 2290; Vermeersch-Creusen, *Epitome Iuris Canonici*, III, 295; Beste, *Introductio in Codicem*, p. 949; Wernz-Vidal, *Ius Canonicum*, VII, 357.

[17] Canon 2298, 2°; Wernz-Vidal, *Ius Canonicum*, VII, 335; Coronata, *Institutiones Iuris Canonici*, IV, 270.

[18] Canon 2298, 2°.

[19] Canon 2298, 6°.

[20] Canon 2298, 4°.

[21] Canon 2303; Wernz-Vidal, *Ius Canonicum*, VII, 375; Coronata, *Institutiones Iuris Canonici*, IV, 274; Beste, *Introductio in Codicem*, p. 952.

[22] Canon 2304; Wernz-Vidal, *Ius Canonicum*, VII, 379; Vermeersch-Creusen, *Epitome Iuris Canonici*, III, 304.

[23] Canon 2305; Wernz-Vidal, *Ius Canonicum*, VII, 385; Coronata, *Institutiones Iuris Canonici*, IV, 275.

In view of the fact that a vindicative penalty may endure perpetually with its consequent deprivation of income for the cleric and that it may endure despite the penitence of the cleric, the Church has wisely made provision for the support of clerics who have incurred vindicative penalties but still remain worthy of support by the Church because of their clerical status. Thus the lesser vindicative penalties—suspension *ab officio* and *a divinis,* deprivation of one's benefice or office, deprivation of some right joined or connected with an office or benefice—do not take away the right of a cleric to receive support, and leave him eligible to regain his office and benefice together with its income.

The vindicative penalty of deposition, which is by its nature perpetual, takes away from a cleric upon whom it is imposed the right to receive support, but also imposes upon the ordinary of such a cleric the obligation of charity to extend support (*subsidium caritativum*) to the deposed cleric if he leads a proper clerical life.[24] But the penalty of deposition renders the cleric ineligible to regain his office, pension or benefice from which he was deposed.[25]

The very severe penalties of perpetual privation of the clerical garb and of degradation deprive the cleric upon whom they are inflicted of any right to receive support, and relieve the bishop of all obligation to support him.[26] The penalties of perpetual privation of the clerical garb and of degradation are by their nature of perpetual duration, and render the cleric upon whom they are imposed ineligible to regain any office, pension or benefice.[27]

The reason why a cleric who has become suspended through the imposition of a vindicative penalty has a right to receive support from the Church is that he still belongs to the ranks of the clergy, and although he is judged not worthy of performing the duties of an office, the dignity of the clerical state demands that he be supported. It has been the constant teaching of the Church that a cleric, for the honor of his sacred character, should not be forced to beg or to work at an unbecoming trade—"it is not becoming for

---

[24] Canons 2303, § 2; 2304, § 1.

[25] Canon 2303, § 1.

[26] Canons 2304, § 2; 2303, § 1.

[27] Canons 2304, § 1; 2305, § 1; 2303, § 1; Findlay, *Deposition and Degradation of Clerics,* pp. 142, 171, 203.

those who are enrolled in the divine ministry to beg or to exercise any sordid trade to the disgrace of their Order."[28]

The mind of the Church concerning the support of delinquent priests is illustrated in a decision of the Sacred Congregation of Bishops and Regulars in the year 1893. Two neighboring bishops requested the Sacred Congregation to determine which diocese owed support to a delinquent priest. There was no question about the duty of some Ordinary to support such a priest who apparently was not guilty of a crime entailing perpetual deprivation of the clerical habit or degradation.[29] The Sacred Congregation decided which bishop owed support to the cleric and enjoined him to supply it.

The general law of the Church regarding the support of clerics who have suffered a vindicative penalty (excepting deposition,

---

[28] Conc. Trident., sess. XXI, *de ref.*, c. 2.

[29] S.C. Ep. et Reg., *Colonien, seu Limburgen.*, 24 febr., 1893—*ASS*, XXV (1893), 627.

The privileges enjoyed by a cleric are conferred on him not in consideration of his personal merit or by way of reward, but in recognition of the dignity of the clerical state. They are the *privilegium canonis* (canon 119), the *privilegium fori* (canon 120), the *exemptio a muneribus publicis* (canon 121), and the *beneficium competentiae* (canon 122). Since these privileges are accorded for the benefit of the clerical state, the individual cleric cannot renounce them (canon 123). The Church alone can, for a just cause, deprive a cleric of these privileges, and is understandably loath to exercise this right.

Apart from the general privileges are the rights and obligations which belong to a cleric in virtue of his status in Orders and his tenure of an office. For instance, a priest in good standing has a right to say Mass (canons 804, 805), and a pastor has a right to assist at the marriage of his parishioners, baptize them, etc. (canon 462). The Church can for a reason deprive a cleric of the exercise of these rights or of his office without depriving him of his clerical privileges. Hence a priest can be suspended (thus deprived of his income) and still enjoy his clerical privileges.

In addition to the other rights of clerics, every cleric in major Orders (a subdeacon, deacon or a priest) has a right to support from his ordinary (canon 980). The cleric loses this right to receive support only when he commits such a crime that he suffers the severe penalties of deposition, perpetual privation of the ecclesiastical habit, or degradation (canons 2303, 2304, 2305). Thus a priest can suffer the penalty of suspension which deprives him of his specific income, but he still has a right to receive support from his ordinary in virtue of his reception of sacred orders.

perpetual privation of the clerical garb, and degradation) is contained in canon 2299, § 3:

> Nequit clericus privari beneficio aut pensione cuius titulo ordinatus fuit, nisi aliunde eius honestae sustentationi provideatur, salvo praescripto can. 2303, 2304.

Of course a cleric could not be deprived of his patrimony, if that was the title on which he was ordained, inasmuch as such a deprivation is not within the competency of ecclesiastical jurisdiction.

It will be noted that the Church is not concerned about minor financial losses resulting from the imposition of lesser vindicative penalties, such as forbidding a cleric to preach[80] or suspending him from the performance of sacred functions (*suspensio a divinis*), which would entail the loss of stole fees and Mass stipends. Deprivation of revenue is a legitimate penalty, and the Church can impose a fine as a penalty.[81] The Church is concerned, however, with securing for a cleric, if he be deserving of it, enough income for his support, even if that cleric has contravened the laws of the Church, but later has proved himself penitent or at least has not suffered the penalty of degradation or the perpetual deprivation of the clerical garb.

Hence, although canon 2299, § 3, states only that an ordinary is bound to supply a respectable support for a cleric who has been deprived of a benefice or a pension which served as a title for his ordination (except for the cases involved in canons 2303 and 2304), this rule of support applies also to priests who have been ordained on the title of service of the diocese.[82] The reason why a bishop must support clerics who have been deprived of a benefice or a pension through the imposition of a vindicative penalty applies also to priests ordained on the title of service of the diocese or of the mission—respect for the dignity of the clerical state and the fact that the clerics have not been guilty of sufficiently serious crimes

---

[80] Canon 2299, § 2; Coronata, *Institutiones Iuris Canonici,* IV, 271.

[81] Canon 2291, 12°; Wernz-Vidal, *Ius Canonicum,* VII, 358.

[82] Pastors of parishes in the United States are considered to have benefices. A good summary of the decisions on this matter is found in Beste, *Introductio in Codicem,* pp. 228, 714.

to incur the deprivation of all the privileges of the clerical state. Clerics ordained on the title of service of the diocese have as much right to support as clerics ordained on the title of benefice or pension.

To how much support is a cleric entitled when through a vindicative penalty he has become deprived of his benefice, his pension or the income accruing to him from ordination on the title of service of the diocese? Canon 2299, § 3, states that he is owed a respectable support, *honesta sustentatio.* This is a measure of support which will enable him to take care of his needs in a convenient manner, so that he will have no need of begging or of engaging in unclerical work for the purpose of supporting himself. Therefore, the amount of this support should not be a mere pittance that would reduce him to threadbare poverty. It should be enough to take care of the ordinary needs of a cleric, but not enough to permit the enjoyment of comforts which a priest in good standing could expect—such as a vacation in the summer or the ownership of an automobile. He should receive adequate housing and food besides enough to clothe himself decently and respectably, to obtain medical care, to purchase books for study, and to enjoy such ordinary and commonplace conveniences as cigarettes, newspapers and occasional recreation.

Obviously, a cleric to whom this respectable support, *honesta sustentatio,* is owed should not receive as much as the cleric in good standing who has a right to a fiitting support, *congrua sustentatio,* commensurate with his merits and position. He should. on the other hand, receive more than the minimum support which an Ordinary, in charity, should accord to a deposed cleric;[33] the Ordinary should not, however, accord such generous support to such a cleric that he would appear to be encouraging delinquency or incompetency.

Although an Ordinary is bound to furnish support to a cleric who has been deprived of his benefice or pension (if such deprivation is not the result of deposition, perpetual deprivation of the clerical garb, or degradation), he is absolved from this duty if the cleric

---

[33] Canon 2303, § 2; Coronata, *Institutiones Iuris Canonici,* IV, 273; Wernz-Vidal, *Ius Canonicum,* VII, 375.

has other means of support. These other means of support could be private funds or income from some work of the ministry which the cleric is permitted to perform, such as that of preaching, of serving as an assistant pastor in a parish, or of assisting in the work of an ecclesiastical tribunal, etc.[34] Thus a cleric could be removed from a benefice, or could suffer the deprivation of an ecclesiastical pension, and yet be permitted to do work that would befit his clerical status and that would amply support him; for instance, a priest who by means of a vindicative penalty has been removed from his parochial benefice could be assigned as an assistant pastor to a different parish, and thus be supported.

Vindicative penalties may be temporary or perpetual,[35] but for the period of their duration the ordinary has the duty to furnish a respectable support to the cleric who has thus been punished, unless, as has been stated before, the cleric has suffered the penalty of deposition, of perpetual deprivation of the ecclesiastical garb, or of degradation. The ordinary, however, can require the cleric suffering the penalty to reside in the place designated by him.

SECTION 3. SUPPORT OF DEPOSED CLERICS

If, unfortunately, a cleric is guilty of a crime for which he suffers deposition, he is deprived of the benefice or pension he enjoyed, even if either of these served as a title for his ordination, and is also deprived of any office to which he was appointed.[36] Nevertheless, if such a deposed cleric is really in want, the ordinary is in charity to provide at least a minimum livelihood, so that

[34] Coronata, *Institutiones Iuris Canonici,* IV, 271.

[35] Canon 2298.

[36] Canon 2303, § 1. The penalty of deposition can be imposed only for the commission of certain crimes; these crimes are: 1) apostasy, heresy or schism (canon 2314, § 1); 2) profanation of the Sacred Species (canon 2320); 3) violation of corpses or graves (canon 2328); 4) abortion (canon 2350, § 1); 5) serious violations of personality, liberty, property (canon 2354); 6) grave delicts against the Sixth Commandment (canon 2359, § 2); 7) violations of the laws concerning the wearing of the ecclesiastical garb (canon 188, 7°); 8) unlawful possession of ecclesiastical offices, benefices, dignities (canon 2394, 1°, 2°); 9) continuation in office after the pronouncement of a decree of deprivation or removal (canon 2401).

the cleric will not be forced to beg or to engage in a trade with consequent dishonor to the clerical state.[37]

The ordinary is required by an obligation arising from charity to provide this sustenance according to his own judgment. The deposed cleric has no right in justice to such support. The duty of the ordinary to provide this minimum support is no less compelling for the reason that it is urged by charity rather than by justice. The basic reason on which rests the ordinary's duty in charity to furnish support is not the consideration of pity for the plight of the deposed cleric, but of esteem for the dignity of the clerical state. The reason which requires that the cleric who suffers a lesser vindicative penalty shall receive a *honesta sustentatio* is also the reason which demands that a deposed cleric shall receive at least a minimum support, a *sustentatio caritativa*—the dignity of the clerical state, which would be dishonored if the cleric needed to do unbecoming work or to beg for support.[38]

The deposed cleric qualifies for this support owed to him because of his clerical dignity in view of his own respect for that dignity—by his penitence for his disgraceful conduct. Therefore it should be given only as long as the deposed cleric obeys the command of his ecclesiastical superior and leads a decent clerical life. If he fails to do this, his claim for charitable support ceases.[39] As long as a deposed cleric leads a decent clerical life he also has the right to wear the ecclesiastical garb and shares in the clerical privileges.

If the deposed cleric has sufficient funds for his support from his private means or from any other legitimate source, he has no right to any charitable subsidy from his ordinary. The duty of the ordinary is not one of contributing to the comfort of the deposed cleric, but one of preventing dishonor to the clerical state by allowing the cleric to be reduced to beggary. It is a duty of a negative character, of prevention of further harm, rather than

[37] Canon 2303, § 2; Vermeersch-Creusen, *Epitome Iuris Canonici,* III, 300; Coronata, *Institutiones Iuris Canonici,* IV, 259; Eduard Eichmann, *Das Strafrecht des* CODEX IURIS CANONICI (Paderborn, 1920), p. 119.

[38] Findlay, *Deposition and Degradation of Clerics,* p. 167; Sipos, *Enchiridion Iuris Canonici,* p. 947.

[39] Canon 2304, § 1.

any duty of directly fostering the welfare of the deposed cleric. Hence, if a deposed cleric enjoys a patrimony or any other source of income sufficient for his support, he has no right to a charitable subsidy.[40]

How much support is owed to a deposed cleric? What amount is due as a *sustentatio caritativa?* The measure of this charitable support should definitely be notably lower than the fitting support that is due not only to a cleric who is in good standing but also to a cleric who has incurred a lesser vindicative penalty. The ordinary must supply funds to provide the essentials of life—adequate food, sufficient housing, proper clothing, medical care, and books suitable for reading and study. This support would also include such minor and commonly accepted luxuries as tobacco and occasional recreation.[41] If these things are supplied today in secular penal institutions, it must be accepted that with greater reason they should likewise be supplied to repentant clerics.

This charitable support or subsidy should be given by the ordinary not in such generous measure that the cleric does not suffer some penalty or deprivation of income; it should not be so much as a pension. Too great generosity on the part of the ordinary could create a semblance of approbation or encouragement of the delinquency.[42] Although in extraordinary circumstances it would be permissible for an ordinary to be very generous to a deposed cleric, it would certainly not be judicious to adopt this course as a policy. However, since the determination of the amount of the charitable support is left to the prudent judgment of the ordinary, he could certainly treat each case separately and without reference to any predetermined policy.

The ordinary may accord this charitable support to a deposed cleric on the condition that the cleric reside in some specified locality or remain at some designated institution.[43] The cleric has no right to demand that this charitable support be given him

[40] Findlay, *Deposition and Degradation of Clerics,* p. 169.

[41] Smith, *Elements of Ecclesiastical Law,* III, 95-97.

[42] Sipos, *Enchiridion Iuris Canonici,* p. 1002.

[43] Canon 2301; Coronata, *Institutiones Iuris Canonici,* IV, 272; Wernz-Vidal, *Ius Canonicum,* VII, 367; Vermeersch-Creusen, *Epitome Iuris Canonici,* III, 301.

in a place of his own choosing. Naturally, peculiar circumstances of health may render it necessary or highly advisable that the deposed cleric be allowed to live in a certain locality. The ordinary would be evading the purpose of the law if he ordered a deposed but penitent cleric to go to a place so harsh and forbidding in its regime that he knew the cleric would leave and thus free the ordinary of his legal obligation of support.

If an ordinary orders a deposed cleric to go to a house of penance or an institution which is not located in his diocese, he must first secure the permission of the ordinary of that place, or, if the house belongs to an exempt religious congregation or order, he must secure the permission of the religious superior.[44] The caution of the law[45] that the ordinary should be temperate in the determination of the time a cleric should stay in a house of penance is particularly apt in this country; it is very doubtful that such a command is enforceable in the civil law.[46]

If however a diocese is in such straitened financial circumstances that it cannot afford assistance to a deposed cleric, it would not be possible to prove that the ordinary is bound to afford such assistance at the cost of severe inconvenience or strain on the financial resources of the diocese. Such a situation may be rare, but it could arise if a deposed cleric were in need of extraordinary medical attention (because of a malignant, chronic disease) over a long period of time; in such a case it seems that the ordinary could rightfully plead inability to sustain such an expense. Under these circumstances it appears allowable for the Ordinary to have the deposed cleric avail himself of the public clinical and public institutional treatment that would efficiently though not very comfortably meet the cleric's needs. Clearly, the deposed cleric has no

[44] Canon 2301. Such houses of penance are generally erected with the understanding that the ordinaries of the surrounding dioceses will be permitted to send clerics there.

[45] Canons 2303; 2214, § 2.

[46] Because of this difficulty, some Concordats specifically empower the Church to regulate such houses of penance, e.g., Article 28 of the Concordat with Germany, signed in 1933.—Ioannes Restrepo-Restrepo, *Concordata Regnante Sanctissimo Domino Pio PP. XI Inita* (Romae: Pontificia Universitas Gregoriana, 1934), p. 587.

right to demand the type of medical treatment that he prefers. However, except for such unusual cases, it is very difficult to conceive how a diocese could not afford to a deposed cleric the minimum sustenance demanded by the Code.

SECTION 4. SUPPORT OF CLERICS SUFFERING TEMPORARY DEPRIVATION OF THE ECCLESIASTICAL GARB

In order that the Ordinary may have an effective method of correcting a scandalous situation and of effectively punishing a cleric without inflicting the very severe and perpetual vindicative penalties, the Ordinary is empowered by the Church to deprive a cleric temporarily of the right to wear the ecclesiastical garb; this temporary deprivation, while it lasts, imposes the prohibition of exercising the sacred ministry in any manner, and deprives the punished cleric of the clerical privileges.[47] This regulation, new in the Code, leaves the cleric in possession of his office, but prohibits him from exercising his power of Orders or of jurisdiction.[48]

Inasmuch as the penalty of temporary deprivation of the ecclesiastical garb is embodied in a new law, the full scope of its application and effects remains uncertain. Since penal laws must be given a strict interpretation, it is evident that this law does not take away from a cleric the income due to his office; hence, if he is a pastor and is punished with the temporary deprivation of the right to wear the ecclesiastical garb, he may continue to receive his salary. A cleric punished with this penalty could not, however, receive the income derived from acts of the sacred ministry, since in the law it is forbidden to him to perform them. However, it seems very strange that a cleric could suffer a penalty which takes away, for the duration of the penalty, all his clerical privileges, and yet leaves secure for him the income from his office.

---

[47] "Si clericus gravia scandala praebeat et monitus non resipiscat, nec scandalum queat aliter removeri, potest interim privari iure deferendi habitum ecclesiasticum; quae privatio, dum perdurat, secumfert prohibitionem exercendi ministeria quaevis ecclesiastica et privationem privilegiorum clericalium."—Canon 2399; Vermeersch-Creusen, *Epitome Iuris Canonici,* III, 303; Wernz-Vidal, *Ius Canonicum,* VII, 367.

[48] Coronata, *Institutiones Iuris Canonici,* IV, 272.

This new law as contained in canon 2300 constitutes an exception to the general jurisprudence of the Church, which makes perpetual the penalties which deprive a cleric of the privileges of his state. Like the lesser vindicative penalties, this temporary deprivation of the ecclesiastical garb leaves the cleric eligible to regain the exercise of his sacred duties; but unlike the lesser vindicative penalties, it takes away, for the duration of the penalty, the clerical privileges.

This penalty therefore leaves unimpaired the salary of a cleric, and thus introduces no problem concerning his fitting support.

SECTION 5. SUPPORT OF CLERICS SUFFERING PERPETUAL DEPRIVATION OF THE ECCLESIASTICAL GARB (AGGRAVATED DEPOSITION) AND DEGRADATION

If a deposed cleric shows no signs of repentance and continues to lead a scandalous life despite warnings given by his superiors, he can be perpetually deprived of the right to wear the ecclesiastical garb, with the consequence that the ordinary is no longer obliged to give him any charitable support (*subsidium caritativum*).[49] This penalty has been called "aggravated deposition," for it always presupposes that the cleric has been deposed, or that he has incurred the perpetual deprivation of the ecclesiastical garb.[50]

Whatever be the correct appellation of the penalty listed in canon 2304, in effect it deprives the deposed cleric of all sustenance furnished by the Church. The ordinary no longer has a duty, even in charity, to support the incorrigible deposed cleric. The cleric is completely deprived of the privileges of a cleric, and among them is the forfeited right to receive support.

The penalty of degradation, the most severe in the Church, reduces a cleric to the lay state, thus depriving him of his clerical

---

[49] Canon 2304.

[50] The penalty listed in canon 2304 is called a perpetual deprivation of the ecclesiastical garb by the following authors: Augustine, *A Commentary on the Code of Canon Law,* VIII, 261; Blat, *Commentarium Textus Codicis Iuris Canonici* (5 vols. in 6, Lib. V, Romae: Typografia Pontificia, 1924), V, 186; Sipos, *Enchiridion Iuris Canonici,* p. 948.

status with its attendant privileges and rights including the right to receive support.[51] Unlike deposition, which still leaves the delinquent cleric in the clerical state, the penalty of degradation takes away his status as a cleric and juridically makes him a lay person. Such a person has absolutely no claim to support from the Church.

Like the penalty of deposition, degradation can be imposed only by a tribunal of five judges,[52] and only subsequent to the conviction on the charge of the commission of certain delicts.[53] Moreover, like deposition, it is by its nature a vindicative penalty of perpetual duration, from which a dispensation can be granted only under papal authority.[54]

---

[51] Canon 2305; Vermeersch-Creusen, *Epitome Iuris Canonici,* III, 304; Wernz-Vidal, *Ius Canonicum,* VII, 384.

[52] Canon 1576, § 1.

[53] Canon 2305, § 1. The causes for degradation are: 1) adherence to a non-Catholic sect (canon 2314, § 1); 2) violence to the Holy Father (canon 2343, § 1); 3) culpable homicide (canon 2354, § 2); 4) solicitation (canon 2368, § 1); 5) violation of the seal of confession (canon 2368, § 1); 6) attempted marriage (canon 2388, § 1).

[54] Canon 2289.

CONCLUSIONS

The canonical concept of the fitting support, *congrua sustentatio,* of the secular clergy means that measure of maintenance which provides a living proper to the clergy in consideration of their dignity and merits according to the economic standards of the locality. Such a fiitting support includes, therefore, in addition to the essentials of adequate housing, food and clothing, a proper allowance for medical care, study, moderate recreation, donations to charitable causes, prudent provision for the future (unless an adequate pension system is in effect in the diocese), and support of the dependent members of one's family if such support is not available from other near-relatives.

The amount constituting this fitting support differs among clerics, since it depends upon such variables as the ecclesiastical dignity and merits of the cleric as well as the circumstances of the parish and the region. It is the duty of the ordinary to determine the amount constituting the fitting support of the clergy. The clergy are to eschew all ostentatious and luxurious living regardless of the prosperous economic conditions of their region. The surplus beneficial income of a cleric must be devoted to charitable or to pious causes.

The proper care of souls is not to be made subservient to the appropriate standard of living owed to the clergy under normal circumstances; the principle, *salus animarum suprema lex,* is applicable also to the claim of the clergy to fitting support. Thus, for the sake of the spiritual good of the faithful, an ordinary can appoint a pastor to a poor parish which is incapable of properly supporting the pastor but is capable of providing for him the minimum support. This minimum support, according to the traditional teaching of the Church and as specified in the legislation of the III Plenary Council of Baltimore, comprises all necessary current living expenses.

A cleric of the secular clergy secures a right to a fitting support by his ordination to sacred Orders. Regardless of the kind of duty to which the cleric is appointed by his ordinary—e.g., pastoral work, curial duties, graduate studies, administrative work—he is owed a fitting support by the ordinary.

A cleric retains his right to a fitting support as long as he is in good standing. If a cleric is forced to retire from the active ministry because of ill health or advanced age, the ordinary is still obliged to provide him with a fitting support.

Provision for the proper support of retired priests can be made according to a number of methods. The preferable method, established by the Code, is the granting of a suitable pension from the income of the parish from which the cleric retires; this method was intended primarily for regions where the majority of the clergy were ordained on the title of benefice, and consequently this method is not well adapted to general use in our country. Other methods of providing support for the clergy, better adapted to the condition of the Church in this country, were proposed by the III Plenary Council of Baltimore in 1884, but the first two methods proposed by the Council have been abrogated through canon 1505. The methods abrogated through canon 1505 were the establishment of a fund for the support of indigent priests by means either of a tax on the parishes or of a tax on the income of the clergy in relatively affluent circumstances. The third method proposed by the III Plenary Council was the establishment of a clerical mutual-aid society; this method has not proved effective or practicable in many dioceses. Another possible method, and apparently the most feasible, is the establishment of a fund for retired priests from the proceeds of a voluntary collection for this purpose in the parishes of the diocese. If all these methods prove ineffective or impracticable, the ordinary may petition for an indult from the Holy See to impose a moderate tax on the parishes for the erection of a fund to provide support for indigent priests.

A cleric loses his right to support only upon conviction for those crimes which entail the application of the severe penalties of the perpetual deprivation of the ecclesiastical garb or of degradation. Although a deposed cleric has no right in justice to receive support from the Church, the ordinary is obliged by charity and respect for the dignity of the clerical state to accord to a deposed cleric a minimum support.

The attitude in the United States towards the support of the clergy has been conditioned by the not far-distant missionary history of our country with the consequence that not all the canonical provisions for the support of the clergy have been realized. There has been a tendency to overlook, possibly for the reason submitted, the priest's duty of supporting or of helping to support dependent near-relatives; the duty of a priest in such circumstances naturally involves a right to receive enough income to enable him to discharge that duty. In some dioceses there has also been a tendency to disregard the duty to provide the fitting support owed to a priest engaged in graduate study in response to the command of his ordinary. However, in most of the dioceses in the eastern part of the United States the clergy are adequately supported. It is estimated that an annual aggregate income of about $2,400 is necessary for the proper support of a pastor in a busy parish if he must use a car in his pastoral work; an assistant pastor, who presumably has fewer social and charitable obligations as well as a smaller medical expense than a pastor, needs an income of about $1,800 a year if he must use a car in his work. A priest may have a right to more than these amounts if his personal circumstances require a greater income. These amounts should be sufficient to enable the priests to save something for disability or eventual retirement, but certainly not enough to dispense with assistance from the diocese in the event of long disability or retirement.

The greatest handicap to securing a fitting support for all the clergy in a diocese which has many poor parishes is the variance between the canonical legislation governing the disposition of income of benefices and the present conditions in such dioceses; the canonical legislation restricts the use of the income from a benefice (as a parish) to the needs of the beneficiary and the benefice. Thus an ordinary cannot direct that part of the surplus income of a wealthy parish be used in payment of the salaries or pensions of the clergy of nearby poor parishes. Wherefore the eminent canonist Coronata suggests at least a change in canon 1429, so that the ordinary could permissibly assign to a retired priest a pension drawn from the surplus income of any wealthy parish in the diocese.

* * * * *

If a general observation is permitted at the end of this work, it should be noted that the Catholic clergy in our country have earned an enviable record in their disposition of the income of the Church. This admirable record has been earned not only by the zealous pioneer priests—including the indomitable Spanish, French and English priests—but by the clergy of our own time. While the income of the Church has increased enormously, the income of the clergy has remained at a very modest level. In many of the wealthy parishes the salaries of the clergy constitute only three per cent of the income of the parish. The income of the Church has been used principally for the construction of an excellent parochial and educational system that has preserved the faith of our Catholic people in the midst of an increasingly materialistic culture. Seldom has the Church witnessed in its history such a general wise and pious use of great wealth.

The learned and saintly Alcuin (735-804) made the claim that, although he had been given the use of 20,000 serfs, he had never used one for his personal comfort. Many bishops and priests in the present territory of the United States could justly make the same claim about the wealth that has been entrusted to them by the faithful. The present material prosperity of the Church in the United States is not only a monument to the generosity of the Catholic laity, but it is a testimonial to the spirit of abnegation and generosity of the clergy, which elicited such generosity through the assurance that such contributions would be scrupulously devoted to the cause of the faith.

APPENDIX I

Manner of Computing and Arranging a Pension

First, the pension granted to the retiring pastor or assistant pastor is not deducted from the salary of the incoming beneficiary, but is drawn from the amount of the parish income which is left after the parish expenses and irregular income have been deducted.[1] The expenses of the parish include those required for the normal maintenance of the parish buildings, the allotting of the stipends of founded Masses, the payments of insurance, of ecclesiastical assessments, of the interest on the debt of the parish, and of pensions already levied on the parish.[2]

The salary of the pastor would not be included in the parish expenses, but the salaries of the assistant pastors would be included in view of the difference in the nature of their salaries.[3] The irregular income of the parish includes stole fees, donations and whatever is comprised under incidental fees or perquisites (*iura casualia*).[4] In most dioceses in the United States the items grouped under irregular income are not computed in the parish income when the parish report is submitted to the ordinary. The financial report of the parish submitted to the ordinary could be used as a basis for computing this net income of the parish from which the pensions would be deducted.

The amount deducted from the parish income for the pension or pensions should not exceed a third of the net income, and must likewise leave enough for the fitting support of the newly appointed beneficiary, the pastor.[5]

The pensions granted to pastors or vicars who have retired from a parish can be imposed on a parish benefice at any time. The law does not place any limitation concerning the time when the pensions may be imposed, and grave difficulty would be encountered if a pension could be levied only at the time of appointment of the new incumbent.[6]

---

[1] ". . . quae [pensiones] tamen ne excedant tertiam partem reditus paroeciae, quibusvis deductis expensis et incertis reditibus."—Canon 1429, § 2.

[2] S. A. Gass, *Ecclesiastical Pensions,* The Catholic University of America Canon Law Studies, n. 157 (Washington, D. C.: The Catholic University of America Press, 1942), pp. 142-143; Pasquale Vito, *Questioni Canoniche di materie reguardanti i nostri tempi secondo il Codice di diritto canonico* (5 vols., Napoli: Raffaele Picone, 1926-1932), IV, 149, note.

[3] Confer Chapter VIII, p. 202, and Chapter IX, pp. 232-233.

[4] Gass, *Ecclesiastical Pensions,* p. 144.

[5] Canon 1429, §§ 1, 2.

[6] Canon 1429, §§ 1, 2; Gass, *Ecclesiastical Pensions,* p. 123.

An apparent obstacle which in the law was thought to prevent the acceptance of the resignation of a pastor upon the condition that a pension be accorded him was removed by a decision of the Sacred Congregation of the Council.[7] It is clear that an ordinary can accept the resignation of a pastor with the understanding that the pastor will receive a pension from the income of that benefice.

In determining the amount of a pension, it seems far preferable to establish a percentage tax on the parish income rather than to set a fixed sum, for once the sum is established no power other than the Holy See can directly increase the pension.[8]

---

[7] It was objected that the Ordinary could not accept the resignation of a pastor upon condition that a pension be granted him from that benefice, since canon 1486 states that the Ordinary cannot accept the resignation of a benefice with a condition affecting its revenue. The Sacred Congregation of the Council decided that such a "condition" was not one that was prohibited by the law of canon 1486 since in fact the reservation of the pension follows not from the condition upon which the pastor resigns, but through the act whereby the ordinary establishes the pension.—S.C.C., *Dioecesis N.* (*Renuntiationis paroeciae*), 11 nov. 1922—*AAS,* XV (1923), 454-456.

[8] S.R.Rota, *Vercellen.* (Pensionis), 18 dec. 1928, coram R.P.D., Francisco Parrillo, Dec. LVI—*Sacrae Romanae Rotae Decisiones seu Sententiae quae iuxta Legem Propriam et Constitutionem "Sapienti Consilio" Pii PP. X prodierunt, cura eiusdem S. Tribunalis editae* (Romae, 1912-) XX (1928), 492-498.

APPENDIX II

SYSTEMS OF SUPPORT OF THE SECULAR CLERGY IN SOME OTHER COUNTRIES

AUSTRIA

In Austria the salaries of the clergy are paid by the State. The following is an outline of the regulations for the payment of salaries in the Archdiocese of Vienna; the salary of each cleric is composed of a basic amount (according to the dignity and duties of the cleric) and a supplement computed according to the years of service. This supplement (*Vorrückungsbetrag*) is increased every two years for a period of twenty-two years; thus a priest who has served for twenty-two years receives eleven supplements or eleven times the amount of the biennial supplement listed below. The amounts listed below are monthly rates; the monetary unit is the Schilling (S.).

Status	*Basic Salary*	*Biennial Supplement* (Vorrückungsbetrag)
Dignitary of the Cathedral Chapter	S.650	S.30
Member of the Cathedral Chapter	S.600	S.30
Pastor	S.500	S.18
Cathedral assistant	S.450	S.15
Assistant pastor	S.400	S.12
Priests engaged in administrative work:		
1st group	S.550	S.30
2nd group	S.500	S.22.50
3rd group	S.450	S.15

(The value of the Austrian Schilling, as of March, 1950, is about four cents.)

Members of religious orders who are pastors receive S.550 per month; those who are assistant pastors receive S.450 per month. These members of religious orders do not receive a biennal supplement.[1]

Thus, according to the salary-rates listed above, a priest who has been a pastor for ten years would receive S.590 per month (basic salary of S.500 plus 5 biennial supplements for the ten years of service).

In addition to the remunerations listed a further payment is made to those

---

[1] The information was supplied by courtesy of the Secretariate of the Archdiocese of Vienna in a communication under date of November 29, 1948. The communication contained a copy of the *Besoldungsordnung* (Salary Regulations) for the secular clergy of the Archdiocese of Vienna besides other pertinent information.

clerics who fill certain offices or perform certain duties. The following is a list of the additional payments rendered to clerics for such duties:

Vicar General	S.400 per month
Dean	S. 50 per month
Secretary of the Deanery	S. 25 per month
Priest performing additional pastoral duties	S. 30 per month

Clerics who are engaged as teachers in schools are also recompensed for their services. This compensation ranges, according to the type of school, from twelve to twenty-four Schillings per month for twelve hours of teaching duty per month. Most of the clerics engaged in such work are instructors in religion.

Certain deductions are also made from the salaries of the clerics for the purpose of supplying contributions for beneficial funds. The following deductions are made each month:

For the Clerical Sick Fund	S.10
For the welfare fund for the domestic help:	
Pastors	S.15
Assistant pastors	S. 8

The Clerical Sick Fund is intended apparently for the relief of priests who have suffered an illness which does not necessitate retirement, since adequate provision is made for the support of priests who have retired because of superannuation or illness.

A priest becomes eligible for a pension if he has reached the age of seventy or if illness has forced him to retire from the active ministry. The amount of the pension is reckoned from the aggregate salary of the priest (counting his basic salary and biennial supplement, but not any additional remuneration) in accordance with the following rule: the pension-rate of a priest begins in his first year of service at 41 per cent of his aggregate salary, and increases 1 per cent each year until he has served forty years and has thus attained to a pension-rate of 80 per cent of his aggregate salary. The maximum pension-rate attainable is 80 per cent, regardless of the number of years spent in the active ministry in excess of forty years. A priest who is retired because of sickness receives the pension-rate to which he is entitled in view of his years of service, but the ordinary is empowered to raise his pension-rate in order to afford him the income necessary for his proper support.

Thus the pension of a pastor who has retired after serving a parish for forty years is calculated in the following manner:

basic salary	S.500
biennial supplement	S.198
	S.698

80 per cent (maximum pension-rate) of the aggregate salary, S.698—S.558.40 per month. If the same pastor had served for some years as a dean, his pension would nevertheless remain the same, since the additional remuneration granted for such duties is not computed in the aggregate salary from which the pension is reckoned.

It is evident that the system of support employed in the Archdiocese of Vienna is very equitable, but it shows that equity generally involves a good deal of labor and painstaking effort.

BELGIUM

The following is a communication from the Embassy of Belgium, Washington, D. C., under date of December 3, 1948, concerning the support of the clergy in Belgium by the Government.

> Pursuant to the terms of Article 117 of the Belgian Constitution, the salaries and retirement pensions of the priests of the recognized religions are supported by the Treasury and are inscribed on the annual budget.
>
> The annual salaries of the Catholic clergy, paid by the State, follow the scale hereunder:

Archbishop	373,500 francs
Bishop	298,800 francs
Vicar General of Archdiocese	85,590 francs
Vicar General of Diocese	76,680 francs
Canon of Archdiocese	61,230 francs
Canon of Diocese	56,640 francs
Rector[2]	54,750 francs
Priest in charge	40,710 francs
Chaplain	37,200 francs
Vicar[3]	37,200 francs

> ($1.00 is equivalent to 43.87 Belgian francs)
>
> The salaries do not vary according to the age of the priests or to the importance of the dioceses or parishes.
>
> The retirement pensions of clergymen have been codified by the law of July 21, 1844.
>
> The annual pension is equivalent to the mean salary of the retired priest during the last five years of service.
>
> To be entitled to the full pension, a priest must have reached the age of 65 and have served for a minimum of 30 years.
>
> The clergymen who have not reached their sixty-fifth year but who are obliged to leave their duties on account of infirmities will be entitled to a pension inasmuch as they have served for at least 10 years. These pensions are calculated as follows: for ten years' service, half the full pension plus 1/60 of it for each year of service for those who have served more than 10 and less than 20 years;
> for twenty years, 2/3 of the full pension plus 1/30 of it for each

---

[2] The "Rector" is a pastor.

[3] The "Vicar" is an assistant pastor.

year of duty for those who have served more than 20 and less than 30 years;
for thirty years of service, the full pension.

The Treasury normally grants subsidies for reparations to cathedrals and parish churches amounting to 60 per cent or 30 per cent of the total cost depending upon whether the churches concerned are classified (as) monuments or not.

The necessary appropriations for the payment of salaries to the clergy are inscribed on the budget of the Ministry of Justice; the credits granted for retirement pensions are inscribed on the budget of the Ministry of the Budget and the subsidies for reparations of churches are inscribed on the budget of the Ministry of Public Works.

EIRE

In the dioceses in Eire[4] the support of the clergy according to the benefice-system is maintained. The pastors and assistants are supported through the voluntary offerings of the people and through stole fees. No fixed amount is assigned to the pastors or assistant pastors as their salary. The amount of the income of the clergy depends upon the amount of the income of the parish. However, in the few instances in which assistant pastors live in the same house with the pastor (generally the pastor and assistant pastors live in separate homes) the assistant pastor is accorded a nominal salary of £22 a year. In addition to his nominal salary, such assistant pastors receive voluntary offerings.

In parishes in which there are separate homes for the pastor and the assistant pastors, there is a fixed rate of division of the offerings and stole fees. The division is made on the basis of two parts to the pastor and one part to the assistant pastor. Thus in parishes in which there is one assistant pastor, the pastor receives two-thirds of the offerings and stole fees, while the assistant pastor receives one-third; in parishes in which there are two assistant pastors, the pastor receives one-half, and the assistant pastors each receive one-fourth of the offerings and stole feels, etc.

The arrangements for affording pensions to retired pastors differ according to dioceses. In the Diocese of Limerick, a retired priest is paid an amount determined by the ordinary from the income of the parish from which the priest retired, and if this amount does not total £208, he is given from a Sick Clergy Fund a supplementary allowance which makes his pension equal to that amount. In the Diocese of Dublin there is a Diocesan Clerical Fund, composed of contributions deriving from the clergy and through bequests, and it is employed for the support of retired priests. If at the end of the year there is a balance in the Fund, this money is divided *pro rata* among the priests who have incurred hospital expenses during the preceding year.

---

[4] This information was supplied by the courtesy of the Archdioceses of Dublin and Limerick through communications under date of October 21, 1948, and October 20, 1948, respectively.

ENGLAND

The support of the clergy in England is supplied through the payment of a fixed salary and through a division of the Christmas and Easter collections among the pastor and assistant pastors.

The amount of the fixed salaries is low. The pastor may draw a salary of £100 a year if the other claims against the parish have been met, including the salary to be paid to the assistant pastor. The assistant pastor receives an annual salary of either £30 or £40 according to the circumstances of the parish. In many instances the amount of the salary of the assistant pastor has remained unchanged since its establishment in the year 1874!

The method of providing support for retired priests is not uniform. In the former "London District" of penal times, comprising the dioceses of Westminster, Brentwood, Southwark and Portsmouth, there are two clerical beneficent Funds which a cleric may join if he is under thirty-five years of age and in good health. If the clerical member maintains his payments to these two Funds and becomes permanently invalided he will receive an annual pension of £155. The two Funds are maintained separately to avoid certain difficulties that might result from a centralized administration. In the case of invalided priests who are not members of these clerical beneficent Funds, the ordinary extends whatever help he can afford.

As of July, 1948, every priest must pay the contribution due under the National Health Insurance Act. The amount of the contribution is six shillings and four pence per week, which amount is paid, by decision of the English bishops, from the parochial funds. In case of illness a priest will be paid fifteen shillings per week, and when he has reached the age of sixty years he becomes eligible to draw the old age pension. The old age pension provides for a payment of twenty-six shillings per week, provided that the recipient receives no more than one pound of earned income per week. However, since Mass stipends are now considered as earned income according to the income tax regulations of England, it is assumed that the income from Mass stipends will be considered as earned income for retired priests. Thus retired priests who can celebrate Mass would be ineligible for any support from the National Health Insurance Fund, since the stipend for Masses, at least in the Archdiocese of Westminster,[5] is five shillings.

FRANCE

The system in France of providing support for the clergy is rather singular. The following is an outline of the system employed in the Archdiocese of Paris.[6]

---

[5] This information was supplied through the kindness of the Chancery of the Archdiocese of Westminster.—Letter from the Archbishop's House, Westminster, London, November 8, 1948.

[6] The information was supplied through the courtesy of the Secretariate of the Archdiocese of Paris.—Letter of Emmanuel Cardinal Suhard of Paris to the Pastors, Paris, January 20, 1948.

Most of the clergy receive a fixed salary from the Chancery; some few receive their income from other sources. The Archdiocesan Chancery receives its funds mainly from the proceeds of the collection, called *Denier du Culte,* solicited from each family by the parish priest.

The following is a list of the salaries paid as of January, 1948, to the clergy in the Archdiocese of Paris who are not receiving from any other source the minimum amount indicated:

Assistant pastors (lowest-salaried)	70,800 francs
Second assistant pastors	72,050 francs
First assistant pastors	73,300 francs
Administrators formerly assistant pastor	72,800 francs
Administrators formerly second assistant pastor	74,050 francs
Pastor, without assistance	86,300 francs
Pastor with 1, 2 or 3 assistant pastors	87,550 francs
Pastor with more than 3 assistants	88,800 francs

(As of January 15, 1948, the rate of exchange was 300 French francs for one dollar.)

The support for retired priests is furnished from the funds of a Clerical Mutual Aid Society (*Caisse d'Entr' Aide du Clergé*). The date of payment to this Society is graduated according to the amount of the salary of the cleric; 55,000 francs of the salary of the cleric is exempt from assessment for this Society. The rate of assessment of the portion of the salary which is not exempt is as follows:

salaries of 55,000 to 60,000 francs	10 per cent
salaries of 60,000 to 80,000 francs	15 per cent
salaries of 80,000 to 100,000 francs	20 per cent
salaries over 100,000 francs	25 per cent

Thus a priest who receives a salary of 74,050 francs is expected to remit 2,857.5 francs to the Clerical Mutual Aid Society (15 per cent of 19,050 francs). The first listing on the above scale is currently not operative, since the minimum salary has been fixed at an amount above 60,000 francs.

Unfortunately there is not at hand any information on the precise amount of the pension paid to retired clerics, but it seems reasonable to assume that in accordance with the prevalent custom in the Continental countries the amount of the pension would be proportioned to the salary received at the time of retirement.

It should also be noted that the Government of France undertakes the maintenance and repair of the churches and cathedrals which are considered national monuments.

BIBLIOGRAPHY

Sources

Acta Apostolicae Sedis, Commentarium Officiale, Romae, 1909—

Acta et Decreta Concilii Plenarii Baltimorensis III, 2. ed., Baltimorae, 1894.

Acta et Decreta Concilii Plenarii Americae Latinae, Romae, 1902.

Acta et Decreta Sacrorum Conciliorum Recentiorum, Collectio Lacensis, 7 vols., Friburgi Brisgoviae: Herder, 1870-1892.

Acta et Decreta Synodi Dioecesanae Toletanae Primae, Toleti: Cancelleria Curiae Dioecesanae, 1941.

Acta Sanctae Sedis, 41 vols., Romae, 1865-1908.

Baluzius, S., *Capitularia Regum Francorum,* 2 vols., Parisiis, 1780.

Bruns, H. T., *Canones Apostolorum Conciliorum Saeculorum IV-VII,* 2 vols., Berolini, 1839.

Bullarum Diplomatum et Privilegiorum Sanctorum Romanorum Pontificum, Taurinensis Editio, 24 vols. in 25, Augustae Taurinorum, 1857-1872.

Codex Iuris Canonici Pii X Pontificis Maximi iussu digestus Benedicti Papae XV auctoritate promulgatus, praefatione, fontium annotatione et indice analytico-alphabetico ab E.mo Petro Card. Gasparri auctus, Romae: Typis Polyglottis Vaticanis, 1917.

Codicis Iuris Canonici Fontes, cura Emi Petri Card. Gasparri editi, 9 vols., Romae (postea Civitate Vaticana): Typis Polyglottis Vaticanis, 1923-1939 (Vols. VII-IX, ed. cura et studio Emi Iustiniani Card. Serédi.)

Collectanea S. Congregationis de Propaganda Fide, 2 vols., Romae, 1907.

Collectio Sirmondensis, Concilia Antiqua Galliae, 3 vols., Parisiis, 1629.

Concilii Plenarii Baltimorensis II Acta et Decreta, 2. ed., Baltimorae, 1894.

Corpus Iuris Canonici, ed. Lipsiensis secunda, post Aemilii Ludovici Richteri curas . . . instruxit Aemilius Friedberg, 2 vols., Lipsiae: Tauchnitz, 1879-1881; ed. anastatice repetita, 1928.

Corpus Iuris Civilis, 3 vols., Vol. III, *Novellae Constitutiones,* ed. stereotypa quinta, recognovit R. Schoell: opus Schoelli morte interceptum absolvit G. Kroll, Berolini: apud Weidmannos, 1928.

Corpus Iuris Civilis, Digesta Iustiniani Augusti—recognoverunt et ediderunt P. Bonfante, C. Fadda, C. Ferrini, S. Riccobono, S. Scialoia, Mediolani: Soc. Editrice Libraria, 1931.

Decisiones Recentiores S. Romanae Rotae (ab anno 1558-1684), ed. P. Farinacius et alii, 19 vols. in 24, Francoforti et Romae, 1623-1703.

Decretum Gratiani, emendatum et notationibus illustratum una cum glossis, 2 vols., Romae, 1582.

Decretales D. Gregorii Papa IX, suae integritati una cum glossis restitutae, Romae, 1582.

Didascalia et Constitutiones Apostolorum, ed. F. X. Funk, 2 vols., Paderborn, 1905.

Gallia Christiana, ed. D. Sammarthanus-P. Piolin, 16 vols., Romae et Parisiis, 1870 ff.

Hardouin, Jean, *Acta Conciliorum et Epistolae Decretales ac Constitutiones Summorum Pontificum*, 12 vols., Parisiis, 1714-1715.

Jaffé, Philippus, *Regesta Pontificum Romanorum ab condita Ecclesia ad annum post Christum natum MCXCVIII*, 2. ed., edd. G. Wattenbach, F. Kaltenbrunner, P. Ewald, S. Loewenfeld, 2 vols. in 1, Lipsiae, 1885-1888.

Liber Synodalis Fargensis I, 1941, Milwaukee: Bruce, 1941.

Magnum Bullarium Romanum, Leo Magnus ad Benedictum XIII, opus Laertii Cherubini, auctum a D. Angelo M. Cherubino, deinde a R.R.P.P. Angelo a Lantusca et Joanne Paulo a Roma, 19 vols., Luxemburgi, 1727.

Mansi, Joannes D., *Sacrorum Conciliorum Nova et Amplissima Collectio*, 53 vols. in 60, Parisiis, 1901-1927.

Monumenta Germaniae Historica, 188 vols., incomplete, Hannoverae, 1826— *Leges in folio*, Vol. I. ed. G. Pertz, Hannoverae, 1835; Neudruck, Leipzig, 1925; *Leges in 4*, Sectio II (*Capitularia Regum Francorum*), Tom. I, ed. A. Boretius, 1883; Tom. II, ed. A. Boretius et V. Krause, 1897; *Legum Sectio III* (*Concilia*), Tom. I, ed. F. Mason, 1893; Tom. II, *Concilia Aevi Karolini*, Pars I, ed. A. Werminghoff, Berolini, 1906; *Epistolae Selectae*, Tom. I (ed. M. Tangl, Berolini, 1916); *Epistolae*, Tom. II, Pars II, *Registrum Epistolarum Gregorii* I, ed. Lud. Hartmann, 1895; *Epistolae Karolini Aevi*, Tom. IV, ed. E. Duemmler, Berolini, 1895; *Scriptores*, Vol. X, ed. G. H. Pertz, Hannoverae, 1852: Neudruck, Leipzig, 1925.

Potthast, A., *Regesta Pontificum Romanorum inde ab anno post Christum natum MCXCVIII ad annum MCCCIV*, 2 vols., Berolini, 1874-1875.

Praxis Missionalis in Vicariatu Apostolico de Ichang, Wuchang; the Franciscan Press, 1935.

Sacrae Romanae Rotae Decisiones seu Sententiae quae iuxta Legem Propriam et Constitutionem "Sapienti Consilio" Pii PP. X prodierunt, cura eiusdem S. Tribunalis editae, Romae, 1912—

Statuta Dioecesis Angelorum et S. Didaci, St. Louis: Herder, 1927.

Statuta Dioecessi Montereyensis-Fresnensis, Fresno: St. Columbia Guild, 1929.

Statuta Dioecesis Seattlensis, Seattle: Metropolitan Press, 1938.

Statuta of the Diocese of Harrisburg, Harrisburg: Curiae Diocesis, 1943.

Thesaurus Resolutionum S. Congregationis Concilii, 167 vols., Romae, 1718-1908.

AUTHORS

Augustine, Charles A., *A Commentary on the New Code of Canon Law,* 8 vols., St. Louis: Herder, Vol. IV, 1920; Vol. IV, 3. ed., 1925; Vol. VI, 3. ed., 1931; Vol. VIII, 1922.

Barbosa, Augustinus, *Collectanea Doctorum in Ius Pontificium Universum,* 6 vols., Lugduni, 1659.

———, *Repertorium Iuris Civilis et Canonici,* Lugduni, 1675.

———, *Iuris Ecclesiastici Universi Libri III,* Lugduni, 1660.

Barrett, John D. M., *A Comparative Study of the Councils of Baltimore and the Code of Canon Law,* The Catholic University of America Canon Law Studies, n. 83, Washington, D. C.: The Catholic University of America, 1932.

Bargilliat, M., *Droits et Devoirs des Curés et des Vicaires Paroissaux,* Paris, 1920.

Bastien, Pierre, *Directoire Canonique,* Abbaye de Maredsous, 1904.

Battandier, Albert, *Guide Canonique pour les Constitutions des Instituts à Voeux Simples,* 6. ed., Paris: Gabalda, 1923.

Bernardus Papiensis, *Summa Decretalium,* ed. E. Laspeyres, Ratisbonae, 1860.

Beste, Udalricus, *Introductio in Codicem,* 3. ed., Collegeville: St. John's Abbey Press, 1946.

Blat, Albertus, *Commentarium Textus Codicis Iuris Canonici,* 5 vols. in 6, Romae: Typographia Pontificia, Lib. III, pars I, 2. ed., 1924; Lib. V, 1924.

Bonal, A., *Institutiones Canonicae,* 2 vols., Parisiis, 1898.

Bouix, D., *Tractatus de Parocho,* 3. ed., Parisiis, 1880.

Bouscaren, T. Lincoln, *The Canon Law Digest,* 2 vols., Vol. I, 5. ed., 1934, Vol. II, 1943, Milwaukee: Bruce.

Brys, J., *Juris Canonici Compendium,* Vol. I, 10. ed. (2. post codicem), Bruges: Desclée, 1947.

Buckland, W. W., *A Textbook of Roman Law,* Cambridge: Cambridge University Press, 1932.

Cappello, Felix M., *Summa Iuris Canonici,* 3 vols., Romae: Universitas Gregoriana, Vol. I, 4. ed., 1945; Vol. II, 4. ed., 1945; Vol. III, 2. ed., 1940.

———, *Tractatus Canonico-Moralis de Sacramentis,* 3 vols. in 6, Romae: Marietti, Vol. I, 3. ed., 1938; Vol. II, pars I, 3. ed., 1938; Vol. II, pars II, 1932; Vol. II, pars III, 1935; Vol. III, pars I, 4. ed., 1939; Vol. III, pars II, 4. ed., 1939.

Chelodi, Joannes, *Ius Canonicum de Personis,* 3. ed., Vicenza: Società Anonima Typografica, 1942.

Connolly, N. P., *The Canonical Erection of Parishes,* The Catholic University of America Canon Law Studies, n. 114, Washington, D. C.: The Catholic University of America, 1938.

Coronata, Matthaeus Conte a, *Institutiones Iuris Canonici,* 2. ed., 5 vols., Taurini: Marietti, Vol. II, 2. ed., 1939; Vol. IV, 2. ed., 1945.

———, *Tractatus Canonicus de Sacramentis,* 3 vols., Vol. II, Taurini-Romae: Marietti, 1945.

Corazzini, G., *La Parrocchia,* Torino, 1900.

Cujaccius, J., *Omnia Opera,* 13 vols. in 12, Prati, 1840.

D'Achery, Lucas, *Spicilegium sive collectio veterum aliquot scriptorum,* 2. ed., 3 vols., Parisiis, 1723.

D'Angelo, Sosio, *Tasse e Pensioni nel Codice di Diritto Canonico,* 2. ed., Torino: L.I.C.E., 1927.

De Brabandére, P., *Compendium Juris Canonici,* 2 vols., Brugis, 1866-1869.

De Clercq, Carlo, *La Législation Religieuse Franque de Clovis à Charlemagne,* Louvain: Bibliothéque de l'Université, 1936.

De Luca, Cardinalis, Joannes Baptista, *Theatrum Veritatis et Justitiae,* 15 vols. in 9, Coloniae Agrippinae, 1706.

De Meester, A., *Juris Canonici et Iuris Canonico-Civilis Compendium,* nova editio, 3 vols. in 4, Vol. III, pars I, Brugis: Desclée, 1926.

De Rosa, Thomas, *De Recta Distributione Reddituum Beneficiorum Ecclesiasticorum. Saecularium,* Neapoli, 1682.

Du Cange, Carolus de Fresne, *Glossarium Mediae et Infimae Latinitatis,* 9. ed., 10 vols., Paris: Librairie des Sciences et Arts, 1938.

Eichmann, Eduard, *Das Strafrecht des* Codex Iuris Canonici, Paderborn, 1920.

Endlicher, Stefan, *Die Gesetze des heiligen Stefan,* Wien, 1849.

Fagnanus, Prosper, *Ius Canonicum seu Commentaria Absolutissima in Quinque Libros Decretalium,* 4 vols., Venetiis, 1696.

Ferguson, John M., *Landmarks of Economic Thought,* Longmans, Green and Co.: New York, 1938.

Ferraris, Lucius, *Bibliotheca Canonica, Iuridica, Moralis, Theologica, necnon Ascetica, Polemica, Rubricistica, Historica,* 9 vols., Romae, 1885-1899.

Findlay, Stephen A., *Canonical Norms Governing the Deposition and Degradattion of Clerics,* The Catholic University of America Canon Law Studies, n. 130, Washington, D. C.: The Catholic University of America Press, 1941.

Fliche, A.-Martin, V., *Histoire de l'Eglise,* 9 vols., incomplete, Paris: Bloud et Gay, 1935—

Garcia, Nicolaus, *De Beneficiis Ecclesiasticis,* Venetiis, 1618.

Gass, S. A., *Ecclesiastical Pensions,* The Catholic University of America Canon Law Studies, n. 157, Washington, D. C.: The Catholic University of America Press, 1942.

Gonzalez-Tellez, Emmanuel, *Commentaria Perpetua in Singulos Textus Quinque Librorum Decretalium Gregorii IX,* 5 vols. in 4, Venetiis, 1699.

Gougaud, H., *Les Chrétientés Celtiques,* Paris, 1911.

Grandclaude, E., *Jus Canonicum,* 3 vols., Parisiis, 1882-1883.

Guilday, Peter, *A History of the Councils of Baltimore,* New York: Macmillan, 1932.

——, *Life and Times of John Carroll,* 2 vols., New York, 1922.

Hannan, Jerome D., *The Canon Law of Wills,* Philadelphia: The Dolphin Press, 1935.

Hefele, K.-LeClercq, H., *Histoire des Conciles de l'Eglise,* 10 vols. in 19, Paris: Letouzey et Ané, 1907-1938.

Heimbucher, Max, *Die Orden und Kongregationen,* 2. ed., 3 vols., Paderborn, 1907-1908.

Hergenröther, Giuseppe, *Storia Universale della Chiesa,* Italian translation by Enrico Rosa, 6. ed., 6 vols., Firenze: Libreria Editrice Fiorentina, 1930.

Heston, E. L., *The Alienation of Church Property in the United States,* The Catholic University of America Canon Law Studies, n. 132, Washington, D. C.: The Catholic University of America Press, 1941.

Hostiensis, Cardinalis (Henricus de Segusio), *Commentaria in Quinque Decretalium Libros,* 5 vols. in 3, Venetiis, 1581.

Hughes, Thomas, *History of the Society of Jesus in North America, Colonial and Federal,* 2 vols., New York, 1908.

Imbart de la Tour, P., *Les Paroisses Rurales du V au XI Siècle,* Paris, 1900.

Ioannes, Andreae, *Commentaria Novella in Quinque Decretalium Libros,* 6 vols. in 5, Venetiis, 1581.

——, *In Sex Decretalium Libros Novella Commentaria,* 6 vols. in 5, Venetiis, 1585.

Leage, R. W., *Roman Private Law,* 2. ed., C. H. Ziegler, London: Macmillan Co., 1937; reprint, 1946.

Lèsne, Emile, *Histoire de la Propriété Ecclésiastique en France,* 3 vols., Lille, 1922.

Leurenius, Petrus, *Forum Ecclesiasticum in quo Ius Canonicum Universum Librorum ac Titulorum Ordine explanatur,* 5 vols. in 4, Venetiis, 1729.

Levet, A., *Bénéfice de Competence,* Paris, 1927.

Many, S., *Praelectiones de Sacra Ordinatione,* Parisiis, 1905.

McBride, J. T., *The Incardination and Excardination of Seculars,* The Catholic University of America Canon Law Studies, n. 145, Washington, D. C.: The Catholic University of America Press, 1941.

Migne, Jacques Paul, *Patrologiae Cursus Completus, Series Graeca,* 161 vols., Parisiis, 1857-1855.

——, *Patrologiae Cursus Completus, Series Latina,* 221 vols., Parisiis, 1844-1855.

Noldin, H.-Schmitt, A., *Summa Theologiae Moralis,* 24. ed., 3 vols., Oeniponte: Rauch, 1936.

O'Brien, K. A., *The Nature of Support of Diocesan Priests in the United States of America,* The Catholic University of America Canon Law Studies, n. 286, Washington, D. C.: The Catholic University of America, 1949.

Panormitanus, Abbas (Nicolaus de Tudeschis), *Commentaria in Quinque Libros Decretalium,* 5 vols. in 7, Venetiis, 1588.

Pirhing, Ernricus, *Ius Canonicum Universum secundum titulos Decretalium Distributum Nova Methodo Explicatum,* 5 vols. in 4, Dilingae, 1674-1678.

Poulet, Charles-Raemers, Sidney, *A History of the Catholic Church,* 2 vols., St. Louis: Herder, 1945.

Pyrrhus, Corradus, *Praxis Beneficiaria,* Venetiis, 1735.

Raymond de Peñafort, St., *Summa,* Veronae, 1744.

Rebuffus, Petrus, *Tractatus Congruae Portionis Beneficiorum Vicariis maxine Debitae brevis et admodum utilis ac in forensi iudicio usu veniens,* Coloniae Agripinae, 1572.

Regatillo, Eduardus, *Institutiones Iuris Canonici,* 2 vols., Vol. I, 2. ed., Santander: Sal Terrae, 1946.

Reiffenstuel, Anacletus, *Ius Canonicum Universum,* 5 vols. in 7, Parisiis, 1864-1870.

Restrepo-Restrepo, Ioannes, *Concordata Regnante Sanctissimo Domino Pio PP. XI Inita,* Romae: Pontificia Universitas Gregoriana, 1934.

Rufinus, Magister, *Summa Decretorum,* ed. H. Singer, Paderbornae, 1902.

Schmalzgrueber, Franciscus, *Ius Ecclesiasticum Universum,* 5 vols. in 12, Romae, 1843-1845.

Shea, John Gilmary, *The Catholic Church in Colonial Days,* New York, 1886.

Sipos, Stephanus, *Enchiridion Iuris Canonici,* 3. ed., Pecs: Haladas, 1936.

Smith, S. B., *Elements of Ecclesiastical Law,* 3 vols., Vol. III, New York, published 1888.

Stutz, Ulrich, *The Proprietary Church as an Element of Mediaeval Germanic Ecclesiastical Law,* in *Studies in Mediaeval History, Mediaeval Germany (911-1252),* translated by Geoffrey Barraclough, 2 vols., Oxford: Blackwell, 1938.

Summa Theologica, 6 vols., Taurini: Marietti, 1932.

Thomassinus, Ludovicus, *Vetus et Nova Ecclesiae Disciplina circa Beneficia et Beneficiarios,* 10 vols., Moguntiaci, 1787.

Van Espen, Z. B., *Ius Ecclesiasticum Universum,* 5 vols., Lovanii, 1753.

Van Hove, A., *Commentarium Lovaniense in Codicem Iuris Canonici,* Vol. I, Tom. 1, *Prolegomena ad Codicem Iuris Canonici,* 2. ed., Mechliniae et Romae: Dessain, 1945.

Vecchiotti, Septimius, *Institutiones Canonicae,* 19. ed., 3 vols., Augustae Taurinorum, 1886.

Vermeersch, Arturus-Creusen, Josephus, *Epitome Iuris Canonici,* 6. ed., 3 vols., Mechliniae-Romae: Dessain, Vol. I, 1937; Vol. II, 1940; Vol. III, 1946.

Vito, Pasquale, *Questioni Canoniche di materie riguardanti i nostri tempi secondo il Codice di diritto canonico,* 5 vols., Napoli: Raffaele Picone, 1926-1932.

Wernz, F. X., *Ius Decretalium,* 6 vols., Vol II, 3. ed., Romae et Prati, 1913.

Wernz, F. X., *Ius Decretalium,* 6 vols., Vol. II, 3. ed., Romae et Prati, 1913. 7 tomes in 8, Romae: Universitas Gregoriana, Vol. II, 3. ed., 1943; Vol. IV, pars 1, 1934; Vol. IV, pars 2, 1935; Vol. VII, 1937.

Woywood, Stanislaus, *A Practical Commentary on the Code of Canon Law,* revised by Callistus Smith, 10. ed., 2 vols., New York: Joseph F. Wagner, 1946.

Zacchia, Lanfrancus, *De Salario,* Romae, 1666.

Articles

Allen, William F., "Parish-Benefice Revenue," *The Jurist,* VIII (1948), 323-332.

Hannan, Jerome D., "The Cleric's Last Will," *The Jurist,* VIII (1948), 41-61.

"Hearings Relative to the Social Security Act Amendments of 1939 before the Committee on Ways and Means," House of Representatives, Seventy-Sixth Congress, First Session, revised printing, Washington, D. C.: U. S. Government Printing Office, 1939.

Lèsne, E., "Les Origines de la Prébende," *Revue Historique de Droit* (fourth series), VIII (1929), 242-290.

——, "Evêché et Abbaye," *Revue d'Histoire de l'Eglise de France,* V (1914), 44.

Perels, E., "Die Ursprünge des karolingischen Zehntrechtes," *Archiv für Urkundenforschung,* IV (1911), 203.

Pope Pius X, Letter to the Apostolic Delegate for the United States, *The Ecclesiastical Review,* XL (1909), 329.

Riccobono, S., "Cristianesimo e Diritto Privato," *Rivista di Diritto Civile,* I (1911), 15.

Stutz, U., "Das karolongische Zehntgebot, zugleich ein Betrag zur Erklärung von c. 7 und 13 des Kapitulars von Heristall," *Zeitschrift der Savigny-Stiftung für Rechtsgeschichte, Germanistische Abteilung,* XXIX (1908), 180.

——, "Ausgewählte Kapitel aus der Geschichte der Eigenkirche und ihres Rechtes," *Zeitschrift der Savigny-Stiftung, Kanonistische Abteilung,* LVII (1937), 1-85.

——, "The proprietary Church as an Element of Mediaeval Germanic Ecclesiastical Law," *Studies of Mediaeval History, Mediaeval Germany (911-1252),* translated by G. Barraclough, II, 35-70.

Van Hove, A., "Le Concordat entre le Saint-Siége et le Gouvernement Italien," *Nouvelle Revue Théologique,* LVI (1929), 518-548.

Periodicals

American Ecclesiastical Review, Vols. I-XXXII, Philadelphia, 1889-1905; from 1905: *The Ecclesiastical Review,* Vols. XXXIII-CIX, Philadelphia, 1905-1943; from 1944: *The American Ecclesiastical Review,* Washington, D. C., Vol. CX, 1944—

Archiv für katholisches Kirchenrecht, Innsbruck, 1857-1861; Mainz, 1862—

Archiv für Urkundenforschung, Berlin and Leipzig, 1908—

Jurist, The, Washington, 1941—

Nouvelle Revue Théologique, Paris, 1869—

Revue Historique de Droit, Paris, 1921—

Revue d'histoire de l'Eglise de France, Paris, 1910—

Rivista di Diritto Civile, Milano, 1911—

Zeitschrift der Savigny-Stiftung für Rechtsgeschichte, Germanistische Abteilung, Weimar, 1880—

Zeitschrift der Savigny-Stiftung für Rechtsgeschichte, Kanonistische Abteilung, Weimar, 1911—

Letters and Autographs

Besoldungsordnung, Curia of the Archdiocese of Vienna, September 1, 1947.

Letter from the Archbishop's House, Westminster, London, November 8, 1948.

Letter from the Archbishop's Palace, Limerick, Eire, October 20, 1948.

Letter from the Chancellery, Archdiocese of Dublin, Eire, October 21, 1948.

Letter from the Curia of the Archdiocese of Malines, Belgium, January 17, 1949.

Letter from the Embassy of Belgium, Washington, D. C., December 3, 1948.

Letter of Emmanuel Cardinal Suhard of Paris to the Pastors, Paris, January 20, 1948.

Instructions Pratiques, Archdiocese of Paris, October 14, 1947.

Abbreviations

AAS—Acta Apostolicae Sedis
ASS—Acta Sanctae Sedis
Collectanea—Collectanea S.C. de Propaganda Fide
Coll. Lac.—Collectio Lacensis
Fontes—Codicis Iuris Canonici Fontes cura . . . Gasparri editi
JE—Jaffé-Ewald, *Regesta Pontificum Romanorum*
JK—Jaffé-Kaltenbrunner, *Regesta Pontificum Romanorum*
JL—Jaffé-Loewenfeld, *Regesta Pontificum Romanorum*
Mansi—*Sacrorum Conciliorum Nova et Amplissima Collectio*
MGH—Monumenta Germaniae Historica
MPG—Migne, *Patrologia, Series Graeca*
MPL—Migne, *Patrologia, Series Latina*

BIOGRAPHICAL NOTE

Philip Matthew Hannan was born in Washington, D. C., on May 20, 1913. He completed his primary education at the Immaculate Conception Parish School and attended St. John's College, also in Washington, for his high school course. He entered St. Charles College, Catonsville, Maryland, in 1931, and upon the completion of his sophomore year of college there was enrolled in Basselin College, Catholic University of America, in 1933. After securing his M.A. in philosophy from the Catholic University of America in 1936, he entered the North American College in Rome the same year, and was ordained in Rome on December 8, 1939. Upon his return from Rome in June, 1940, he was engaged in parish work and service in the U. S. Army as a chaplain until he enrolled in the School of Canon Law at the Catholic University of America in 1946. He received the degree of the Baccalaureate in Canon Law in June, 1947, and the degree of the Licentiate in Canon Law in June, 1948.

INDEX

CANON LAW STUDIES*

1. FRERIKS, REV. CELESTINE A., C.PP.S., J.C.D., Religious Congregations in Their External Relations, 121 pp., 1916.
2. GALLIHER, REV. DANIEL M., O.P., J.C.D., Canonical Elections, 117 pp., 1917.
3. BORKOWSKI, REV. AURELIUS L., O.F.M., J.C.D., De Confraternitatibus Ecclesiasticis, 136 pp., 1918.
4. CASTILLO, REV. CAYO, J.C.D., Disertacion Historico-Canonica sobre la Potestad del Cabildo en Sede Vacante o Impedida del Vicario Capitular, 99 pp., 1919 (1918).
5. KUBELBECK, REV. WILLIAM J., S.T.B., J.C.D., The Sacred Penitentiaria and Its Relation to Faculties of Ordinaries and Priests, 129 pp., 1918.
6. PETROVITS, REV. JOSEPH J. C., S.T.D., J.C.D., The New Church Law on Matrimony, X-461 pp., 1919.
7. HICKEY, REV. JOHN J., S.T.B., J.C.D., Irregularities and Simple Impediments in the New Code of Canon Law, 100 pp., 1920.
8. KLEKOTKA, REV. PETER J., S.T.B., J.C.D., Diocesan Consultors, 179 pp., 1920.
9. WANENMACHER, REV. FRANCIS, J.C.D., The Evidence in Ecclesiastical Procedure Affecting the Marriage Bond, 1920 (Printed 1935).
10. GOLDEN, REV. HENRY FRANCIS, J.C.D., Parochial Benefices in the New Code, IV-119 pp., 1921 (Printed 1925).
11. KOUDELKA, REV. CHARLES J., J.C.D., Pastors, Their Rights and Duties According to the New Code of Canon Law, 211 pp., 1921.
12. MELO, REV. ANTONIUS, O.F.M., J.C.D., De Exemptione Regularium, X-188 pp., 1921.
13. SCHAAF, REV. VALENTINE THEODORE, O.F.M., S.T.B., J.C.D., The Cloister, X-180 pp., 1921.
14. BURKE, REV. THOMAS JOSEPH, S.T.D., J.C.D., Competence in Ecclesiastical Tribunals, IV-117 pp., 1922.
15. LEECH, REV. GEORGE LEO, J.C.D., A Comparative Study of the Constitution "Apostolicae Sedis" and the "Codex Juris Canonici," 179 pp., 1922.
16. MOTRY, REV. HUBERT LOUIS, S.T.D., J.C.D., Diocesan Faculties According to the Code of Canon Law, II-167 pp., 1922.

---

*All published numbers are available from the Catholic University of America Press, 620 Michigan Ave., N.E., Washington 17, D. C., except the following: Nos. 1-114 inclusive, 116, 118, 120, 121, 122, 123, 136, 153, 162, 182 and 198. But the following numbers, now reissued, are obtainable from *The Jurist*, The Catholic University of America, Washington 17, D. C., namely: Nos. 5, 7, 11, 17, 18, 19, 26, 28, 30, 31, 34, 42, 44, 51, 52 and 61.

17. MURPHY, REV. GEORGE LAWRENCE, J.C.D., Delinquencies and Penalties in the Administration and the Reception of the Sacraments, IV-121 pp., 1923.
18. O'REILLY, REV. JOHN ANTHONY, S.T.B., J.C.D., Ecclesiastical Sepulture in the New Code of Canon Law, II-129 pp., 1923.
19. MICHALICKA, REV. WENCESLAS CYRIL, O.S.B., J.C.D., Judicial Procedure in Dismissal of Clerical Exempt Religious, 107 pp., 1923.
20. DARGIN, REV. EDWARD VINCENT, S.T.B., J.C.D., Reserved Cases According to the Code of Canon Law, IV-103 pp., 1924.
21. GODFREY, REV. JOHN A., S.T.B., J.C.D., The Right of Patronage According to the Code of Canon Law, 153 pp., 1924.
22. HAGEDORN, REV. FRANCIS EDWARD, J.C.D., General Legislation on Indulgences, II-154 pp., 1924.
23. KING, REV. JAMES IGNATIUS, J.C.D., The Administration of the Sacraments to Dying Non-Catholics, V-141 pp., 1924.
24. WINSLOW, REV. FRANCIS JOSEPH, M.M., J.C.D., Vicars and Prefects Apostolic, IV-149 pp., 1924.
25. CORREA, REV. JOSE SERVELION, S.T.L., J.C.D., La Potestad Legislativa de la Iglesia Catolica, IV-127 pp., 1925.
26. DUGAN, REV. HENRY FRANCIS, A.M., J.C.D., The Judiciary Department of the Diocesan Curia, 87 pp., 1925.
27. KELLER, REV. CHARLES FREDERICK, S.T.B., J.C.D., Mass Stipends, 167 pp., 1925.
238. PASCHANG, REV. JOHN LINUS, J.C.D., The Sacramentals According to the Code of Canon Law, 129 pp., 1925.
29. PIONTEK, REV. CYRILLUS, O.F.M., S.T.B., J.C.D., De Indulto Exclaustrationis necnon Saecularizationis, XIII-289 pp., 1925.
30. KEARNEY, REV. RICHARD JOSEPH, S.T.B., J.C.D., Sponsors at Baptism According to the Code of Canon Law, IV-127 pp. 1925.
31. BARTLETT, REV. CHESTER JOSEPH, A.M., LL.B., J.C.D., The Tenure of Parochial Property in the United States of America, V-108 pp., 1926.
32. KILKER, REV. ADRIAN JEROME, J.C.D., Extreme Unction, V-425 pp., 1926.
33. MCCORMICK, REV. ROBERT EMMETT, J.C.D., Confessors of Religious, VIII-266 pp., 1926.
34. MILLER, REV. NEWTON THOMAS, J.C.D., Founded Masses According to the Code of Canon Law, VII-93 pp., 1926.
35. ROELKER, REV. EDWARD G., S.T.D., J.C.D., Principles of Privilege According to the Code of Canon Law, XI-166 pp., 1926.
36. BAKALARCZYK, REV. RICHARDUS, M.I.C., J.U.D., De Novitiatu, VIII-208 pp., 1927.
37. PIZZUTI, REV. LAWRENCE, O.F.M., J.U.L., De Parochis Religiosis, 1927. (Not Printed.)
38. BLILEY, REV. NICHOLAS MARTIN, O.S.B., J.C.D., Altars According to the Code of Canon Law, XIX-132 pp., 1927.

39. Brown, Mr. Brendan Francis, A.B., LL.M., J.U.D., The Canonical Juristic Personality with Special Reference to its Status in the United States of America, V-212 pp., 1927.
40. Cavanaugh, Rev. William Thomas, C.P., J.U.D., The Reservation of the Blessed Sacrament, VIII-101 pp., 1927.
41. Doheny, Rev. William J., C.S.C., A.B., J.U.D., Church Property: Modes of Acquisition, X-118 pp., 1927.
42. Feldhaus, Rev. Aloysius H., C.PP.S., J.C.D., Oratories, IX-141 pp., 1927.
43. Kelly, Rev. James Patrick, A.B., J.C.D., The Jurisdiction of the Simple Confessor, X-208 pp., 1927.
44. Neuberger, Rev. Nicholas J., J.C.D., Canon 6 or the Relation of the Codex Juris Canonici to the Preceding Legislation, V-95 pp., 1927.
45. O'Keefe, Rev. Gerald Michael, J.C.D., Matrimonial Dispensations, Powers of Bishops, Priests, and Confessors, VIII-232 pp., 1927.
46. Quigley, Rev. Joseph, A.M., A.B., J.C.D., Condemned Societies, 139 pp., 1927.
47. Zaplotnik, Rev. Johannes Leo, J.C.D., De Vicariis Foraneis, X-142 pp., 1927.
48. Duskie, Rev. John Aloysius, A.B., J.C.D., The Canonical Status of the Orientals in the United States, VIII-196 pp., 1928.
49. Hyland, Rev. Francis Edward, J.C.D., Excommunication, Its Nature, Historical Development and Effects, VIII-181 pp., 1928.
50. Reinmann, Rev. Gerald Joseph, O.M.C., J.C.D., The Third Order Secular of Saint Francis, 201 pp., 1928.
51. Schenk, Rev. Francis J., J.C.D., The Matrimonial Impediments of Mixed Religion and Disparity of Cult, XVI-318 pp., 1929.
52. Coady, Rev. John Joseph, S.T.D., J.U.D., A.M., The Appointment of Pastors, VIII-150 pp., 1929.
53. Kay, Rev. Thomas Henry, J.C.D., Competence in Matrimonial Procedure, VIII-164 pp., 1929.
54. Turner, Rev. Sidney Joseph, C.P., J.U.D., The Vow of Poverty, XLIX-217 pp., 1929.
55. Kearney, Rev. Raymond A., A.B., S.T.D., J.C.D., The Principles of Delegation, VII-149 pp., 1929.
56. Conran, Rev. Edward James, A.B., J.C.D., The Interdict, V-163 pp., 1930.
57. O'Neill, Rev. William H., J.C.D., Papal Rescripts of Favor, VII-218 pp., 1930.
58. Bastnagel, Rev. Clement Vincent, J.U.D., The Appointment of Parochial Adjutants and Assistants, XV-257 pp., 1930.
59. Ferry, Rev. William A., A.B., J.C.D., Stole Fees, V-136 pp., 1930.
60. Costello, Rev. John Michael, A.B., J.C.D., Domicile and Quasi-Domicile, VII-201 pp., 1930.
61. Kremer, Rev. Michael Nicholas, A.B., S.T.B., J.C.D., Church Support in the United States, VI-136 pp., 1930.

62. ANGULO, REV. LUIS, C.M., J.C.D., Legislation de la Iglesia sobre la intencion en la application de la Santa Misa, VII-104 pp., 1931.
63. FREY, REV. WOLFGANG NORBERT, O.S.B., A.B., J.C.D., The Act of Religious Profession, VIII-174 pp., 1931.
64. ROBERTS, REV. JAMES BRENDAN, A.B., J.C.D., The Banns of Marriage, XIV-140 pp., 1931.
65. RYDER, REV. RAYMOND ALOYSIUS, A.B., J.C.D., Simony, IX-151 pp., 1931.
66. CAMPAGNA, REV. ANGELO, Ph.D., J.U.D., Il Vicario Generale del Vescovo, VII-205 pp., 1931.
67. COX, REV. JOSEPH GODFREY, A.B., J.C.D., The Administration of Seminaries, VI-124 pp., 1931.
68. GREGORY, REV. DONALD J., J.U.D., The Pauline Privilege, XV-165 pp., 1931.
69. DONOHUE, REV. JOHN F., J.C.D., The Impediment of Crime, VII-110 pp., 1931.
70. DOOLEY, REV. EUGENE A., O.M.I., J.C.D., Church Law on Sacred Relics, IX-143 pp., 1931.
71. ORTH, REV. CLEMENT RAYMOND, O.M.C., J.C.D., The Approbation of Religious Institutes, 171 pp., 1931.
72. PERNICONE, REV. JOSEPH M., A.B., J.C.D., The Ecclesiastical Prohibition of Books, XII-267 pp., 1932.
73. CLINTON, REV. CONNELL, A.B., J.C.D., The Paschal Precept, IX-108 pp., 1932.
74. DONNELLY, REV. FRANCIS B., A.M., S.T.L., J.C.D., The Diocesan Synod, VIII-125 pp., 1932.
75. TORRENTE, REV. CAMILO, C.M.F., J.C.D., Las Procesiones Sagradas, V-145 pp., 1932.
76. MURPHY, REV. EDWIN J., C.PP.S., J.C.D., Suspension Ex Informata Conscientia, XI-122 pp., 1932.
77. MACKENZIE, REV. ERIC F., A.M., S.T.L., J.C.D., The Delict of Heresy in its Commission, Penalization, Absolution, VII-124 pp., 1932.
78. LYONS, REV. AVITUS E., S.T.B., J.C.D., The Collegiate Tribunal of First Instance, XI-147 pp., 1932.
79. CONNOLLY, REV. THOMAS A., J.C.D., Appeals, XI-195 pp., 1932.
80. SANGMEISTER, REV. JOSEPH V., A.B., J.C.D., Force and Fear as Precluding Matrimonial Consent, V-211 pp., 1932.
81. JAEGER, REV. LEO A., A.B., J.C.D., The Administration of Vacant and Quasi-Vacant Episcopal Sees in the United States, IX-229 pp., 1932.
82. RIMLINGER, REV. HERBERT T., J.C.D., Error Invalidating Matrimonial Consent, VII-79 pp., 1932.
83. BARRETT, REV. JOHN D. M., S.S., J.C.D., A Comparative Study of the Plenary Councils of Baltimore and the Code of Canon Law, IX-221 pp., 1932.
84. CARBERRY, REV. JOHN J., Ph.D., S.T.D., J.C.D., The Juridical Form of Marriage, X-177 pp., 1934.

85. Dolan, Rev. John L., A.B., J.C.D., The Defensor Vinculi, XII-157 pp., 1934.
86. Hannan, Rev. Jerome D., A.M., S.T.D., LL.B., J.C.D., The Canon Law of Wills, IX-517 pp., 1934.
87. Lemieux, Rev. Delise A., A.M., J.C.D., The Sentence in Ecclesiastical Procedure, IX-131 pp., 1934.
88. O'Rourke, Rev. James J., A.B., J.C.D., Parish Registers, VII-109 pp.. 1934.
89. Timlin, Rev. Bartholomew, O.F.M., A.M., J.C.D., Conditional Matrimonial Consent, X-381 pp., 1934.
90. Wahl, Rev. Francis X., A.B., J.C.D., The Matrimonial Impediments of Consanguinity and Affinity, VI-125 pp., 1934.
91. White, Rev. Robert J., A.B., LL.B., S.T.B., J.C.D., Canonical Ante-Nuptial Promises and the Civil Law, VI-152 pp., 1934.
92. Herrera, Rev. Antonio Parra, O.C.D., J.C.D., Legislacion Ecclesiastica sobra el Ayuno y la Abstinencia, XI-191 pp., 1935.
93. Kennedy, Rev. Edwin J., J.C.D., The Special Matrimonial Process in Cases of Evident Nullity, X-165 pp., 1935.
94. Manning, Rev. John J., A.B., J.C.D., Presumption of Law in Matrimonial Procedure, XI-111 pp., 1935.
95. Moeder, Rev. John M., J.C.D., The Proper Bishop for Ordination and Dimissorial Letters, VII-135 pp., 1935.
96. O'Mara, Rev. William A., A.B., J.C.D., Canonical Causes for Matrimonial Dispensations, IX-155 pp., 1935.
97. Reilly, Rev. Peter, J.C.D., Residence of Pastors, IX-81 pp., 1935.
98. Smith, Rev. Mariner T., O.P., S.T.Lr., J.C.D., The Penal Law for Religious, VII-169 pp., 1935.
99. Whalen, Rev. Donald W., A.M., J.C.D., The Value of Testimonial Evidence in Matrimonial Procedure, XIII-297 pp., 1935.
100. Cleary, Rev. Joseph F., J.C.D., Canonical Limitations on the Alienation of Church Property, VIII-141 pp., 1936.
101. Glynn, Rev. John C., J.C.D., The Promoter of Justice, XX-337 pp., 1936.
102. Brennan, Rev. James H., S.S., M.A., S.T.B., J.C.D., The Simple Convalidation of Marriage, VI-135 pp., 1937.
103. Brunini, Rev. Joseph Bernard, J.C.D., The Clerical Obligations of Canons 139 and 142, X-121 pp., 1937.
104. Connor, Rev. Maurice, A.B., J.C.D., The Administrative Removal of Pastors, VIII-159 pp., 1937.
105. Guilfoyle, Rev. Merlin Joseph, J.C.D., Custom, XI-144 pp., 1937.
106. Hughes, Rev. James Austin, A.B., A.M., J.C.D., Witnesses in Criminal Trials of Clerics, IX-140 pp., 1937.
107. Jansen, Rev. Raymond J., A.B., S.T.L., J.C.D., Canonical Provisions for Catechetical Instruction, VII-153 pp., 1937.
108. Kealy, Rev. John James, A.B., J.C.D., The Introductory Libellus in Church Court Procedure, XI-131 pp., 1937.

109. McManus, Rev. James Edward, C.Ss.R., J.C.D., The Administration of Temporal Goods in Religious Institutes, XVI-196 pp., 1937.
110. Moriarty, Rev. Eugene James, J.C.D., Oaths in Ecclesiastical Courts, X-115 pp., 1937.
111. Rainer, Rev. Eligius George, C.Ss.R., J.C.D., Suspension of Clerics, XVII-249 pp., 1937.
112. Reilly, Rev. Thomas F., C.Ss.R., J.C.D., Visitation of Religious, VI-195 pp., 1938.
113. Moriarity, Rev. Francis E., C.Ss.R., J.C.D., The Extraordinary Absolution from Censures, XV-334 pp., 1938.
114. Connolly, Rev. Nicholas P., J.C.D., The Canonical Erection of Parishes, X-132 pp., 1938.
115. Donovan, Rev. James Joseph, J.C.D., The Pastor's Obligation in Prenuptial Investigation, XII-322 pp., 1938.
116. Harrigan, Rev. Robert J., M.A., S.T.B., J.C.D., The Radical Sanation of Invalid Marriages, VIII-208 pp., 1938.
117. Boffa, Rev. Conrad Humbert, J.C.D., Canonical Provisions for Catholic Schools, VII-211 pp., 1939.
118. Parsons, Rev. Anscar John, O.M.Cap., J.C.D., Canonical Elections, XII-236 pp., 1939.
119. Reilly, Rev. Edward Michael, A.B., J.C.D., The General Norms of Dispensation, XII-156 pp., 1939.
120. Ryan, Rev. Gerald Aloysius, A.B., J.C.D., Principles of Episcopal Jurisdiction, XIII-172 pp., 1939.
121. Burton, Rev. Francis James, C.S.C., A.B., J.C.D., A Commentary on Canon 1125, X-222 pp., 1940.
122. Miaskiewicz, Rev. Francis Sigismund, J.C.D., Supplied Jurisdiction According to Canon 209, XII-340 pp., 1940.
123. Rice, Rev. Patrick William, A.B., J.C.D., Proof of Death in Prenuptial Investigation, VIII-156 pp., 1940.
124. Anglin, Rev. Thomas Francis, M.S., J.C.D., The Eucharistic Fast, VIII-183 pp., 1941.
125. Coleman, Rev. John Jerome, J.C.D., The Minister of Confirmation, VI-153 pp., 1941.
126. Downs, Rev. Joseph Emmanuel, A.B., J.C.D., The Concept of Clerical Immunity, XI-163 pp., 1941.
127. Esswein, Rev. Anthony Albert, J.C.D., Extrajudicial Penal Powers of Ecclesiastical Superiors, X-144 pp., 1941.
128. Farrell, Rev. Benjamin Francis, M.A., S.T.L., J.C.D., The Rights and Duties of the Local Ordinary Regarding Congregations of Women Religious of Pontifical Approval, V-195 pp., 1941.
129. Feeney, Rev. Thomas John, A.B., S.T.L., J.C.D., Restitutio in Integrum, VI-169 pp., 1941.
130. Findlay, Rev. Stephen William, O.S.B., A.B., J.C.D., Canonical Norms Governing the Deposition and Degradation of Clerics, XVII-279 pp., 1941.

131. Goodwine, Rev. John, A.B., S.T.L., J.C.D., The Right of the Church to Acquire Property, VIII-119 pp., 1941.
132. Heston, Rev. Edward Louis, C.S.C., Ph.D., S.T.D., J.C.D., The Alienation of Church Property in the United States, XII-222 pp., 1941.
133. Hogan, Rev. James John, A.B., S.T.L., J.C.D., Judicial Advocates and Procurators, XIII-200 pp., 1941.
134. Kealy, Rev. Thomas M., A.B., Litt.D., J.C.D., Dowry of Women Religious, IX-152 pp., 1941.
135. Keene, Rev. Michael James, O.S.B., J.C.D., Religious Ordinaries and Canon 198, V-164 pp., 1941 (Printed 1942).
136. Kerin, Rev. Charles A., S.S., M.A., S.T.B., J.C.D., The Privation of Christian Burial, XVI-279 pp., 1941.
137. Louis, Rev. William Francis, M.A., J.C.D., Diocesan Archives, X-101 pp., 1941.
138. McDevitt, Rev. Gilbert Joseph, A.B., J.C.D., Legitimacy and Legitimation, X-247 pp., 1941.
139. McDonough, Rev. Thomas Joseph, A.B., J.C.D., Apostolic Administrators, X-217 pp., 1941.
140. Meier, Rev. Carl Anthony, A.B., J.C.D., Penal Administrative Procedure Against Negligent Pastors, XI-240 pp., 1941.
141. Schmidt, Rev. John Rogg, A.B., J.C.D., The Principles of Authentic Interpretation in Canon 17 of the Code of Canon Law, XII-331 pp., 1941.
142. Slafkosky, Rev. Andrew Leonard, A.B., J.C.D., The Canonical Episcopal Visitation of the Diocese, X-197 pp., 1941.
143. Swoboda, Rev. Innocent Robert, O.F.M., J.C.D., Ignorance in Relation to the Imputability of Delicts, IX-271 pp., 1941.
144. Dube, Rev. Arthur Joseph, A.B., J.C.D., The General Principles for the Reckoning of Time in Canon Law, VIII-299 pp., 1941.
145. McBride, Rev. James T., A.B., J.C.D., Incardination and Excardination of Seculars, XX-585 pp., 1941.
146. Krol, Rev. John T., J.C.D., The Defendant in Ecclesiastical Trials, XII-207 pp., 1942.
147. Comyns, Rev. Joseph J., C.Ss.R., A.B., J.C.D., Papal and Episcopal Administration of Church Property, XIV-155 pp., 1942.
148. Barry, Rev. Garrett Francis, O.M.I., J.C.D., Violation of the Cloister, XII-260 pp., 1942.
149. Bolduc, Rev. Gatien, C.S.V., A.B., S.T.L., J.C.D., Les Etudes dans les Religions Clericales, VIII-155 pp., 1942.
150. Boyles, Rev. David John, M.A., J.C.D., The Juridic Effects of Moral Certitude on Pre-Nuptial Guarantees, XII-188 pp., 1942.
151. Canavan, Rev. Walter Joseph, M.A., Litt.D., J.C.D., The Profession of Faith, XII-143 pp., 1942.
152. Desrochers, Rev. Bruno, A.B., Ph.L., S.T.B., J.C.D., Le Premier Concile Plenier de Quebec et le Code de Droit Canonique, XIV-186 pp., 1942.

153. DILLON, REV. ROBERT EDWARD, A.B., J.C.D., Common Law Marriage, X-148 pp., 1942.
154. DODWELL, REV. EDWARD JOHN, PH.D., S.T.B., J.C.D., The Time and Place for the Celebration of Marriage, X-156 pp., 1942.
155. DONNELLAN, REV. THOMAS ANDREW, A.B., J.C.D., The Obligation of the Missa pro Populo, VII-131 pp., 1942.
156. ELTZ, REV. LOUIS ANTHONY, A.B., J.C.D., Cooperation in Crime, XII-208 pp., 1942.
157. GASS, REV. SYLVESTER FRANCIS, M.A., J.C.D., Ecclesiastical Pensions, XI-206 pp., 1942.
158. GUINIVEN, REV. JOHN JOSEPH, C.Ss.R., J.C.D., The Precept of Hearing Mass, XIV-188 pp., 1942.
159. GULCZYNSKI, REV. JOHN THEOPHILUS, J.C.D., The Desecration and Violation of Churches, X-126 pp., 1942.
160. HAMMILL, REV. JOHN LEO, M.A., J.C.D., The Obligations of the Traveler According to Canon 14, VIII-204 pp., 1942.
161. HAYDT, REV. JOHN JOSEPH, A.B., J.C.D., Reserved Benefices, XI-148 pp., 1942.
162. HUSER, REV. ROGER JOHN, O.F.M., A.B., J.C.D., The Crime of Abortion in Canon Law, XII-187 pp., 1942.
163. KEARNEY, REV. FRANCIS PATRICK, A.B., S.T.L., J.C.D., The Principles of Canon 1127, X-162 pp., 1942.
164. LINAHEN, REV. LEO JAMES, S.T.L., J.C.D., De Absolutione Complicis in Peccato Turpi, 114 pp., 1942.
165. MCCLOSKEY, REV. JOSEPH ALOYSIUS, A.B., J.C.D., The Subject of Ecclesiastical Law According to Canon 12, XVII-246 pp., 1942 (Printed 1943).
166. O'NEILL, REV. FRANCIS JOSEPH, C.Ss.R., J.C.D., The Dismissal of Religious in Temporary Vows, XIII-220 pp., 1942.
167. PRINCE, REV. JOHN EDWARD, A.B., S.T.D., J.C.D., The Diocesan Chancellor, X-136 pp., 1942.
168. RIESNER, REV. ALBERT JOSEPH, C.Ss.R., J.C.D., Apostates and Fugitives from Religious Institutes, IX-168 pp., 1942.
169. STENGER, REV. JOSEPH BERNARD, J.C.D., The Mortgaging of Church Property, 186 pp., 1942.
170. WALDRON, REV. JOSEPH FRANCIS, A.B., J.C.D., The Minister of Baptism, XII-197 pp., 1942.
171. WILLETT, REV. ROBERT ALBERT, J.C.D., The Probative Value of Documents in Ecclesiastical Trials, X-124 pp., 1942.
172. WOEBER, REV. EDWARD MARTIN, M.A., J.C.D., The Interpellations, XII-161 pp., 1942.
173. BENKO, REV. MATTHEW ALOYSIUS, O.S.B., M.A., J.C.D., The Abbot Nullius, XIV-148 pp., 1943.
174. CHRIST, REV. JOSEPH JAMES, M.A., S.T.L., J.C.D., Dispensation from Vindicative Penalties, XIV-285 pp., 1943.

175. Clancy, Rev. Patrick M. J., O.P., A.B., S.T.Lr., J.C.D., The Local Religious Superior, X-299 pp., 1943.
176. Clarke, Rev. Thomas James, J.C.D., Parish Societies, XII-147 pp., 1943.
177. Connolly, Rev. John Patrick, S.T.L., J.C.D., Synodal Examiners and Parish Priest Consultors, X-223 pp., 1943.
178. Drumm, Rev. William Martin, A.B., J.C.D., Hospital Chaplains, XII-175 pp., 1943.
179. Flanagan, Rev. Bernard Joseph, A.B., S.T.L., J.C.D., The Canonical Erection of Religious Houses, X-147 pp., 1943.
180. Kelleher, Rev. Stephen Joseph, A.B., S.T.B., J.C.D., Discussions with non-Catholics; Canonical Legislation, X-93 pp., 1943.
181. Lewis, Rev. Gordian, C.P., J.C.D., Chapters in Religious Institutes, XII-169 pp., 1943.
182. Marx, Rev. Adolph, J.C.D., The Declaration of Nullity of Marriages Contracted Outside the Church, X-151 pp., 1943.
183. Matulenas, Rev. Raymond Anthony, O.S.B., A.B., J.C.D., Communication a Source of Privileges, XII-225 pp., 1943.
184. O'Leary, Rev. Charles Gerard, C.Ss.R., J.C.D., Religious Dismissed After Perpetual Profession, X-213 pp., 1943.
185. Power, Rev. Cornelius Michael, J.C.D., The Blessing of Cemeteries, XII-231 pp., 1943.
186. Shuhler, Rev. Ralph Vincent, O.S.A., J.C.D., Privileges of Regulars to Absolve and Dispense, XII-195 pp., 1943.
187. Ziolkowski, Rev. Thaddeus Stanislaus, A.B., J.C.D., The Consecration and Blessing of Churches, XII-151 pp., 1943.
188. Heneghan, Rev. John Joseph, S.T.D., J.C.D., The Marriages of Unworthy Catholics: Canons 1065 and 1066, XVI-213 pp., 1944.
189. Carroll, Rev. Coleman Francis, M.C., S.T.L., J.C.L., Charitable Institutions.
190. Ciesluk, Rev. Joseph Edward, Ph.B., S.T.L., J.C.D., National Parishes in the United States, VI-178 pp., 1944.
191. Coburn, Rev. Vincent Paul, A.B., J.C.D., Marriages of Conscience, XII-172 pp., 1944.
192. Connors, Rev. Charles Paul, C.S.Sp., A.B., J.C.D., Extra-Judicial Procurators in the Code of Canon Law, X-94 pp., 1944.
193. Coyle, Rev. Paul Raymond, A.B., J.C.D., Judicial Exceptions, X-142 pp., 1944.
194. Fair, Rev. Bartholomew Francis, A.B., S.T.L., J.C.D., The Impediment of Abduction, XII-122 pp., 1944.
195. Gallagher, Rev. Thomas Raphael, O.P., A.B., S.T.Lr., J.C.D., The Examination of the Qualities of the Ordinand, X-166 pp., 1944.
196. Gannon, Rev. John Mark, S.T.L., J.C.D., The Interstices Required for the Promotion to Orders, XII-100 pp., 1944.

197. GOLDSMITH, REV. J. WILLIAM, B.C.S., S.T.L., J.C.D., The Competence of Church and State over Marriage—Disputed Points, X-128 pp., 1944.
198. GOODWINE, REV. JOSEPH GERARD, A.B., S.T.B., J.C.D., The Reception of Converts, XIV-326 pp., 1944.
199. KOWALSKI, REV. ROMUALD EUGENE, O.F.M., A.B., J.C.D., Sustenance of Religious Houses of Regulars, X-174 pp., 1944.
200. MCCOY, REV. ALAN EDWARD, O.F.M., J.C.D., Force and Fear in Relation to Delictual Imputability and Penal Responsibility, XII-160 pp., 1944.
201. MCDEVITT, REV. VINCENT JOHN, Ph.B., S.T.L., J.C.L., Perjury.
202. MARTIN, REV. THOMAS OWEN, Ph.D., S.T.D., J.C.D., Adverse possession, Prescription and Limitation of Actions; The Canonical "Praescriptio," XX-208 pp., 1944.
203. MIKLOSOVIC, REV PAUL JOHN, A.B., J.C.L., Attempted Marriages and Their Consequent Juridic Effects.
204. MUNDY, REV. THOMAS MAURICE, A.B., S.T.L., J.C.D., The Union of Parishes, X-164 pp., 1944.
205. O'DEA, REV. JOHN COYLE, A.B., J.C.D., The Matrimonial Impediment of Nonage, VIII-126 pp., 1944.
206. OLALIA, REV. ALEXANDER AYSON, S.T.L., J.C.D., A Comparative Study of the Christian Constitution of States and the Constitution of the Philippine Commonwealth, XII-136 pp., 1944.
207. POISSON, REV. PIERRE-MARIE, C.S.C., A.B., Ph.L., Th.L., J.C.L., Droits Patrimoniaux des Maisons et des Eglises Religieuses.
208. STADALNIKAS, REV. CASIMIR JOSEPH, M.I.C., J.C.D., Reservation of Censures, X-141 pp., 1944.
209. SULLIVAN, REV. EUGENE HENRY, S.T.L., J.C.D., Proof of the Reception of the Sacraments, X-165 pp., 1944.
210. VAUGHAN, REV. WILLIAM EDWARD, J.C.D., Constitutions for Diocesan Courts, X-210 pp., 1944.
211. PARO, REV. GINO, S.T.D., J.C.D., The Right of Papal Legation, X-221 pp., 1944 (Printed 1947).
212. BALZER, REV. RALPH FRANCIS, C.P., J.C.D., The Computation of Time in a Canonical Novitiate, X-227 pp., 1945.
213. DOUGHERTY, REV. JOHN WHELAN, A.B., S.T.L., J.C.D., De Inquisitione Speciali, XII-195 pp., 1945.
214. DZIOB, REV. MICHAEL WALTER, J.C.D., The Sacred Congregation for the Oriental Church, XII-181 pp., 1945.
215. EIDENSCHINK, REV. JOHN ALBERT, O.S.B., B.A., J.C.D., The Election of Bishops in the Letters of Pope Gregory the Great, VIII-200 pp., 1945.
216. GILL, REV. NICHOLAS, C.P., J.C.D., The Spiritual Prefect in Clerical Religious Houses of Study, X-140 pp., 1945.
217. HYNES, REV. HARRY GERARD, S.T.L., J.C.D., The Privileges of Cardinals, XII-183 pp., 1945.

218. McDevitt, Rev. Gerald Vincent, S.T.L., J.C.D., The Renunciation of an Ecclesiastical Office, XIV-179 pp., 1946.
219. Manning, Rev. Joseph Leroy, J.C.D., The Free Conferral of Offices, VII-116 pp., 1945.
220. Meyer, Rev. Louis G., O.S.B., A.B., S.T.B., J.C.D., Alms-Gathering by Religious, XII-163 pp., 1946.
221. O'Donnell, Rev. Cletus Francis, M.A., J.C.D., The Marriage of Minors, XII-268 pp., 1945.
222. Prunskis, Rev. Joseph, J.C.D., Comparative Law, Ecclesiastical and Civil in Lithuanian Concordat, X-161 pp., 1945.
223. Sweeney, Rev. Francis Patrick, C.Ss.R., J.C.D., The Reduction of Clerics to the Lay State, X-199 pp., 1945.
224. Vogelpohl, Rev. Henry John, J.C.D., The Simple Impediments to Holy Orders, XVI-190 pp., 1945.
225. Brockhaus, Rev. Thomas Aquinas, O.S.B., A.B., J.C.D., Religious who Are Known as Conversi, X-127 pp., 1945.
226. Griese, Rev. Nicholas Orville, S.T.D., J.C.D., Marriage and The Procreation of Offspring, XVI-224 pp., 1945.
227. Boudreaux, Rev. Warren Louis, J.C.D., The "ab acatholicis nati" of Canon 1099, § 2, XII-110 pp., 1946.
228. Bowe, Rev. Thomas Joseph, A.B., J.C.D., Religious Superioresses, VIII-206 pp., 1946.
229. Diederichs, Rev. Michael Ferdinand, S.C.J., J.C.D., The Jurisdiction of the Latin Ordinaries over their Oriental Subjects, XIV-153 pp., 1946.
230. Dingman, Rev. Maurice John, A.B., S.T.L., J.C.L., The Plaintiff in Contentious Trials.
231. Frison, Rev. Basil, C.M.F., M.Mus., J.C.D., The Retroactivity of Law, X-221 pp., 1946.
232. Galvin, Rev. William Anthony, M.A., J.C.D., The Administrative Transfer of Pastors, XII-288 pp., 1946.
233. Goracy, Rev. Joseph C., J.C.L., The Diriment Impediment of Major Orders.
234. Hale, Rev. Joseph Francis, M.A., S.T.L., J.C.D., The Pastor of Burial, X-247 pp., 1946 (Printed 1949).
235. Henry, Rev. Joseph Arthur, A.B., J.C.D., The Mass and Holy Communion: Inter-Ritual Law, XII-138 pp., 1946.
236. Linenberger, Rev. Herbert, C.PP.S., J.C.D., The False Denunciation of an Innocent Confession, VIII-205 pp., 1946 (Printed 1949).
237. Lowry, Rev. James Martin, A.B., J.C.D., Dispensation from Private Vows, XII-266 pp., 1946.
238. Lynch, Rev. George Edward, A.B., S.T.L., J.C.D., Coadjutors and Auxiliaries of Bishops, X-107 pp., 1946 (Printed 1947).
239. Lynch, Rev. Timothy, M.S.SS.T., J.C.D., Contracts between Bishops and Religious Congregations, XIV-232 pp., 1946.

240. McClunn, Rev. Justin David, A.B., S.T.L., J.C.D., Administrative Recourse, VII-142 pp., 1946.
241. Lohmuller, Rev. Martin M., A.B., J.C.D., The Promulgation of Law, XII-140 pp., 1947.
242. McGrath, Rev. James, A.B., J.C.D., The Privilege of the Canon, XII-156 pp., 1946.
243. Marbach, Rev. Joseph Francis, A.B., J.C.D., Marriage Legislation for the Catholics of the Oriental Rites in the United States and Canada, XIV-314 pp., 1946.
244. Shimkus, Rev. Bernard Aloysius, A.B., J.C.L., The Determination and Transfer of Rite.
245. Smith, Rev. Vincent Michael, A.B., S.T.L., J.C.L., Ignorance Affecting Matrimonial Consent.
246. Wachtrle, Rev. Paul Anthony, A.B., J.C.L., The Baptism of the Children of Non-Catholics.
247. Crotty, Rev. Matthew M., J.C.D., The Recipient of First Holy Communion, X-142 pp., 1947.
248. Eagleton, Rev. George, J.C.D., The Quinquennial Faculties, Formula IV, XIV-199 pp., 1947 (Printed 1948).
249. Gibbons, Rev. Marion L., C.M., LL.B., J.C.D., Domicile of The Wife Unlawfully Separated from Her Husband, XIV-171 pp., 1947.
250. Kelly, Rev. Bernard M., S.T.L., J.C.D., The Functions Reserved to Pastors, XII-141 pp., 1947.
251. Kilcullen, Rev. Thomas J., LL.M., J.C.D., The Collegiate Moral Person as Party Litigant, X-150 pp., 1947.
252. Lafontaine, Rev. Germain J., W.F., J.C.D., Relations Canoniques entre Le Missionnaire et Ses Superieurs, X-117 pp., 1947.
253. Lane, Rev. Loras T., A.B., S.T.L., J.C.L., Matrimonial Procedure in the Ordinary Court of Second Instance.
254. Lover, Rev. James F., C.Ss.R., J.C.D., The Master of Novices, X-168 pp., 1947.
255. McNicholas, Rev. Timothy J., J.C.L., The Septimae Manus Witness.
256. Marositz, Rev. Joseph J., M.S.C., J.C.D., Obligations and Privileges of Religious Promoted to the Episcopal or Cardinalitial Dignities, XII-180 pp., 1947.
257. Murphy, Rev. Francis J., A.B., J.C.D., Legislative Powers of the Provincial Council, XII-158 pp., 1947.
258. O'Brien, Rev. Romaeus W., O.Carm., J.C.D., The Provincial Superior in Religious Orders of Men, X-294 pp., 1947.
259. Pfaller, Rev. Benedict A., O.S.B., J.C.L., The Ipso Facto Effected Dismissal of Religious.
260. Popek, Rev. Alphonse S., M.A., J.C.D., The Rights and Obligations of Metropolitans, XVIII-460 pp., 1947.
261. Ristuccia, Rev. Bernard J., C.M., J.C.D., Quasi-Religious, XVI-318 pp., 1947 (Printed 1949).

262. SONNTAG, REV. NATHANIEL L., O.F.M.CAP., J.C.D., Censorship of Special Classes of Books, XII-147 pp., 1947.
263. STADLER, REV. JOSEPH N., J.C.L., Frequent Holy Communion.
264. SZAL, REV. IGNATIUS J., J.C.L., The Communication of Catholics with Schismatics.
265. WAGNER, REV. URBAN S., O.F.M. CONV., J.C.D., Parochial Substitute Vicars and Supplying Priests, IX-126 pp., 1947.
266. QUINN, REV. JOSEPH, M.A., J.C.L., Documents Required for the Reception of Orders.
267. BENNINGTON, REV. JAMES CLEMENT, A.B., J.C.L., The Recipient of Confirmation.
268. BLAHER, REV. DAMIAN JOSEPH, O.F.M., A.B., J.C.L., The Ordinary Processes in Causes of Beatification and Canonization.
269. CLUNE, REV. ROBERT BELL, A.B., J.C.L., The Judicial Interrogation of the Parties.
270. COURTMANCHE, REV. BASIL F., A.B., J.C.L., The Total Simulation of Matrimonial Consent.
271. DLOUHY, REV. MAUR JOHN, O.S.B., A.B., J.C.L., The Ordination of Exempt Religious.
272. DONOVAN, REV. JOHN THOMAS, PH.B., S.T.L., J.C.D., The Clerical Obligations of Canons 138 and 140, XII-209 pp., 1948.
273. FREKING REV. FREDERICK W., A.B., S.T.B., J.C.L., The Canonical Installation of Pastors.
274. FULTON, REV. THOMAS B., J.C.L., Prenuptial Investigation.
275. GODLEY, REV. JAMES P., J.C.L., The Time and the Place for the Celebration of Mass.
276. KANE, REV. THOMAS A., A.B., B.S., J.C.D., The Jurisdiction of the Patriarchs of the Major Sees in Antiquity and in the Middle Ages, XII-111 pp., 1948 (Printed 1949).
277. KENNEDY, REV. ANDREW A., J.C.L., The Annual Pastoral Report to the Local Ordinary.
278. KONRAD, REV. JOSEPH GEORGE, J.C.L., Transfer of Religious.
279. KRESS, REV. ALPHONSE, J.C.L., Contumacy in Ecclesiastical Trials.
280. MCCARTNEY, REV. MARCELLUS ANTHONY, O.F.M., M.A., J.C.L., Faculties of Regular Confessors.
281. MCCASLIN, REV. EDWARD PATRICK, M.A., S.T.L., J.C.L., The Division of Parishes.
282. MCELROY, REV. FRANCIS J., A.B., J.C.L., The Privileges of Bishops.
283. QUINN, REV. STEPHEN, M.S.SS.T., J.C.D., Relation between the Local Ordinary and Religious of Diocesan Approval, XII-158 pp., 1948 (Printed 1949).
284. SCHNEIDER, REV. EDELHARD LOUIS, A.D.S., M.A., J.C.D., The Status of Secularized ex-Religious Clerics, X-155 pp., 1948.
285. THOMPSON, REV. CHESTER J., A.B., J.C.L., The Simple Removal from Office.

286. O'Brien, Rev. Kenneth R., A.B., J.C.D., The Nature of Support of Diocesan Priests in the United States, XVI-162 pp., 1949.
287. Metz, Rev. John E., S.T.L., J.C.D., The Recording Judge in the Ecclesiastical Collegiate Tribunal, X-130 pp., 1949.
288. Reinhardt, Rev. Marion J., S.T.L., J.C.L., The Rogatory Commission.
289. Ortega Uhink, Rev. Juan, S.J., J.C.L., *De Delicto Sollicitationis.*
290. Casey, Rev. James V., J.C.L., A Study of Canon 2222, § 1.
291. Allgeier, Rev. Joseph L., J.C.L., The Canonical Obligations of Preaching in Parish Churches.
292. Cahill, Rev. Daniel R., J.C.L., The Custody of the Holy Eucharist.
293. Carr, Rev. Aidan, O.F.M., Conv., S.T.D., J.C.L., Vocation to the Priesthood: Its Canonical Concept.
294. Knopke, Rev. Roch F., O.F.M., J.C.L., Reverential Fear in Matrimonial Cases in Asiatic Countries: Rota Cases.
295. Lavelle, Rev. Howard D., J.C.L., The Obligation of Holding Sacred Missions in Parishes.
296. Michells, Rev. Anthony B., J.C.L., The Constitutive Elements of Parishes.
297. Noone, Rev. John J., J.C.L., Nullity in Judicial Acts.
298. Sheehan, Rev. Daniel E., J.C.L., The Minister of Holy Communion.
299. Statkus, Rev. Francis J., J.C.L., The Minister of the Last Sacraments.
300. Cook, Rev. John P., J.C.L., Ecclesiastical Communities and Their Ability to Induce Legal Customs.
301. Fazzalaro, Rev. Francis J., J.C.L., The Place for the Hearing of Confessions.
302. Hannan, Rev. Philip M., J.C.L., The Canonical Concept of *Congrua Sustentatio* for the Secular Clergy.
303. Quinn, Rev. Hugh G., S.T.L., J.C.L., The Particular Penal Precept.
304. Gallagher, Rev. John F., J.C.L., The Matrimonial Impediment of Public Propriety.
305. Welsh, Rev. Thomas J., J.C.L., The Use of the Portable Altar.

www.ingramcontent.com/pod-product-compliance
Lightning Source LLC
LaVergne TN
LVHW050250080826
844660LV00012B/619

* 9 7 8 0 8 1 3 2 2 4 7 8 7 *